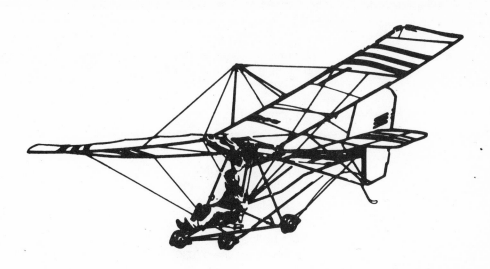

Ultralight Aircraft

The Basic Handbook Of Ultralight Aviation

Michael A. Markowski

Third Edition–Fully Revised, Updated And Expanded

Ultralight Aircraft —
The Basic Handbook of Ultralight Aviation
by Michael A. Markowski

Copyright © 1981, 1982 by Michael A. Markowski

FIRST EDITION
First Printing — August 1981
Second Printing — December 1981
Third Printing — May 1982

SECOND EDITION
First Printing — August 1982
Second Printing — January 1983
Printed in the United States of America

THIRD EDITION
First Printing — October 1983

Published by:
Ultralight Publications, Inc.
Post Office Box 234
Hummelstown, PA 17036

Books by the Author

THE HAND GLIDER'S BIBLE, The Complete Pilot's and Builder's Guide.
THE ENCYCLOPEDIA OF HOMEBUILT AIRCRAFT, Including Powered Hang Gliders.
ULTRALIGHT AIRCRAFT, The Basic Handbook of Ultralight Aviation.

Library of Congress Cataloging in Publication Data

Markowski, Michael A., 1947
Ultralight Aircraft — The Basic Handbook of Ultralight Aviation
(Ultralight Aviation Series, No. 1)
Bibliography
1. Airplanes, Home-built.   2. Hang gliders.
I. Title   II. Series
TL671.2.M333   1982   629.133'3   83-050249
ISBN 0-938716-16-6 Paperback   AACR2
ISBN 0-938716-17-4 Hardcover

On The Cover

The double-surfaced Quicksilver "MXL" features conventional independent, three axis aerodynamic controls and is powered by the Rotax 377 in-line twin of 35 hp. Designed to FAR 103, it offers maximum allowable performance.
Courtesy Eipper Aircraft, Inc., 26531 Ynez Road, Rancho, CA 92390.
(Dave Gustafson photo.)

For my wife, Roberta

When Jonathan Seagull joined the Flock on the beach, it was full night. He was dizzy and terribly tired. Yet in delight he flew a loop to landing, with a snap roll just before touchdown. When they hear of it, he thought, of the Breakthrough, they'll be wild with joy. How much more there is now to living! Instead of our drab slogging forth and back to the fishing boats, there's a reason to life! We can lift ourselves out of ingnorance, we can find ourselves as creatures of excellence and intelligence and skill. We can be free! We can learn to fly!

from Jonathan Livingston Seagull
by Richard Bach

About the Author

Mike Markowski's life literally revolves around flight. He is a graduate aeronautical engineer (specialized in low speed aerodynamics) and FAA licensed private pilot who, since 1971 has devoted his life to the development of ultralight aviation. He was instrumental in initiating hang gliding in the eastern regions of the United States, and began his writing career as editor of the original *Skysurfer* magazine. Prior to that, he was employed as an advanced research engineer for Douglas and Sikorsky aircraft companies, working in the areas of advanced designs and new concepts. Since then, he has built and flown many ultralights of his own design, founded two manufacturing firms, ran a flight school, taught ultralight flight theory at the university level (M.I.T. and others), and is considered an authority on ultralight aviation.

He has lectured to numerous organizations and groups, including the International Symposium on the Technology and Science of Low Speed and Motorless Flight held at M.I.T. He was also responsible for the Forum on Foot-Launched Flight held at the Annual Convention and Fly-In of the Experimental Aircraft Association during the mid-seventies. He has made "star" appearances on national television shows, is sought after for speaking engagements by various groups, and he is often quoted in books, magazines, and newspapers around the world.

Mike is a widely read author, having five books (The Hang Glider's Bible, The Encyclopedia of Homebuilt Aircraft, Ultralight Aircraft, Ultralight Flight and Ultralight Technique) to his credit—classics in their fields—as well as numerous magazine articles.

In addition to writing and flying, Mike is an aeronautical consultant to the ultralight industry for engineering design, as well as marketing, advertising, and public relations. He is also listed as the nation's only Technical Expert in Ultralight Aviation by Attorneys in the Products Liability and Transportation Legal directory and, as such, is active in legal cases. He holds memberships in the Experimental Aircraft Association, Soaring Society of America, United States Hang Gliding Association, the Aircraft Owners and Pilots Association, and the National Association of Sport Aircraft Designers.

It is hoped that this book will foster safety through education as ultralight aviation develops and grows into recreational flying of the future.

Foreword

Ever since I can remember, I've always wanted to fly! As a babe in arms, I oohed and aahed at anything that suspended itself "mysteriously" in the invisible substance we call atmosphere, seemingly defying the law of gravity. Aircraft, birds, and even clouds held an incredible fascination for me — a fascination that continues to grow and flourish with the passage of time.

From the time I was "knee-high-to-a-grasshopper", I have built and flown model airplanes of all types and descriptions. After all, I was too young to be a pilot and modeling offered a great way to learn about the idiosyncrasies of the great ocean of air that surrounds us. I also built and flew kites, and spent many happy hours watching them dance in the wind, as their tethers tugged at my hands as if to seek freedom. Bird watching, too, held an endless fascination for my sky gazing eyes and daydreaming mind.

As time went on, I read "every-book-I-could-get-my-hands-on" related to flight". I simply couldn't get enough of this wonderful stuff. I was determined to learn all I possibly could so I could better understand this incredible "miracle-of-flight". Eventually, I graduated college with a degree in aerospace engineering and got my precious pilot's license. Yet, through it all, I still felt as though something was missing. Sure, flying an airplane was really great, but something was lacking — it fell short of my dreams!

Thinking about those dreams, I suddenly realized that even though I was flying, in the traditional sense of the word, I didn't really "feel" like I was flying — I felt more like I was merely being transported at some distance above the ground. Being contained in an aluminum and plexiglass shell — even though it had wings — didn't allow me to "taste" flight. It wasn't my idea of flying. I couldn't touch the wind. I didn't feel as though I was part of the air. I felt more like an intruder, and I wanted to be more like a bird.

Then one day, back in the early 70's, I stopped to daydream for awhile. I was getting bored designing somebody else's supersonic jet and my mind flashed back to my boyhood and how I wanted to fly like a bird. With my knowledge, I figured I could design my own wings. Wings so light, I could pick them up. Wings so light, I could run with them down hill, lift off and fly, landing gently in the meadow below, I was convinced, bound and determined. I couldn't wait any longer. I would do it!

Ever since that liberating daydream of 1971, I've been deeply involved in ultralight flight. I have designed, built, flown and observed hang gliders and powered ultralights fly, and taken a few notes along the way so that I wouldn't forget what I had done, felt, heard and saw.

It is my intent, with this book, to share some of what I have learned about ultralight flight so that you too may realize your childhood or current dreams of flying — so that you too may experience the true and total freedom that only ultralight flight can provide — so that you may learn to fly yourself more easily, quickly and safely than was possible for me.

I wish you well in your quest for flight — the dream of men through the ages. Be cautious and conservative in your approach to learning and practicing. We are creatures of habit — develop safe ones from the very beginning and your trips through the sky will be many. Learn to walk before you run — taxi before you fly. Sometimes your emotions will want you to disregard your sense of good judgment, but think before you takeoff. Above all, **respect the wind,** and observe the limitations of you and your aircraft. Only then, will the domain of the eagles be yours.

Before you begin your study of this book, I'd like you to read what Wilbur Wright (he and Orville were superb ultralight pilots) had to say about learning to fly: "For the purpose of reducing the danger to the lowest possible point, we usually kept close to the ground. Often a glide of several hundred feet would be made at a height of a few feet or sometimes even a few inches. It was the aim to avoid unnecessary risk. While the high flights were more spectacular, the low ones were fully as valuable for training purposes. Skill comes by the constant repetition of familiar feats rather than be a few over-bold attempts at feats for which the performer is yet poorly prepared."

Acknowledgements

Grateful thanks are extended to the manufacturers of ultralight aircraft and accessories for their cooperation in making material available for inclusion in this book.

Advanced Aviation, Aerodyne, American Aerolights, American Microflight, B & B Aircraft, Cascade Ultralights, Eastern Ultralight, Eipper Aircraft, Gimini International, Goldwing, R. W. Hovey, Kolb Co., Maxair Sports, Midwest Microlites, Mitchell Aircraft, Pterodactyl, Roter, Teratorn Ultraflight, Ultralight Flight, Ultralite Soaring, and many more too numerous to mention.

Special thanks also go out to the following: Art Jones (FAA) for his thoughts, the USHGA, John Weaver (editor of *Ultralight*) and the EAA, Tracy Knauss (publisher of *Glider Rider*) for his opinions, photographs and support of this publishing project, Dan Poynter (author-publisher) for his advice, Park Bierbower (CFI) for proof reading Section Two, and Chuck Slusarczyk (CGS Aviation) for his suggestions and enthusiastic support of my endeavors.

I extend my sincerest thank you to all these fine people and organizations for their contributions to the development of ultralight avaiation, the sport, technology and industry, as well as their contributions to this work.

Introduction

Today, there are many different designs and configurations of ultralight aircraft available, each reflecting the designer's taste and performance goals. Section One of this book is an attempt to present as many aircraft as possible that are available, without any desire to support one or the other. To aid you in selecting an aircraft that best suits your wants, needs and skills, we will discuss such things as construction, performance, stability, control, handling and portability. Three-view drawings and photographs are also presented, wherever possible, to give you a general idea of what each aircraft is all about. However, do not rely only on what is said here. Go out where you can see them fly. Talk to the pilots. Learn as much as you can about each airplane that interests you. Try to get honest opinions from people who actually fly. Don't depend just on a smooth-talking salesman who's trying to make a buck.

It is also recommended that you join your local EAA ultralight chapter. These folks are knowledgeable of aircraft construction and flying techniques and are eager to have you join their ranks. They want to help you build an airworthy craft and get airborne as safely as possible. Ultralight aircraft construction is not all that difficult — many are often described as overgrown model airplanes. Their assembly does, however, require that you be meticulous. There's no place to park to fix something once you're airborne. Every little detail must be exactly correct before you can even think of flying.

No matter what ultralight interests you most, it is of utmost importance that it possesses good handling qualities. It must be stable and easily controlled throughout its entire performance envelope.

Structural integrity should also be a high priority of yours. Any aircraft must be strong enough to withstand the maneuvers it was designed to perform. Then too, it is imperative that you, as a pilot, never exceed your aircraft's performance limitations. Remember, ultralights are very lightly loaded, slow flying aircraft and as such, cannot tolerate much wind or gustiness. They are fair weather flyers! If a small craft warning is up, you should definitely not attempt to fly.

Finally, since there are no certification standards, per se, each ultralight must be proven airworthy on its own merits. True, the best proof of safety and performance lies in the time proven successful flight of the configuration. However, each ultralight built and registered as an experimental aircraft will have to be inspected and certified on an individual basis by the local FAA office before it can be flown. Its final success though, depends on how well you followed the instructions and plans and your use of recognized good construction procedures and techniques.

What It's Like To Fly — A Word From The First Pilots
To give you some idea of what it's like to fly, Orville Wright had this to say

in the Wright Brothers' first official description of powered flight:

"After the Flyer has lifted off the track, Orville wrote, the ground under you is at first a perfect blur, but as you rise the objects become clearer. At a height of one hundred feet you feel hardly any motion at all, except for the wind which strikes your face. If you did not take the precaution to fasten your hat before starting, you have probably lost it by this time.

The operator moves a lever — the right wing rises, and the machine swings about to the left. You make a very short turn, yet you do not feel the sensation of being thrown from your seat, so often experienced in automobile and railway travel. You find yourself facing toward the point from which you started. The objects on the ground now seem to be moving at a much higher speed, though you perceive no change in the pressure of the wind on your face. You know then that you are traveling with the wind.

When you near the starting point, the operator stops the motor while still high in the air. The machine coasts down at an oblique angle to the ground, and after sliding fifty or a hundred feet comes to a rest. Although the machine often lands when traveling at a speed of a mile a minute, you feel no shock whatever, and cannot, in fact, tell the exact moment at which it first touched the ground."

Wilbur also gives a brief description of what is was like to fly. "When you know, after the first few minutes, that the whole mechanism is working perfectly, the sensation is so keenly delightful as to be almost beyond description.... More than anything else the sensation is one of perfect peace, mingled with an excitement that strains every nerve to the utmost, if you can conceive of such a combination."

WARNING — A WORD OF CAUTION

Flight, in and of itself, is not necesarily dangerous, however it is most unforgiving of errors, sloppiness and misjudgment on the part of both the designer and pilot. Whenever a man flies, he accepts the risk that he may be injured or even killed. It is each individual's decision to either accept or reject this risk in light of its potential hazards, challenges and rewards. Flying can be and is done safely every day of the year by paying strict attention to the details.

This book is not intended as a do-it-yourself guide, but merely as a source of information to be used as a reference. If there is anything you don't understand, don't hesitate to ask your flight instructor. It is further recommended that you take flight training in a two-seater ultralight and ground school before you attempt flight on your own. Ultralights are real airplanes, not toys, and they must be treated with respect.

Contents

Section One — Ultralight Aircraft Described

Section Two - Basic Ultralight Flight Manual

Section Three - Ultralight Propulsion

Section Four - Appendicies and Lists 312

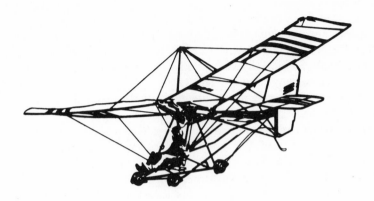

Section One — Ultralight Aircraft Described

Performance Figures - A Word of Caution

The performance figures presented with each aircraft description were supplied by the manufacturer, and no claim is made regarding their exactness. As for most mechanical devices, ultralight performance figures should be subject to the buyer's scrutiny. This is not to imply or suggest that the manufacturer's figures are inaccurate, but rather to enlighten readers and flyers of a few facts.

Without delving into aerodynamic theory, and in keeping with the non-mathematical nature of this book, the reader should understand the significance of stalling. The stall speed of an ultralight is that airspeed or, more precisely, angle of attack where the airflow separates from the upper surface of the wing, results in not only a loss of lift, but also a loss of

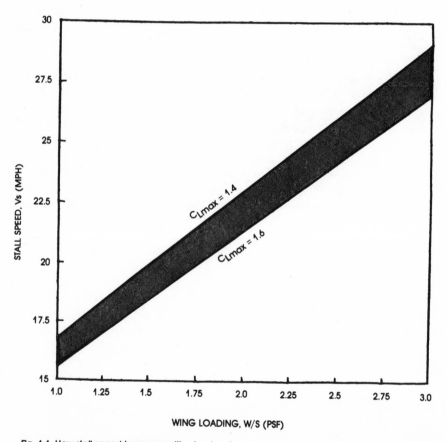

Fig. 1-1. How stall speed increases with wing loading.

controllability. In response to this event, a stalled airplane will drop its nose (lowering the angle of attack), and lose altitude to regain flying speed.

The stall speed is clearly the pilot's most important performance figure. The lower it is, to a certain extent, the more desirable the airplane. A low stall speed translates into the ability to takeoff and land in smaller areas. It also means less energy is carried into the landing, and therefore presents less potential to damage the aircraft or injure the pilot in the event of a mishap. (Note: Keep in mind that a lower stall speed usually means a lower top speed as well, for an unflapped wing.)

Regardless of the stall speeds listed in this book, you might not be able to realize them as such, perhaps because you're not flying under the exact same conditions as did the factory test pilot. For a given aircraft, stall speed depends on two primary items - density altitude (see Koch Chart) and gross weight. Furthermore, that stall speed, as indicated on your airspeed indicator (ASI), could be different due to its precise position on your airplane — it being sensitive to local airflows.

Assuming you are flying at or near sea level (which is where the manufacturer's data should have been reduced to), the stalling speed can be conveniently related to wing loading. Doubling wing loading increases stall speed by a factor of 1.41! Wing loading can be figured simply by dividing total flying weight (sum of aircraft empty weight, pilot clothed weight, plus fuel weight —one gallon weighs 6 pounds) — by the total wing area (for canards, include the canard area as well).

Now, there's one other factor important in determining stall speed, and that is known as the coefficient of lift, CL. Normally, this figure is arrived at by wind tunnel tests, and it depends primarily on the airfoil (wing section), wing planform, plus some other variables. Without getting involved in unnecessary detail, it is sufficient to say that most ultralights seem to exhibit (wing tunnel data is sketchy or non-existent) CL's of somewhere between 1.4 and 1.6. A ribbed Rogallo wing might be able to generate a CL max of 1.4, a rigid single surface ribbed sailcloth wing a CL max of 1.5, while a double surfaced sailcloth or doped wing might produce 1.8.

Assuming an ultralight CL range of 1.4 to 1.6, and selecting a wing loading range of 1.0 to 3.0 pounds per square foot, we can construct a graph that will allow approximation of stalling speed.

Ground Effect and Dynamic Lift Stall

Now if that's all there was to it, we could pack up our bags and go home, however, there's still more to this stall speed game. The previous discussion concerned itself with stalls in "free air" (i.e., at altitudes in excess of one wingspan above the ground). It was also assumed that the stall angle was approached slowly.

When an airplane is within a wingspan of the ground, it experiences a phenomenon known as "ground effect". It could be thought of as a cushioning between the wing and the ground. At any rate, it has the effect of reducing the wing's drag and making it more efficient as a lifting device. (Aeronautical engineers say it increases the effective aspect ratio.) Practically speaking, ground effect might have the result of lowering stall speed by maybe a mile per hour below the free air value.

The ground effect is especially noticeable when the wheels are less than a foot above the ground. Here, it takes less power to fly at a given speed, and can cause an airplane to float, overshooting the intended landing spot. Operating an ultralight with marginal climb capability and/or at a high density altitude, could lead to this: after rotation and while a few feet above the ground, no problem is noticed in acceleration and initial climb. Suddenly, at an altitude of say 10 feet, the aircraft refuses to climb any more and the plane can't clear the obstacles at the end of the field — clearly a dangerous situation.

Dynamic lift stall occurs when the wing is pitched at a faster than normal rate, causing a momentary increase on CL above its steady state free air value. This can be done at the instant before touchdown, and might bring the stall speed down a mile per hour, or so, below the free air value. If the wing is pitched too abruptly while at an altitude of say 3 feet, the aircraft could drop suddenly after the dynamic lift affects are gone, resulting in a crash.

Dynamic lift stall can also occur because of a sudden pull-up and turn an otherwise gentle stalling ultralight into a violently stalling beast.

In summary then, know what your free air stall speed is, as indicated on your ASI, and always fly well above it. Always carry a margin to help you fly through those unexpected gusts that always seem to come from nowhere. Remember too, that stall speed goes up when you are in a turn — a banked wing will stall at a higher speed than a level wing! Speed up appropriately before banking.

Yes, touchdown speed can be lowered by taking advantage of ground effect and high pitch rate dynamic lift, but why risk it!

Other Performance Factors

All performance figures are affected by atmospheric conditions (see Koch Chart in the flight manual section), and gross weight. Basically, the higher your density altitude and/or the higher your gross weight, the less performance you'll be able to realize. Rate of climb is particularly affected by the above.

The manufacturer's figures were certainly done under ideal conditions, with a well tuned engine. Don't be too disappointed if you can't duplicate the factory's figures exactly.

Advanced Aviation — *Cobra*

The Cobra is a cable braced, double surfaced, high wing monoplane with three axis aerodynamic controls actuated via a center-mounted stick and rudder pedals. Roll is controlled by spoilers. Power is provided by the Cuyuna UL II-02 with a planetary reduction drive gearbox. A rigid seat is mounted atop a tricycle undercarriage.

The Cobra may be purchased as a bolt-together assembly kit or assembled by your dealer. The do-it-yourself version requires only the basic tools found around most households. All rigging cables are cut to proper length and preswaged at the factory. The ladder frame wing is constructed primarily of aluminum tubing, as is most of the airframe. All flying surfaces are presewn of 3.9 oz. stabilized dacron sailcloth, available in a three color pattern. All hardware is aircraft quality, and the kit contains all parts necessary to build the entire air vehicle.

The tricycle landing gear features twin arched tubes for shock absorption. A nose wheel brake is standard equipment. The airplane sits upright, even when unoccupied.

The powerplant is designed specifically for ultralights, and comes with a 90-day warranty. The reduction driven prop produced 225 pounds of static

Fig. 1-2. The Cobra is Advanced Aviation's three axis aerodynamic control model.

thrust. It is laminated from hardwood and protected by a clear finish. The complete power package is test run at the factory before shipping.

Entry to the seat is somewhat cramped, due to the spacing of the down tubes, but once in, the bucket is comfortable. Rudder and elevator control is smooth and responsive, while the spoiler affected roll control was somewhat slow on the prototype. Subsequent production units were to have enhanced roll control, however.

Optional items include custom wing patterns, wheel pants and pontoons.

Specifications

Wingspan	35 ft.
Length	17 ft. 6 in.
Height	9 ft. 3 in.
Wing Area	155 sq. ft.
Engine Make, Model, HP	Cuyuna UL II-02, 35 hp.
Prop Diameter/Pitch	54 in./27 in.
Reduction Ratio	2-to-1, planetary gear box
Fuel Capacity/Consumption	5 gal./2 gph.
Gross Weight	525 lbs.
Empty Weight	245 lbs.
Useful Load	280 lbs.
Wing Loading	3.38 psf.
Power Loading	15 lb./hp.
Design Load Factors	+5, -3
Construction Time	40 man-hrs.
Field Assembly Time	25 min.
Pricing	$5195

Flight Performance

Velocity Never Exceed	70 mph.
Top Level Speed	63 mph.
Cruise Speed	55 mph.
Stall Speed (in free air)	26 mph.
Sea Level Climb Rate	800 fpm. @ 38 mph.
Takeoff Run	100 ft.
Dist. Req'd. to clear 50 ft.	N.A.
Landing Roll	100 ft.
Service Ceiling (100 fpm. climb)	N.A.
Range at Cruise	100 mi.
L/D (Glide Ratio)	9-to-1 @ N.A. mph.
Minimum Sink Rate	N.A.

Cobra
Advanced Aviation, Inc.
Rt. 7, Box 569
Orlando, FL 32805
(305) 298-2920
Kerry Richter

Advanced Aviation — *Huski*

The Huski is a single engine, single surfaced, high wing monoplane consisting of cable braced aluminum tubing construction. It is controlled by a hybrid system of aerodynamic controls and weight shift. Fore and aft body movements control pitch, while lateral movements deflect rudder and spoilers.

The tricycle landing gear features spring loaded cable "shock absorbers" and a steerable nose gear. The Huski uses the Cuyuna 430 in direct drive, while a Huski II is available with a reductions drive for improved performance. Both air vehicles are transportable on a small trailer or in the back of a pick-up truck.

Specifications

Wingspan	33 ft. 6 in.
Length	16 ft. 9 in.
Height	9 ft. 9 in.
Wing Area	166 sq. ft.
Engine Make, Model, HP	Cuyuna 430-0, 30 hp.
Prop. Diameter/Pitch	36 in/16 in.
Reduction Ratio	Direct drive
Fuel Capacity/Consumption	3 gal./1.5 gph.
Gross Weight	440 lbs.
Empty Weight	190 lbs.
Useful Load	250 lbs.
Wing Loading	2.65 psf.
Power Loading	14.67 lb/hp.
Design Load Factors	+4, -3
Construction Time	N.A.
Field Assembly Time	30 min.
Pricing	$3995.

Flight Performance

Velocity Never Exceed	60 mph.
Top Level Speed	45 mph.
Cruise Speed	35-40 mph.
Stall Speed (in free air)	22 mph.
Sea Level Climb Rate	700 fpm. @ 29 mph.
Takeoff Run	100 ft.
Dist. Req'd. to clear 50 ft.	N.A.
Landing Roll	100 ft.
Service Ceiling (100 fpm. climb)	N.A.

Range at Cruise   80 mi.
L/D (Glide Ratio)   6-to-1
Minimum Sink Rate   N.A.

Huski
Advanced Aviation, Inc.
Rt. 7, Box 569
Orlando, FL 32805
(305) 298-2920
Angel Matos

Aerodyne Systems — Vector 627SR

The Vector 627SR is very similar in outward appearance to the venerable 610. Due to the increased power of the Rotax 377 over the Zenoah, the airframe was "beefed-up". The keel was squared off and enlarged, while the tail section was reinforced, and the rear span lengthened and strengthened. The engine mount was also necessarily re-designed to accommodate the new powerplant.

Perhaps the most unique feature of this latest Vector is its "SR" designation, which stands for "stick and rudder". Unlike the "610", which has coupled spoiler and rudder functions, the "627SR" features foot pedal operated rudders, while the stick controls spoilers and elevators. The "SR" designation means the air vehicle has a fully independent, three-axis aerodynamic control system. This is a boon to licensed pilots, and should enhance the aircraft's crosswind capabilities.

NOTE: (The factory informs us that an "SR" option is also available for the "610". In fact, the pilot can change from a coupled control system to a fully independent one in a matter of minutes. It is claimed this feature allows the neophyte to learn on the supposedly easier coupled system, then switch to the independent system as his experience level grows.)

The powerplant for this new bird is the Austrian built Rotax. It was chosen for several reasons, not the least of which is the fact that it has time proven use in the Ski-Doo line of snowmobiles. In fact, the factory claims a 400 hour TBO (time before overhaul). It is also claimed to produce a lower, mellower tone than some other two-strokes — it's described as more like a "hum".

Fig. 1-3. The Vector 627SR was the first US ultralight to receive German certification.

Other attributes of the powerplant include: natural cylinder head ventilation enhanced with a cooling fan; a spring mounted "floating" type muffler; a factory equipped Bing carburetor; and, a dual point ignition system, Uniroyal HTD cog-belt reduction drive. The power system is a bolt together package requiring six hours of assembly time via a factory supplied tool kit.

The Vector is the first US-built ultralight to meet German certification standards, and was awarded a German certificate of airworthiness.

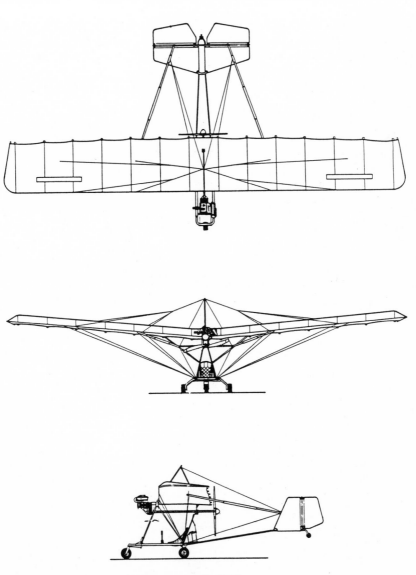

Fig. 1-4. Three-view drawing of the Aerodyne Vector 627SR.

Specifications

Wingspan	35 ft. 10 in.
Length	18 ft. 7 in.
Height	8 ft. 4 in.
Wing Area	154 sq. ft.
Engine Make, Model, HP	Rotax 377, 32 hp. @ 6250 rpm.
Prop. Diameter/Pitch	54 in/26 in.
Reduction Ratio	2.32-to-1
Fuel Capacity/Consumption	5 gal./2.5 gph.
Gross Weight	500 lbs.
Empty Weight	252 lbs.
Useful Load	248 lbs.
Wing Loading	3.25 psf.
Power Loading	16.6 lb/hp.
Design Load Factors	+5.8, -2.9 ultimate load
Construction Time	38 man-hrs.
Field Assembly Time	45 min.
Pricing	$5,495.

Flight Performance

Velocity Never Exceed	63 mph.
Top Level Speed	55 mph.
Cruise Speed	50 mph. @ 75% power
Stall Speed (in free air)	27 mph.
Sea Level Climb Rate	1000 fpm. @ 35 mph.
Takeoff Run	100 ft.
Dist. Req'd. to clear 50 ft.	300 ft.
Landing Roll	75 ft.
Service Ceiling (100 fpm. climb)	N.A.
Range at Cruise	100 mi.
L/D (Glide Ratio)	8-to-1

Vector 627SR
Aerodyne Systems, Inc.
194 Millers Falls Road
Turners Falls, MA 01376
(413) 863-9736
Chris Frado

American Aerolights — Eagle Series

The Eagle represents a family of air vehicles of canned pusher configuration with a Rogallo type sailwing. It borrows heavily from hang glider technology and features similar portability. Each member of the family is sold only as a "ready-to-field assemble" unit, flight tested at the factory.

The airframe consists primarily of bolted-together, wire-braced aluminum tubing, and is stated by the factory as being stronger than most hang gliders. The main wing is a bowsprit rigged Rogallo sailwing with airfoil shaped aluminum ribs retained in pockets sewn into the upper surface. The keel tube extends forward and supports a canard with elevator. The bottom of the keel picks up the under-carriage and tricycle landing gear. The gas tank and powerplant are mounted to the rear of the undercarriage, while a shaft driven prop is at the tail end. A rudder is mounted at each wing tip.

Fig. 1-5. The American Aerolights Eagle features a nearly unstallable canard.

The Eagle can be purchased in several different combinations of powerplant and control system. The Eagle B models feature a hybrid control system consisting of handlebar actuated tip rudders, and harness activated elevator augmented by weight shift for pitch control. The 215-B is powered by the Cuyuna 215R, while the 430-B is powered by the 430R. Performance and price increase accordingly with the larger engine.

The Eagle XL models feature a fully independent, three-axis aerodynamic flight control system. The pilot is seated in a padded, contoured fiberglass seat, restrained by lap and shoulder belts. A right side stick controls spoilers and elevator, while foot pedals control the tip rudders and nosewheel. A T-handled throttle is mounted on the pilot's left.

The Eagle Two-Place is not an ultralight by FAA definition and therefore, it must be registered as an amateur-built aircraft and operated by someone with at least a student pilot license. It features dual rudder pedals operating the tip rudders, and centrally mounted stick. The nosewheel is steered by a separate small stick mounted between the seats. The aircraft is powered by the 50 hp. Rotax 503 two-cycle engine.

The Eagles have a sensitive pitch response, but even in the most violent stalls attempted by the factory, the canard resisted any angle of attack below 10°. The aircraft actually mushes at a high sink rate, as opposed to a clean break type stall. Test flights in the most aft CG position resulted in a noticeable increase in sink rate and a mild porpoising of the nose — a typical canard characteristic.

In general, the flight characteristics can be described as docile and predictable. The factory has even demonstrated successive takeoffs and landings with no pilot input — all of which were safe, if not perfect. The Eagle has a fairly tight turning radius and an ability to "hang-in-there". It can also climb and soar with the engine off, in tenuous lift conditions where high performance sailplanes might find difficulty.

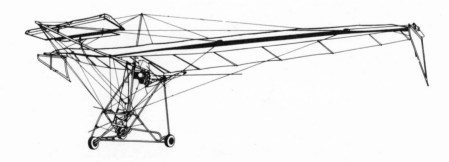

Fig. 1-6. The American Aerolights Eagle in cutaway.

The Eagle folds-up into a hang glider-like package that can actually be carried on the shoulders, as well as a car top. The landing gear and powerplant would, of course, be disconnected from the flying surfaces assembly. The frame can be further disassembled to 12-foot lengths for air transport as "excess baggage".

A network of dealers and a training program support the Eagle's distribution.

Eagle 215-B
American Aerolights, Inc.

Specifications

Wingspan	35 ft.
Length	15 ft.
Height	10 ft.
Wing Area	180 sq. ft.
Engine Make, Model, HP	Cuyuna 215, single cylinder, 20 hp.
Prop. Diameter/Pitch	54 in/24 in.
Reduction Ratio	2.4-to-1
Fuel Capacity/Consumption	4.0 gal./1.5 gph.
Gross Weight	380 lbs.
Empty Weight	175 lbs.
Useful Load	180 lbs., + full fuel
Wing Loading	2.1 psf. @ gross
Power Loading	19 lb/hp. @ gross
Design Load Factors	+ 8, -2.5
Construction Time	Zero man-hrs.
Field Assembly Time	45 min., 15 minutes from trailer
Pricing	$4,595. ready-to-fly

Flight Performance (150 lb. pilot, standard conditions)

Velocity Never Exceed	55 mph.
Top Level Speed	46 mph.
Cruise Speed	32 mph. @ 70% power
Stall Speed (in free air)	25 mph.
Sea Level Climb Rate	550 fpm. @ 30 mph.
Takeoff Run	75 ft.
Dist. Req'd. to clear 50 ft.	N.A.
Landing Roll	50 ft.
Service Ceiling (100 fpm. climb)	11,000 ft.
Range at Cruise	80 mi.
L/D (Glide Ratio)	7-to-1 @ 30 mph.
Minimum Sink Rate	300 fpm. @ 26 mph.

Eagle 430-R
American Aerolights, Inc.

Specifications

Wingspan	35 ft.
Length	15 ft.
Height	10 ft.
Wing Area	180 sq. ft.
Engine Make, Model, HP	Cuyuna 430, two-cylinder, 35 hp.
Prop. Diameter/Pitch	54 in/36 in.
Reduction Ratio	2.2-to-1
Fuel Capacity/Consumption	4.0 gal./1.5 gph.
Gross Weight	535 lbs.
Empty Weight	210 lbs.
Useful Load	300 lbs., full fuel
Wing Loading	2.9 psf. @ gross
Power Loading	15.3 lb/hp. @ gross
Design Load Factors	=6, -2.5
Construction Time	Zero man-hrs.
Field Assembly Time	45 min, 15 minutes from trailer
Pricing	$5,095. ready-to-fly

Flight Performance (150 lb. pilot, standard conditions)

Velocity Never Exceed	55 mph.
Top Level Speed	55 mph.
Cruise Speed	37 mph.
Stall Speed (in free air)	27 mph.
Sea Level Climb Rate	750 fpm. @ 34 mph.
Takeoff Run	75 ft.
Dist. Req'd. to clear 50 ft.	N.A.
Landing Roll	75 ft.
Service Ceiling (100 fpm. climb)	17,500 ft.
Range at Cruise	95 mi.
L/D (Glide Ratio)	7-to-1 @ 34 mph.
Minimum Sink Rate	400 fpm. @ 30 mph.

Eagle XL 215
American Aerolights, Inc.

Specifications

Wingspan	35 ft.
Length	15 ft.
Height	9 ft.
Wing Area	177 sq. ft.

Engine Make, Model, HP	Cuyuna 215, single cylinder, 20 hp.
Prop. Diameter/Pitch	54 in/24 in.
Reduction Ratio	2.4-to-1
Fuel Capacity/Consumption	4.0 gal./1.5 gph.
Gross Weight	420 lbs.
Empty Weight	225 lbs.
Useful Load	170 lbs., full fuel
Wing Loading	2.4 psf. @ gross
Power Loading	21 lb/hp. @ gross
Design Load Factors	+6, -2.5
Construction Time	Zero man-hrs.
Field Assembly Time	60 min., 15 min. from trailer
Pricing	$5,395. ready-to-fly

Flight Performance (150 lb. pilot, standard conditions)

Velocity Never Exceed	55 mph.
Top Level Speed	47 mph.
Cruise Speed	34 mph. @ 75% power
Stall Speed (in free air)	25 mph.
Sea Level Climb Rate	450 fpm.
Takeoff Run	200 ft.
Dist. Req'd. to clear 50 ft.	N.A.
Landing Roll	50 ft.

Fig. 1-7. The Eagle XL is controlled solely by aerodynamic means.

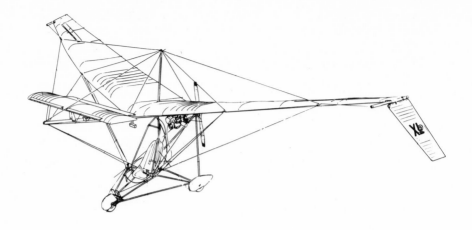

Fig. 1-8. Perspective drawing of the Eagle XL.

Service Ceiling (100 fpm. climb)	10,000 ft.
Range at Cruise	85 mi.
L/D (Glide Ratio)	7-to-1 @ 29 mph.
Minimum Sink Rate	280 fpm. @ 27 mph.

Eagle XL
American Aerolights, Inc.

Specifications

Wingspan	35 ft.
Length	15 ft.
Height	9 ft.
Wing Area	177 sq. ft.
Engine Make, Model, HP	Cuyuna 430, two-cylinder, 35 hp.
Prop. Diameter/Pitch	54 in/36 in.
Reduction Ratio	2.2-to-1
Fuel Capacity/Consumption	4.0 gal./2.0 gph.
Gross Weight	545 lbs.
Empty Weight	248 lbs.
Useful Load	240 lbs. w/full fuel
Wing Loading	3.1 psf. @ gross
Power Loading	15.6 lb/hp. @ gross
Design Load Factors	+6, -2.5
Construction Time	Zero man-hrs.
Field Assembly Time	60 min., 15 minutes from trailer
Pricing	$5,595. ready-to-fly

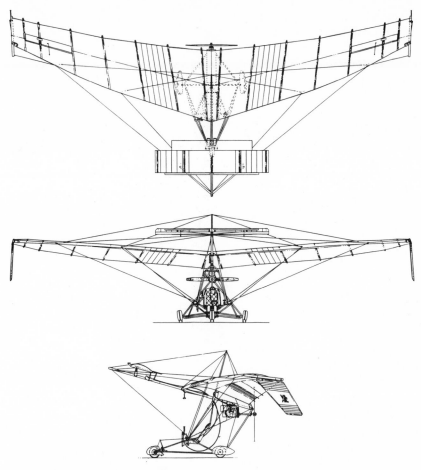

Fig. 1-9. Three-view drawing of the Eagle XL.

Flight Performance (150 lb. pilot, standard conditions)

Velocity Never Exceed	55 mph.
Top Level Speed	50 mph.
Cruise Speed	37 mph. @ 55% power
Stall Speed (in free air)	26 mph.
Sea Level Climb Rate	750 fpm. @ 30 mph.
Takeoff Run	125 ft.
Dist. Req'd. to clear 50 ft.	N.A.
Landing Roll	50 ft.
Service Ceiling (100 fpm. climb)	17,500 ft.
Range at Cruise	95 mi.
L/D (Glide Ratio)	7-to-1 @ 30 mph.
Minimum Sink Rate	300 fpm. @ 28 mph.

Eagle 2-Place
American Aerolights, Inc.

Specifications

Wingspan	35 ft.
Length	15 ft.
Height	10 ft.
Wing Area	177 sq. ft.
Engine Make, Model, HP	Rotax 503, two-cylinder, 50 hp.
Prop. Diameter/Pitch	58 in/27 in.
Reduction Ratio	2.05-to-1
Fuel Capacity/Consumption	4 gal./2 gph.
Gross Weight	650 lbs.
Empty Weight	275 lbs.
Useful Load	350 lbs. w/full fuel
Wing Loading	37 psf. @ gross
Power Loading	13 lb/hp. @ gross
Design Load Factors	+5, -2.5
Construction Time	75 man-hrs.
Field Assembly Time	75 min., 15 min. from trailer
Pricing	$6,295. kit

Flight Performance (Based on two 150 lb. people, standard conditions)

Velocity Never Exceed	55 mph.
Top Level Speed	50 mph.

Fig. 1-10. The Eagle Two Place is used by dealers to train students.

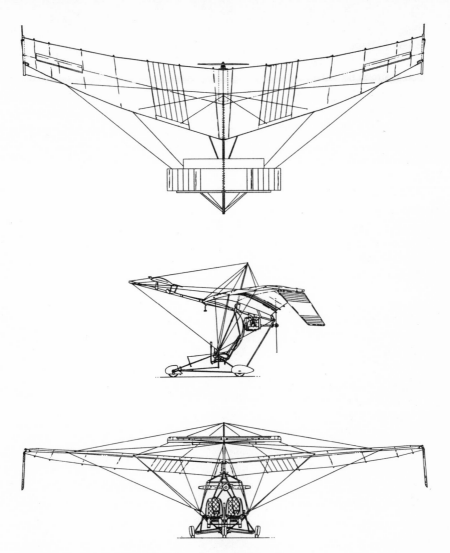

Fig. 1-11. Three-view drawing of the stick-controlled Eagle Two Place.

Cruise Speed	45 mph. @ 75% power
Stall Speed (in free air)	34 mph.
Sea Level Climb Rate	450 fpm. @ 38 mph.
Takeoff Run	250 ft.
Dist. Req'd. to clear 50 ft.	N.A.
Landing Roll	250 ft.
Service Ceiling (100 fpm. climb)	8,000 ft.
Range at Cruise	75 mi.
L/D (Glide Ratio)	5-to-1 @ 33 mph.
Minimum Sink Rate	500 fpm. @ 36 mph.

Eagle 2-Place
American Aerolights, Inc.
700 Comanche Rd.
Albuquerque, NM 87107
(505) 822-1417
Emory Ellis, Sales Manager

American Aerolights — *Falcon*

The Falcon is a strut-braced, high wing monoplane canard with a completely faired, open cockpit fuselage. It features a tricycle landing gear with a steerable nosewheel and three-axis aerodynamic controls including canard, elevator, tip rudders, and full span ailerons. Its high glide ratio allows engine-off soaring. It is available only as a completely ready-to-fly air vehicle.

The airframe makes use of advanced technology materials. The fuselage owes its light weight and strength to composites of kevlar, graphite and epoxy. The strut-braced, laminar flow wings consist of a D-cell leading edge, foam composite ribs, and an antidrag diagonal of aluminum tubing. The wing is covered with "Tedlar", a spage-age alloy of teflon and mylar. It is nearly impervious to the elements, and affords the pilot with improved upward visibility.

The Falcon is powered by the single cylinder Rotax of 27 hp., which still enables the craft to cruise at 60 mph at a 40 mpg economy. The ship stalls at 26 mph and climbs at 600 fpm at sea level, with takeoff and landing requiring less than 300 feet. The crosswind capability is reportedly good. Field assembly/disassembly requires 15 minutes and the craft can be transported by trailer.

The air vehicle comes complete with the electronic Aerogage instrument panel, cabin heat, steerable nosewheel and brake, in-flight restarting, cockpit-operated choke, padded seat, and shoulder harness and seatbelt. The fuselage is available in four colors.

Fig. 1-12. The Falcon features built-up composite construction of aluminum and fiberglass.

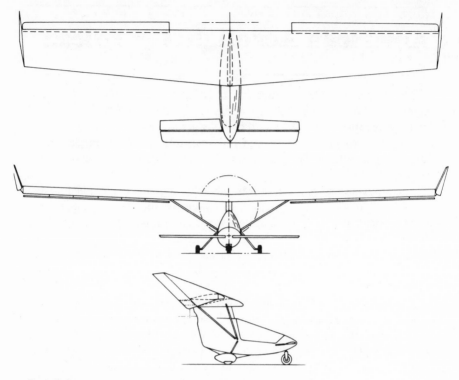

Fig. 1-13. Three-view drawing of American Aerolights Falcon prototype.

Specifications

Wingspan	36 ft.
Length	10 ft. 6 in.
Height	5 ft.
Wing Area	165 sq. ft.
Engine Make, Model, HP	Rotax 277, single cylinder, 28 hp.
Prop. Diameter/Pitch	N.A.
Reduction Ratio	2.1-to-1
Fuel Capacity/Consumption	5.0 gal./0.8 gph.
Gross Weight	515 lbs.
Empty Weight	250 lbs.
Useful Load	235 lbs. w/full fuel
Wing Loading	3.1 psf. @ gross, 2.5 w/standard pilot
Power Loading	18.4 lb/hp. @ gross, 14.8 w/standard pilot
Design Load Factors	+6, -3
Construction Time	50 man-hrs.
Field Assembly Time	20 min.
Pricing	$7,500. ready-to-fly

Flight Performance (150 lb. pilot, standard conditions)

Velocity Never Exceed	75 mph.
Top Level Speed	63 mph.
Cruise Speed	63 mph. @ 80% power
Stall Speed (in free air)	26 mph.
Sea Level Climb Rate	500 fpm. @ 36 mph.
Takeoff Run	250 ft.
Dist. Req'd. to clear 50 ft.	N.A.
Landing Roll	200 ft.
Service Ceiling (100 fpm. climb)	15,000 ft.
Range at Cruise	280 mi.
L/D (Glide Ratio)	16-to-1 @ 36 mph.
Minimum Sink Rate	250 fpm. @ 32 mph.

Falcon
American Aerolights, Inc.
700 Comanche Rd.
Albuquerque, NM 87107
(505) 822-1417
Emory Ellis, Sales Manager

American Microflight — Vampire

The Vampire is a shoulder wing, pod and twin boom pusher. It features a totally enclosed engine, tricycle landing gear, fully cantilevered wing, and pilot pod.

The Vampire's construction is unique to the ultralight world, but very similar to conventional aircraft practice. The constant chord wing is made entirely of aluminum, including the skin. The airfoil is an 18% thick laminar flow section, giving plenty of depth for the channel section span with extruded aluminum caps. The ribs are .012 inch thick, machine-stamped from 2024-T3 Alclad, fastened to the spar via special two-sided bonding tape and minimal rivits. The skins are fastened similarly to the ribs, forming a D-cell leading edge and box section behind the spar. Ailerons and flaps share the trailing edge and are hinged to the rear spar, which is also a channel section.

The tail surfaces are built similar to the wing, and supported by twin aluminum tubes jutting aft the wing center section. Twin fins and rudders take

Fig. 1-14. The Vampire offers top performance in a sleek, sophisticated shape.

care of yaw stability and control, while a separate stabilizer and elevator head up the longitudinal department.

The underslung fuselage, or pod, is constructed of fiberglass supported by an aluminum tube frame, housing both the engine and pilot in a streamlined form. The pilot can opt for either a completely enclosed cabin or an open cockpit.

Power is provided by 20 hp solo ultralight engine, but the 26 hp NGL 342 is also available. The solo engine turns a 54 inch prop via a reduction drive, while the NGL is run directly to a 30 incher.

The performance is termed sprightly, even with the prototype's undeveloped engine. The air vehicle responds like a conventional airplane, and would not be recommended for beginners.

The Vampire is readily folded for trailer transportation. The wing panels fold back along side the tail booms in under five minutes, while all control linkages remain intact. It is not a do-it-yourself kit, and is sold only ready to fly to licensed pilots. The price includes pilot orientation and checkout before delivery is made.

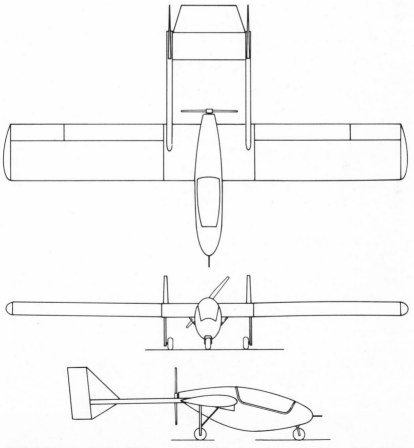

Fig. 1-15. Three view drawing of the Vampire reveals streamlined shape and various control surfaces, including flaps.

Specifications

Wingspan	30 ft. 10 in
Length	17 ft 6 in.
Height	4 ft 8 in.
Wing Area	128 sq. ft.
Engine Make, Model, HP	Solo, 20 hp.
Prop. Diameter/Pitch	54 in.
Reduction Ratio	3.0-to-1
Fuel Capacity/Consumption	5 gal./1.5 gph.
Gross Weight	500 lbs.
Empty Weight	250 lbs.
Useful Load	250 lbs.
Wing Loading	3.9 psf.
Power Loading	25 lb/hp.
Design Load Factors	+6, −6 yield
Construction Time	Factory Built
Field Assembly Time	5-10 min.
Pricing	$6,950.

Flight Performance

Velocity Never Exceed	85 mph.
Top Level Speed	63 mph.
Cruise Speed	55 mph.
Stall Speed	25 mph.
Sea Level Climb Rate	500 fpm.
Takeoff Run	300 ft.
Dist. Req'd. to clear 50 ft.	N.A.
Landing Roll	200 ft.
Service Ceiling	N.A.
Range at Cruise	150 mi.
L/D (Glide Ratio)	N.A.

Vampire
American Microflight, Inc.
7654 E. Acoma Drive
Scottsdale Airport
Scottsdale, AZ 85260
(602) 951-9772
Bill Sadler

B & B Aircraft — *Sand Piper*

Sand Piper

B & B Aircraft Company
Newberg, Oregon 97132 U.S.A.

Fig. 1-17. The Sand Piper features a strut-braced built-up wing and inverted V-tail.

Fig. 1-18. Artist's line drawing shows San Pipers basic structure.

The Sand Piper is a strut-braced, high wing monoplane with tricycle landing gear and three axis aerodynamic controls.

The wing is constructed of a composite of aluminum tube spars and foam ribs, and is covered with heat shrink dacron. Flaperons are hinged to the rear spar, providing both lift and roll control. The fuselage is a 3 inch square aluminum tube with a vertical mast and tail boom. Aircraft hardware is used throughout for fastening.

The tail is an inverted "V" with ruddervators controlling pitch and yaw. The factory claims this system enhances the air vehicle's safety in that spins are said to be very difficult to do accidentally. Contact B & B for further details.

Specifications

Wingspan	31 ft. 4 in.
Length	15 ft. 8 in.
Height	6 ft. 0 in.
Wing Area	171 sq. ft.
Engine Make, Model, HP	Rotax 377, 38 hp.
Prop Diameter/Pitch	52 in./34 in.
Reduction Ratio	1.8-to-1
Fuel Capacity/Consumption	5 gal./1.8 gph.
Gross Weight	521 lbs.
Empty Weight	251 lbs.
Useful Load	270 lbs.
Wing Loading	3.05 psf
Power Loading	13.71 lb/hp
Design Load Factors	+9, -6
Construction Time	80 man-hrs
Field Assembly Time	35 min
Pricing	$5,495

Flight Performance
(421 lbs)

Velocity Never Exeed	90 mph
Top Level Speed	63 mph
Cruise Speed	60 mph

Stall Speed (in free air)	22 mph
Sea Level Climb Rate	950 fpm
Takeoff Run	100 ft.
Dist. Req'd to clear 50 ft.	NA
Landing Roll	60 ft.
Service Ceiling (100 fpm climb)	NA
Range at Cruise	NA
L/D (Glide Ratio)	11-to-1 @ 44 mph
Minimum Sink Rate	NA

Sand Piper
B & B Aircraft Co., Inc.
P.O. Box 930
Newburg, OR 97132
(503) 538-8855
R. Miller

Birdman Enterprises — WT-11 Chinook

The Chinook is a high wing cabin monoplane with pusher engine, a single tube tail boom, and taildragger landing gear. It features a cruciform tail, and conventional three-axis aerodynamic controls. The rear of the cabin has space for a second seat and dual controls, allowing conversion to a trainer.

The wing is a two-span ladder type frame with internal drag wire trussing. It is supported by streamlined lift and jury struts. It is covered with a 3.9 oz. dacron envelope with aluminum ribs in pockets, and is drawn tight at the root to eliminate sagging. The airfoil sections is maintained by securing the ribs to the spars and the cover to the rib end.

The roll control system is of the wing warp style. The outboard ribs are fitted with a fringe and control horn which flex the wing cover to achieve roll. Cables are routed to a differential bellcrank on the inboard compression struts, and a quick-disconnect pushrod links the system to the fuselage.

The tail surfaces make use of a sealed-gap elevator and rudder hinge system in which the main spar of elevator and rudder post act like the pin in a piano hinge. The fin and rudder, and stabilizer/elevator envelopes are interlocked on their respective spars to form a smooth, tight surface.

The fuselage, undercarriage and cabin assembly are built as a unit around a 4 inch diameter aluminum tube, acting as a lower "spine". The body of the ultralight is an elongated sentagonal cross-section which is a compromise between a triangularized and rounded "streamline" form. All major load-bearing members terminate in a strong cluster joint to transfer under-carriage, seat, wing and fuselage loads throughout the structure.

The curved members of the forward fuselage form a semi-teardrop shape for lower drag. The junction between wing and body is nearly 90° with a sealing strip for improved airflow. The cabin area is large, and includes an upholstered seat, center mounted control stick, and adjustable rudder pedals. The windshield is gently curved to reduce the chance of glare, and side panels extend from shoulder to toe to provide near-open cockpit visibility. The rear cabin or baggage area behind the seat has large windows for rearward vision.

A portion of the cabin floor is covered to allow easier entry and exit, and control cables are routed close to the floor along the centerline where they are out of the way, but readily visible for inspection. A center-mounted panel enables the mounting of full instrumentation without restricting visibility.

The elevator cables are routed through the tailboom, while the rudder cables run along the outside to the tailpost, and also move the steerable, bungee-suspended tailwheel. The main wheels incorporate a caged axle and bungee suspension to absorb shocks.

The wing panels and struts are attached to the fuselage with six aircraft grade bolts, enabling removal by one person for storage or transport. The

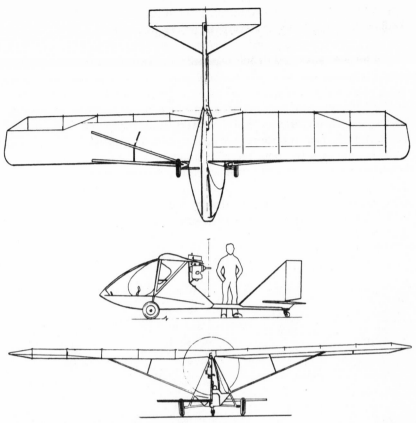

Fig. 1-19. Three-view drawing of the Chinook.

wings may be fitted alongside the fuselage for best use of space.

The factory test pilot had the following comments regarding the Chinook and its flight characteristics: The cabin isn't cramped. Ground handling is easy. Cabin noise level is low. Power was adequate for a good climbout. The elevator and rudder are very responsive, but smooth. The ailerons are less sensitive but good. No vibrations were noticed at any rpm. The ultralight holds its speed well, and will fly at low throttle settings. The transition from power-on to power-off is very smooth with no pitching tendencies. Deadstick landing is just as easy as with the engine idling. Visibility is good. It cruises at 50, and stalls, power-off at 23-25 mph with full up elevator. The Chinook stall straight ahead, with no tendency to drop a wing.

Spins were attempted, but not attainable. With the nose held high and the power off, the ailerons and rudder will hit hard as soon as the stall came on. The air vehicle broke to the right as if to spin, then after a quarter-turn, it mushed to a level attitude and settled into a wide righty mushy turn, airspeed stayed at 40 mph, and this continued until the control input was released.

A spin was also tried by entering from a snap roll. The ultralight snapped about 270° and quit, nose down then mushed, into the same flat turn. Spins were tried both left and right.

Some turning stalls were also tried. The ultralight was held in a steep turn, (roughly 70° bank). As speed dropped to 35 mph, the nose dropped slightly until the craft was flying again. This was done left and right.

During his tests, the pilot watched the airframe for wobbles and distortions, and saw none. The Chinook was put through a very wide speed range and some fairly heavy loads with no rattles, flutters or vibrations.

The Chinook was also put through some basic aerobatics during its testing. Loop, stall turns and tail slides were fairly easy. Rolls were possible, but everything had to be done just right to complete the last quarter. Snap rolls only make it to about the 270° point, where the air vehicle usually breaks from the stall. Inverted flight is good under power, but the glide is poor without power.

In general, the test pilot summarizes by saying that the Chinook is a solid, forgiving, predictable ultralight that is pleasant to fly.

Specifications

Wingspan	32 ft. 0 in.
Length	17 ft. 6 in.
Height	5 ft. 8 in.
Wing Area	140 sq. ft.
Engine Make, Model, HP	Rotax, 277, 28 hp.
Prop. Diameter/Pitch	48 in/30 in.
Reduction Ratio	2-to-1
Fuel Capacity/Consumption	5 gal./1 gph. cruise
Gross Weight	625 lbs.
Empty Weight	230 lbs.
Useful Load	395 lbs.
Wing Loading	3.1 psf.
Power Loading	15.3 lb/hp.
Design Load Factors	+5.5, -3
Construction Time	80 man-hrs.
Field Assembly Time	10 min. (Wings)
Pricing	$6,000. US, $7,495. Canadian

Flight Performance

Velocity Never Exceed	85 mph.
Top Level Speed	63 mph.
Cruise Speed	50-55 mph. @ 65% power
Stall Speed (in free air)	23-25 mph.
Sea Level Climb Rate	700-900 fpm. @ 35 mph.
Takeoff Run	100 ft. 2500 ft. (ASL)
Dist. Req'd. to clear 50 ft.	200 ft. 2500 ft. (ASL)
Landing Roll	100 ft.
Service Ceiling (100 fpm. climb)	18,500 ft.
Range at Cruise	150-200 mi.

L/D (Glide Ratio)   10-to-1 @ 35 mph.
Minimum Sink Rate   350 fpm. @ 32 mph. 2500 ASL (175
                                   Pilot)

Chinook WT-11
Birdman Enterprises LTD.
7939 Argyll Road
Edmonton, Alberta, Canada T6C 4A9
(403) 466-5370 or 466-2579
Jim Reimchen

Cascade Ultralights — Kasperwing 1-80

The Kasperwing 1-80 ultralight is a direct descendant of the Kasper BKB sailplane, invented and patented by Witold Kasper during the late '50's and early '60's. The airframe was originally based on the Fledgling hang glider, chosen as a research and development vehicle because of its simplicity, high strength, portability, and ease of modification or repair.

The first prototype was built from scratch during mid-1976 utilizing the stock sweep, dihedral, and airfoil configuration of the Fledge — except for the wingtip controls, which were designed around the aerodynamic principles suggested by Witold Kasper. Systematic flight testing and modifications allowed an understanding of the significance that each Kasper concept contributed to the aircraft's performance. The primary result was a wing that would not stall or spin. It was also stable about all three axis at all speeds, and had a sink rate of 160 fpm with a 150 pound pilot.

In keeping with the Kasper "vortex lift" theory, the wing could be flown with hands-off stability in a vertical descent. Yaw and roll control proved to be totally independent of the craft's forward speed.

Having proved the theory of extended aerodynamics with the glider, it was decided to add power. A low thrust line was chosen to minimize the problem

Fig. 1-20. The Kasperwing has the unique ability to perform nearly vertical descents under complete control.

of pitchovers when flying through turbulence. The centers of gravity and drag were also kept close together resulting in minimized drag and easier ground handling.

After several engines were tried, the designer settled on the 250cc Honda Odyssey of 23 hp. It delivers 170 pounds of static thrust through a 50" x 24" prop at 3,000 rpm, resulting in a 60 mph top speed and a climb rate of 650 fpm. Average engine life wide-open is 100 hours — more if the throttle is used conservatively. The throttle and mixture controls are located on a quadrant on the right side of the pilot frame, while the ignition is mounted on the steering yoke.

In order to realize the flight performance predicted by Kasper's theories, a special harness was developed to permit faster weight shifting than a hammock could allow. This enabled the pilot to make the precise CG (trim) changes necessary to properly control the craft and perform vertical descents and safe landings.

The wingtips were originally controlled by twist grips or dual sticks, but this proved to be awkward or confusing to some pilots. A butterfly wheel steering yoke was designed, incorporated the functions of two independent controls, and has the added feature of positively opening and closing the tips at any airspeed or altitude.

Aside from the overall performance and handling characteristics of the Kasperwing, its most unique feature is its ability to "mush" or fly below the stall without spinning or dropping the nose. The machine can literally "parachute" vertically at about 600-800 fpm riding on a span-wise vortex of

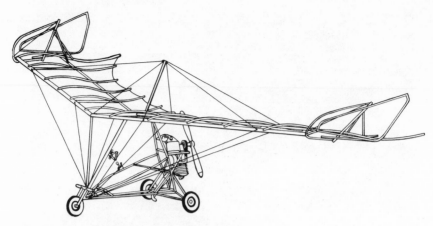

Fig. 1-21. Cutaway of Kasperwing shows basic construction.

air which shears off at the leading edge of the wing, forming a low pressure area — a phenomenon known as "vortex lift".

Because of the unique wingtip design, the machine can be turned and otherwise controlled in a vertical descent — the controls remain responsive independent of forward speed. This situation is similar to what a bird does when approaching a branch and "hovering down".

Complete kits, including engine and reduction drive, are available from Cascade. The wing is of presewn dacron sailcloth, ready to slip on over the airframe. All tubing, hardware, cable and necessary miscellaneous materials and components are included, along with step-by-step assembly and flying instructions. Kits, however, do not come with the harness or instruments, which are optional.

Other options offered are: a streamlined fairing with "clam shell" opening feature, composed of lightweight fiberglass and a lexan windshield — this should boost performance 20-30%; and still under development are leading edge devices for enhanced vortex generation. These two items ought to result in an L/D of 15-to-1 at 27 mph, a minimum sinking speed of 160 fpm, and an increase in cruise to 45 mph at 50% power.

The airplane is not recommended for novices.

Specifications

Wingspan	35 ft. 0 in.
Length	12 ft. 8 in.
Height	7 ft. 6 in.
Wing Area	180 sq. ft.
Engine Make, Model, HP	Zenoah, 23 hp.
Prop. Diameter/Pitch	54 in/27 in.
Reduction Ratio	2.5-to-1
Fuel Capacity/Consumption	2.5 gal./1 gph.
Gross Weight	395 lbs.
Empty Weight	175 lbs.

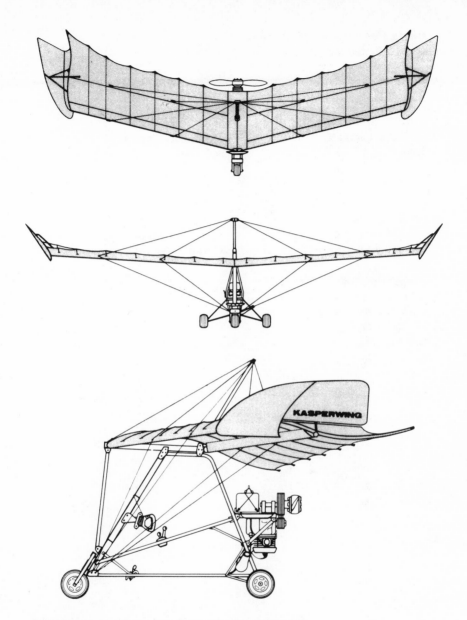

Fig. 1-22. Three-view drawing of the Kasperwing without pilot fairing.

Useful Load	220 lbs.
Wing Loading	2.2 psf.
Power Loading	16.5 lb/hp.
Design Load Factors	+7, -4
Construction Time	40 man-hrs.
Field Assembly Time	30 min.
Pricing	$4,450. (kit) $5,250. (assembled)

Flight Performance (150 pound pilot at sea level)

Velocity Never Exceed	N.A.
Top Level Speed	60 mph.
Cruise Speed	40 mph. @ 50% power
Stall Speed (in free air)	20 mph.
Sea Level Climb Rate	800 fpm. @ 28 mph.
Takeoff Run	75 ft.
Dist. Req'd. to clear 50 ft.	N.A.
Landing Roll	50 ft.
Service Ceiling (100 fpm. climb)	15,000 ft.
Range at Cruise	100 mi.
L/D (Glide Ratio)	10-to-1 @ 23 mph.
Minimum Sink Rate	200 fpm @ 18 mph.

Kasperwing 1-80
Cascade Ultralights, Inc.
1490-19th Ave. N.W.
Issaguah, WA 98027
(206) 392-0386
Leslie Grossruck

CGS Aviation — *Hawk B*

The Hawk is a single engine high wing monoplane with totally enclosed cabin and conventional three-axis aerodynamic controls.

The airplane is constructed primarily of aluminum tubing with a truss type fuselage and ladder frame wing. Two struts tie each wing panel to the fuselage. Landing gear can be taildragger, tricycle or pontoons, depending on personal requirements.

The Hawk's control system is unique to the ultralight industry in that the double surfaced wing incorporates both ailerons and three-position flaps. For takeoff the flaps can be lowered 15° to increase the coefficient of lift and decrease the takeoff distance. The flaps can be lowered further still for glide path control and to reduce landing speed.

The empennage is a standard cruciform with separate fin, rudder, stabilizer and elevator. The moveable surfaces are large and provide ample control at low speeds, especially since they are fully immersed in the propwash. Structurally, the tail surfaces are cantilevered aluminum tubing frames.

The powerplant is the popular Kawasaki 440 with reduction drive. It features a quiet efficient muffler and, turns a large diameter laminated wooden propeller.

The Hawk handles much like a J-3 Cub and affords a rolleage cockpit for added pilot protection, as well as a seatbelt-shoulder harness restraint system

Fig. 1-23. CGS Hawk has been referred to as an ultralight in lightplane clothing.

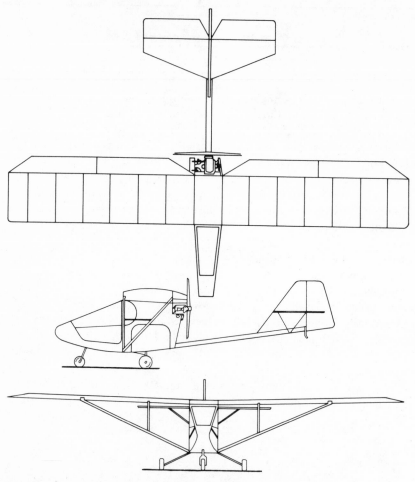

Fig. 1-24. Three-view drawing of the Hawk reveals its lightplane kinship.

The kit comes complete with engine. Optional accessories include: CMT, EGI, altimeter, ASI, tach, compass, wheel pants, position and strobe lights, cabin heater, electric start, dope and fabric wings, and Spitfire Liquid Cooled engine. The aircraft can be flown with the canopy on or off and is available from CGS Aviation, Inc.

Specifications

Wingspan	28 ft. 10 in.
Length	20 ft. 8 in.
Height	6 ft. 10½ in.
Wing Area	135 sq. ft.
Engine Make, Model, HP	Kawasaki 440, 35 hp.
Prop Diameter/Pitch	60 in./27 in.
Reduction Radio	2.37-to-1
Fuel Capacity/Consumption	5 gal./1.5 gph.

Gross Weight	530 lbs.
Empty Weight	251 lbs.
Useful Load	279 lbs.
Wing Loading	3.3 psf.
Power Loading	15.14 lb/hp
Design Load Factors	+4, -3
Construction Time	100 man-hrs.
Field Assembly Time	25 min.
Pricing	$6,345

Flight Performance

(460 pounds, calm, sea level)

Velocity Never Exceed	80 mph.
Top Level Speed	60 mph.
Cruise Speed	55-60 mph. @ 75% power
Stall Speed (in free air)	26 mph. with full flaps
Sea Level Climb Rate	600 fpm. @ 45 mph.
Takeoff Run	150 ft.
Dist. Req'd. to clear 50 ft.	N.A.
Landing Roll	95 ft. with full flaps
Service Ceiling (100 fpm. climb)	N.A.
Range at Cruise	150 mi.
L/D (Glide Ratio)	8.85-to-1 @ 42 mph.
Minimum Sink Rate	250 fpm. @ 30 mph.

Hawk Model B
CGS Aviation, Inc.
1305 Lloyd Road
Wickliffe, OH 44092
(216) 943-3064
Sales Manager

D

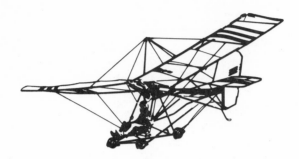

Diehl Aero-Nautical — XTC

Fig. 1-25. The XTC canard is a true amphibian, complete with center hull and retractable landing gear.

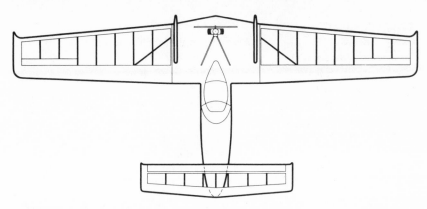

Fig. 1-26. Top view drawing of the XTC reveals its canard configuration.

The XTC is an amphibious, mid-wing canard with retractable landing gears and steerable nosewheel. It features three-axis controls via a side stick and is constructed of composite materials.

Kits are manufactured using aircraft materials and specifications, according to the factory. The fiberglass fuselage and wing sections are pre-molded, while the landing gear and control assemblies are prefabricated. It is claimed the aircraft can be built with everyday shop tools in a few weekends. Construction time is estimated at 100 man-hours.

The factory requires all prospective owners to take flight training prior to flying the XTC. Options include both ballistic and hand deployed parachutes.

Specifications

Wingspan	32 ft. 0 in.
Length	15 ft. 2 in.
Height	4 ft. 9 in.
Wing Area	150 sq. ft.
Engine Make, Model, HP	KFM 107 ER, 25 hp.
Prop Diameter/Pitch	52 in/22 in.
Reduction Radio	2.1-to-1
Fuel Capacity/Consumption	5 gal./.8 gph.
Gross Weight	500 lbs.
Empty Weight	247 lbs.
Useful Load	253 lbs.
Wing Loading	3.2 psf.
Power Loading	20 lb/hp.
Design Load Factors	+4, -4
Construction Time	100 man-hrs.
Field Assembly Time	15 min.
Pricing	$6,000. +

Flight Performance

Velocity Never Exceed	80 mph.

Top Level Speed

Cruise Speed

Stall Speed (in free air)

Sea Level Climb Rate

Takeoff Run

Dist. Req'd. to clear 50 ft.

Landing Roll

Service Ceiling (100 fpm. climb)

Range at Cruise

L/D (Glide Ratio)

Minimum Sink Rate

63 mph.

55 mph. @ 65% power

25 mph.

600 fpm. @ 40 mph.

100 ft.

400 ft.

200 ft.

Unknown

150 mi.

14-to-1 @ 40 mph.

250 fpm. @ 37 mph.

XTC
Diehl Aero-Nautical
1855 No. Elm
Jenks, OK 74037
(918) 299-4445
Dan Diehl

Eastern Ultralight — Snoop Series

The Snoops are cable braced, high wing monoplanes with tricycle landing gear, steerable nosewheel and three-axis aerodynamic controls. They are powered by the Cuyuna UL II-02, and come with a tuned exhaust.

The wings constructed on the ladder frame principle with leading and trailing edge spars, compression members and a diagonal. Cables from the pilot cage support lift loads, while a kingpost and cables support landing loads. The aluminum framed tail surfaces are supported by both tubing and cable to the pilot cage and kingpost.

The engine is mounted at the nose and drives a pusher propeller via a reduction unit at the wing's root trailing edge. The pilot sits at the center of gravity, eliminating the need to worry about trim changing with various weight pilots.

The basic Snoop model incorporates spoilerons for roll control, plus rudder and elevator for yaw and pitch. The wing is single surfaced, and allows a top level speed of 50 mph, with cruise in the 40 to 45 mph range. It is more suited to the beginning ultralight flyer.

The Snoop Plus is more for the experienced ultralight pilot and licensed pilot as well. It features a double surfaced wing with ailerons and flaps. Top

Fig. 1-27. The Snoop features a single surface wing with spoilers.

level speed is 63 mph, with cruise from 55 to 60 mph.

Options available include: choice of custom color finished airframe, floats, skis, nose fairing, windshield, complete cockpit enclosure, wheel pants, communications package, lifting package, and electric start. Accessory items include: flight suits, jackets, T-shirts, hats, patches, tote bags, wind socks, wing and tail covers, prop covers, and engine covers.

"SNOOP"

Specifications

Wingspan	33 ft.
Length	16 ft. 2 in.
Height	8 ft. 6 in.
Wing Area	165 sq. ft.
Engine Make, Model, HP	Cuyuna UL II-02 35 hp.
Prop Diameter/Pitch	54 in./27 in.
Reduction Ratio	2-to-1
Fuel Capacity/Consumption	3 gal./1½ gph.
Gross Weight	518 lbs.
Empty Weight	238 lbs.
Useful Load	280 lbs.
Wing Loading	3.1 psf.
Design Load Factors	5½ + 3½
Construction Time	30 man-hrs.
Field Assembly Time	45 min.
Pricing	$4,790

Fig. 1-28. The Snoop+ features a double surface wing with flaps and ailerons.

Flight Performance

Velocity Never Exceed	55 mph.
Top Level Speed	50 mph.
Cruise Speed	40-45 mph. @ 60% power
Stall Speed (in free air)	18 mph.
Sea Level Climb Rate	600 fpm.
Takeoff Run	50 ft.
Dist. Req'd. to clear 50 ft.	150 ft.
Landing Roll	100 ft.
Service Ceiling (100 fpm. climb)	N.A.
Range at Cruise	80 mi.
L/D (Glide Ratio)	7-to-1 @ 25 mph.
Minimum Sink Rate	N.A.

"SNOOP PLUS"

Specifications

Wingspan	30 ft.
Length	16 ft. 2 in.
Height	8 ft. 6 in.
Wing Area	150 sq. ft.
Engine Make, Model, HP	Cuyuna UL II-02
Prop Diameter/Pitch	54 in/27 in.
Reduction Ratio	2-to-1
Fuel Capacity/Consumption	3 gal./1½ gph.
Gross Weight	534 lbs.
Empty Weight	254 lbs.

Useful Load	280 lbs.
Wing Loading	3.5 psf.
Power Loading	N.A.
Design Load Factors	+5½, -3½
Construction Time	40 man-hrs.
Field Assembly Time	45 min.
Pricing	$5,790.

Flight Performance

Velocity Never Exceed	63 mph.
Top Level Speed	60 mph.
Cruise Speed	55 mph.
Stall Speed (in free air)	26 mph.
Sea Level Climb Rate	800 fpm.
Takeoff Run	100 ft.
Dist. Req'd. to clear 50 ft.	250 ft.
Landing Roll	150 ft.
Service Ceiling (100 fpm. climb)	N.A.
Range at Cruise	110 mi.
L/D (Glide Ratio)	5-to-1 @ 25 mph.
Minimum Sink Rate	N.A.

"SNOOP PLUS"
Eastern Ultralights
P.O. Box 424
Chatsworth, NJ 08019
(609) 726-1193
Donald L. Minner

Eipper Aircraft — Quicksilver Series

Fig. 1-29. The Eipper Quicksilver "E" couples weight shift to rudder and trim-vator controls. Pilot sits in moveable harness.

The Quicksilver is a tricycle landing geared, high wing, pusher monoplane which evolved from a hang glider by the same name, but there the similarity ends. Today's models feature a robust airframe and come with various control systems from weight shift augmented by rudder and elevator, all the way to conventional three-axis controls. It is without doubt, the largest selling design family today, and many other brands are copied from it. In fact, the term "ripsilver" has been coined by enthusiasts for other designs of similiar construction.

The Quicksilver's airframe can only be described as simple and basic, to the point of being an almost irreduceable minimum. It is your basic end loaded tension structure. The airframe consists primarily of anodized aluminum tubing structures held together by stainless steel cables, and covered with pre-sewn dacron sailcloth. The wing is constructed in a ladder type frame of leading and trailing edge tubes, with compression members serving as "rungs". A kingpost above the center of the wing supports the wing and tail against negative flight and landing loads. Fittings consist of stainless steel tangs and brackets, and injection molded saddles and plugs. The Quicksilver is available factory-built, or as a complete kit featuring no-weld, bolt-together assembly. A unique adjustable kingpost eliminates the need for turnbuckles or other wire tensioning devices.

A couple of aluminum tubing triangles jut down from the wing center section (root tube), surrounding the pilot. The rear triangle picks up the main landing gear, while the front one is mid-way between the mains and nosewheel. A series of triangles make up the undercarriage and spring suspension system. Two more tubular triangles are attached to the trailing edge and run aft to support the tail group. The entire lower airframe is interconnected via stainless steel cables.

The engine is hung below the root tube and drives a pusher propeller via an extension drive shaft and multi V-belt drive. The reduction drive is mounted at the rear of the root tube, turning the propeller between the longerons leading to the tail.

The Quicksilver "E"

The Quicksilver "E" is Eipper's least expensive model. It is powered by the single cylinder, 20 hp. Cuyuna "215" driving a 52 inch propeller via a V-belt reduction drive. It is controlled by the so-called "Variable C.G. Flight Control System" as pioneered in the original hang glider version. It consists essentially of a pilot weight shift harness, connected to the rudder and "trimavator" via control lines. This control system could be described as natural, in that the pilot moves his body in the direction he wants to go. It is also mechanically very simple, with a minimum of cables, pulleys and hinges.

Flight control is quite simple. Pitch control is accomplished by fore and aft movements while turning is done by side to side movements. The pilot's harness is connected to the moveable rudder and trimavator control surfaces via lines. A weight shift to the left turns the rudder to the left, yawing and rolling the air vehicle into a left turn. The yaw induces a roll via the ship's dihedral, a roll which is augmented by the pilot's weight being under the left wing. Once the bank is established, the pilot returns to the center and continues turning until he shifts to the right to level the wings, before re-centering. A small movement simultaneously aft brings the trimavator up to keep the ultralight's nose in the proper attitude throughout the turn. The "E's" large dihedral and low inertia make rolls light and quick.

Shifting forward lowers the nose and causes the aircraft to accelerate to a higher airspeed, and vice versa. Since the pilot can constitute over half of the total flight system's gross weight, body shift coupled to aerodynamic controls can be quite effective. Pitch control can remain relatively constant regardless of airspeed, even down to the stall. This is a distinct peculiarity of weight shift, due to the extra pitching moments that only weight shift can generate.

The "E" model's landing gear is unique, being called a "Tricycle-Tail Gear" landing gear system. It combines the tricycle undercarriage with a tail skid and works well because of the pilot's weight shifting capabilities. For taxiing on rough ground or making sharp turns, the pilot shifts aft, lifting the non-steerable nose wheel, and moves into the taildragger mode. He then swings into the desired turn direction, guns the engine and the prop blast swings the aircraft around. Takeoffs and straight taxiing are done in the tricycle mode, with the pilot's weight forward for improved acceleration and crosswind resistance.

The flight characteristics of the Quicksilver can only be described as docile and forgiving. In fact, it just might be the most docile of all the ultralights. Full

Fig. 1-30. The Quicksilver "MX" is the world's most popular ultralight. It features a single surface wing with pedal operated spoilers, and stick controlled rudder and elevator.

throttle and about 60 feet of ground roll gets you airborne at around 20 mph, and you'll climb at 300 fpm, depending on your weight. Stalls are straightforward, and proceeded by adequate warning. The airplane will not drop a wing or spin. The landing approach speed can vary between 25 and 30 mph, depending on wind conditions, but it is always advisable to carry a little extra airspeed. Since the stall speed is so low, a light headwind will make landing seem almost like a hover, allowing landings in very small areas. In general, this hybrid control system has proven to be quite adequate and the air vehicle is inherently stable with no apparent vices.

The Quicksilver "E" constitutes only a small fraction of Eipper's sales, since it appeals mostly to those with hang glider experience. Also, the advent of the two-seat trainer "ultralight," with conventional three-axis controls, all but spells the end to this model. It is, however, still available, and represents a bridge between our hang glider origins and modern day ultralights.

Quicksilver "MX"

The "MX" (multi-axis) version of the Quicksilver is currently the largest selling ultralight in the world. It is somewhat "beefier" than the "E" model, and is powered by the Rotax "377" of 33.5 hp. It shares the "E" model's single surface wing.

The heart of the "MX" is its control system which is activated by a side-mounted joystick and pedals. The stick is connected to the elevator via a pushrod and to the rudder through a housed "teleflex" cable. Roll control is normally induced by a rudder affected yaw, courtesy of the dihedral. Additional roll control is achieved with wing-mounted spoilers activated by the foot pedals. The spoilers may be deflected individually for a quicker roll rate with appropriate rudder. They may also be used to steepen descents or to

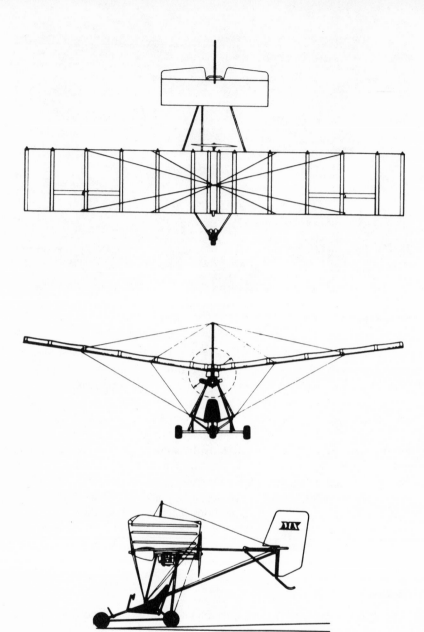

Fig. 1-31. Three-view drawing of the Quicksilver "MX".

make precision landings. The control system was evidently human engineered, for the positioning and actuation feel natural. To top it off, the pilot sits in a fully padded, naugahyde covered, fiberglass seat for support and comfort.

Like the Quicksilver "E", the "MX" features the same "Tricycle-Tailgear", combining the taxiing stability of the tricycle, and the manuverability of the

Fig. 1-32. Quicksilver "MXL" is Eipper's top-of-the-line model. Designed to the maximum allowable limits of FAR 103, it features a pedal operated rudder, and stick controlled elevator and spoilers. Is favored by licensed pilots.

taildragger. For taxiing on rough ground or making sharp turns, the pilot simply pulls back on the stick to lift the nosewheel and move into the taildragger mode. Propwash flowing over the tail surfaces allows the rudder to turn the air vehicle as up elevator is simultaneously applied. Takeoffs and landings are, of course, made in the tricycle gear mode. A single nosewheel brake is standard, while main wheel brakes can be added as an accessory.

The "MX" needs less than 70 feet to become airborne, and climbs out at 800 fpm. Stalls are straightforward and, preceeded by plenty of warning. The Quicksilver will not drop a wing, and its characteristics can be described as generally forgiving. Final approach speed is around 30 mph, and she stalls at about 24 mph. It cruises at 46 mph on 75% power.

The kit comes neatly packaged with all hardware shrink-wrapped on cardboard parts boards, and appropriately identified. Assembly requires 40 man-hours, with basic hand tools. All precision machining, drilling, cable swaging and major fabrication is done at the factory. Assembly is simply a bolt-together operation. The wing and tail surface coverings are pre-sewn stabilized dacron sailcloth, reinforced where needed, that are simply slipped on over the frames. No gluing or doping is required.

Options include the following items: 1) Ten special color schemes using various colors, such as: red, orange, gold, yellow, light green, dark green, light blue, dark blue, purple, white, brown or black. 2) Custom sails at additional cost. 3) Color coordinated nylon storage covers for the wing, tail, engine and propeller. 4) Retrofit kit to change control system over to pedal actuated rudder and stick actuated spoilers and elevator. 5) Pontoons to give your Quicksilver off-water capability. 6) Other accessories, including: snow skis, wheel pants, parachutes, and main wheel brakes.

Quicksilver "MXL"

The "MXL" is Eipper's top-of-the-line ultralight. It is similar to the "MX" but, features several modifications that enhance performance as well as a more conventional control system.

The most obvious difference is the double surfaced, shorter span wing. This ups the top speed about 10 mph, and reduces the fuel consumption. The climb rate is also improved, going from 800 fpm to 850 fpm.

Licensed pilots should be right at home in the "MXL". The control stick controls spoilers and elevator, while the rudder pedals control the rudder. Turns are easily made with the stick, while the roll rate can be enhanced with rudder. Unlike ailerons though, there is no adverse aileron yaw. The deflected spoiler reduces the lift of its wing panel, while creating the proper yaw force as well, making for basically coordinated turns. As it turns out though, rudder application alone will roll the aircraft just fine, even though the dihedral is only half of the "MX's".

In general, the "MXL" is more sensitive and offers more performance than the "MX". For that reason, it is not recommended for beginners as an entry level ultralight. The kit is packaged just like the "MX" and the same options and accessories are also available, as well.

Quicksilver "MX-II"

The "MX-II" is not really an ultralight, according to the FAA definition. It must be registered as an experimental aircraft and operated by a licensed pilot. It's primary purpose is for dual instruction of prospective ultralight pilots, but it could also be used by a licensed pilot for pleasure flying. It is heavier than the other Quicksilvers, and powered by a larger engine. Its stall speed is still 27 mph, but the top speed is only 45 mph. Performance with two on board is generally decreased, but adequate enough to serve as a trainer before one moves into the "hotter" ships.

Quicksilver® "E"®

Specifications

Wingspan	32 ft. 0 in.
Length	18 ft. 1 in.
Height	9 ft. 8 in.
Wing Area	160 sq. ft.
Engine Make, Model, HP	Cuyuna 215, 20 hp.
Prop Diameter/Pitch	52 in/32 in.
Reduction Ratio	2-to-1
Fuel Capacity/Consumption	3.5 gal./2.0 gph.
Gross Weight	227 lbs.
Empty Weight	210 lbs.
Useful Load	220 lbs.
Wing Loading	2.1 psf.

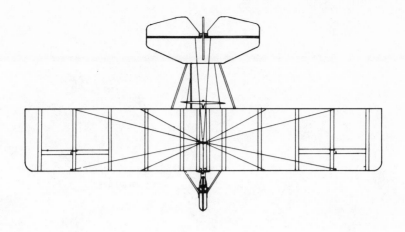

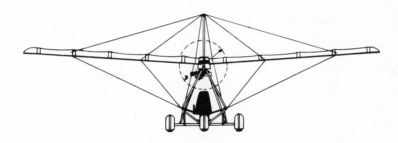

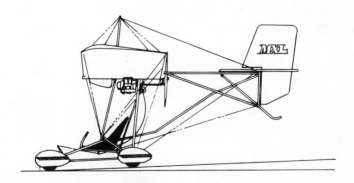

Fig. 1-33. Three-view drawing of the Quicksilver "MXL".

Power Loading	19 lb/hp.
Design Load Factors	+ 4.8 - 1.5
Construction Time	40 man-hrs.
Field Assembly Time	30 min.
Pricing	$3.995 F.O.B.

Fig. 1-34. The Quicksilver "MX-II" is built solely for the purpose of training students.

Flight Performance

Velocity Never Exceed	45 mph.
Top Level Speed	42 mph.
Cruise Speed	32 mph. @ 75% power
Stall Speed (in free air)	17 mph.
Sea Level Climb Rate	300 fpm
Takeoff Run	60 ft.
Dist. Req'd. to clear 50 ft.	210 ft.
Landing Roll	75 ft.
Service Ceiling (100 fpm climb)	14,000 ft.
Range at Cruise	68 mi.
L/D (Glide Ratio)	6.4-to-1
Minimum Sink Rate	300 fpm.

Quicksilver®MX®

Specifications

Wingspan	32 ft. 0 in.
Length	18 ft. 1 in.
Height	9 ft. 8 in.
Wing Area	160 sq. ft.
Engine Make, Model, HP	Rotax, Model 377, 33.5 hp.
Prop Diameter/Pitch	52 in/32 in.
Reduction Ratio	2-to-1
Fuel Capacity/Consumption	5 gal./2 gph. @ 55% power
Gross Weight	260 lbs.
Empty Weight	235 lbs.
Useful Load	290 lbs.
Wing Loading	3.28 psf.
Power Loading	15.6 lb/hp.

Stall Speed (in free air)	27 mph.
Sea Level Climb Rate	850 fpm. @ 41 mph.
Takeoff Run	75 ft.
Dist. Req'd. to clear 50 ft.	250 ft.
Design Load Factors	+5.8, -3.5
Construction Time	40 man-hrs.
Field Assembly Time	30 min.
Pricing	$4,950 F.O.B.

Flight Performance

Velocity Never Exceed	63 mph.
Top Level Speed	52 mph. @ Sea Level
Cruise Speed	.46 mph. @ 75% power
Stall Speed (in free air)	24 mph.
Sea Level Climb Rate	800 fpm @ 37 mph.
Takeoff Run	69 ft.
Dist. Req'd. to clear 50 ft.	220 ft.
Landing Roll	60 ft.
Service Ceiling (100 fpm. climb)	14,000 ft.
Range at Cruise	523 mi.
L/D (Glide Ratio)	7.8-to-1 @ 36 mph.
Minimum Sink Rate	450 fpm @ 36 mph.

Quicksilver® MXL®

Specifications

Wingspan	30 ft. 0 in.
Length	18 ft. 1 in.
Height	9 ft. 8 in.
Wing Area	150 sq. ft.
Engine Make, Model, HP	Rotax, Model 377, 33.5 HP
Prop Diameter/Pitch	52 in/32 in.
Reduction Ratio	2-to-1
Fuel Capacity/Consumption	5 gal./2 gph. @ 55% power
Gross Weight	268 lbs.
Empty Weight	252 lbs.
Useful Load	298 lbs.
Wing Loading	3.67 psf.
Power Loading	16.42 lb/hp.
Design Load Factors	+5.8 -3.5
Construction Time	40 man-hrs.
Field Assembly Time	30 min.
Pricing	$5,695 F.O.B.

Flight Performance

Velocity Never Exceed	74 mph.
Top Level Speed	61 mph.
Cruise Speed	54 mph. @ 75% power

Landing Roll	75 ft.
Service Ceiling (100 fpm climb)	14,000 ft.
Range at Cruise	61.4 mi.
L/D (Glide Ratio)	8.0-to-1 @ 41 mph.
Minimum Sink Rate	500 fpm. @ 41 mph.

Quicksilver® MXII®

Specifications

Wingspan	32 ft. 0 in.
Length	18 ft. 1 in.
Height	9 ft. 8 in.
Wing Area	160 sq. ft.
Engine Make, Model, HP	Rotax, Model 503, 46 hp.
Prop Diameter/Pitch	52 in/34 in.
Reduction Ratio	2-to-1
Fuel Capacity/Consumption	6.5 gal/2.1 gph. @ 55% power
Gross Weight	36/lbs.
Empty Weight	300 lbs.
Useful Load	400 lbs.
Wing Loading	4.375 psf.
Power Loading	15.38 lb/hp.
Design Load Factors	+5.8, -3.5
Construction Time	40 man-hrs.
Field Assembly Time	30 min.
Pricing	$6,495 F.O.B.

Flight Performance

Velocity Never Exceed	73 mph.
Top Level Speed	45 mph.
Cruise Speed	41 mph. @ 75% power
Stall Speed (in free air)	27 mph.
Sea Level Climb Rate	350 fpm. @ 39 mph.
Takeoff Run	100 ft.
Dist. Req'd. to clear 50 ft.	300 ft.
Landing Roll	100 ft.
Service Ceiling (100 fpm. climb)	14,000 ft.
Range at Cruise	63.4 mi.
L/D (Glide Ratio)	4.9-to-1 @ 40 mph.
Minimum Sink Rate	800 fpm. @ 40 mph.

Quicksilver® MXII®
Eipper Aircraft, Inc.
16531 Ynez Road
Rancho, CA 92390
(714) 676-3228
Eric R. Gilliatt, Marketing and Advertising Manager

F

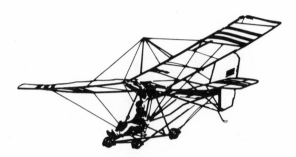

Fisher Flying Products — FP-101

Fig. 1-35. The Fisher FP-101 resembles an old Aeronca lightplane.

The "FP-101" is a high wing cabin monoplane, patterned after the Aeronca lightplane. It features conventional three-axis controls and tail-dragger landing gear. The airframe is primarily of wood and it is covered with fabric and doped.

The basic feature of this design is its use of geodetic structures. These consist essentially of a series of triangles formed by diagonal members between the airframe outline members. This technique is used in the spar, ribs, tail surfaces and fuselage, and offers excellent torsional rigidity. The designer says that "anybody that has ever built a balsawood model airplane can build the FP-101."

The landing gear is pre-welded at the factory and is fastened to the fuselage with six bolts. A shock cord suspension helps absorb bumps, but unless you touch down as slowly as possible, you will bounce.

The wing struts are aluminum tubing with jury struts. Both main struts are bolted to the rear landing gear legs and, of course, the underside of the wing.

The cabin is fairly roomy and features a center mounted stick, and rudder pedals. The instrument panel has plenty of room for the necessary instruments. A lexan windshield tames the blast from the prop.

The prototype stalled at 18 mph, making the air vehicle more susceptible to gusts. Since then, a clipped wing version has been made available with a higher stall speed, the ability to handle greater winds, and higher cruising speeds. Optional items include: brakes, electric start, wheel pants, and side curtains. The standard kit engine is the 40 hp Kawasaki, but other could be used. The airframe kit can be purchased without the engine.

Specifications

Wingspan	34 ft. 10 in. (29 ft. optional)
Length	16 ft. 6 in.
Height	5 ft. 8 in.
Wing Area	140 sq. ft.
Engine Make, Model, HP	40 hp. Kawasaki
Prop Diameter/Pitch	54 in/27 in.
Reduction Ratio	2.4-to-1
Fuel Capacity/Consumption	5 gal./2 gph.
Gross Weight	520 lbs.
Empty Weight	245 lbs.
Useful Load	275 lbs.
Wing Loading	3.5 psf. at 500 lb.
Power Loading	10.3 lb/hp.
Design Load Factors	+5, -2.5
Construction Time	200 man-hrs.
Field Assembly Time	10-20 min.
Pricing	$3,290 (airframe only $1,850)

Flight Performance

Velocity Never Exceed	70 mph.

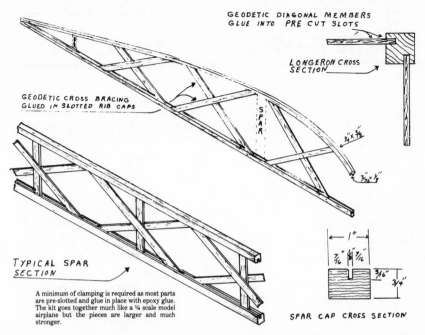

GEODETIC DIAGONAL MEMBERS
GLUE INTO PRE CUT SLOTS

LONGERON CROSS
SECTION

GEODETIC CROSS BRACING
GLUED IN SLOTTED RIB CAPS

SPAR

¼" x ¾"

³⁄₃₂" x ½"

TYPICAL SPAR
SECTION

A minimum of clamping is required as most parts
are pre-slotted and glue in place with epoxy glue.
The kit goes together much like a ¼ scale model
airplane but the pieces are larger and much
stronger.

1"

³⁄₁₆" ³⁄₁₆"

³⁄₁₆"

¾"

SPAR CAP CROSS SECTION

Fig. 1-36. A couple of drawings depicting the geodetic construction of the FP-101.

Top Level Speed	60 mph.
Cruise Speed	45-50 mph. @ 75% power
Stall Speed (in free air)	18 mph.
Sea Level Climb Rate	850 fpm @ 30 mph.
Takeoff Run	75-100 ft. short grass
Dist. Req'd. to clear 50 ft.	N.A.
Landing Roll	100 ft.
Service Ceiling (100 fpm. climb)	N.A.
Range at Cruise	90 mi. approx.
L/D (Glide Ratio)	11-to-1
Minimum Sink Rate	N.A.

FP-101
Fisher Flying Products
R #2, Box 282
South Webster, OH 45682
(614) 778-3185
Lana or Mike Fisher

Flight Designs — Jetwing ATV

The Jetwing is a weight shift controlled Trike suspended from a Demon hang glider. The wing is a double surfaced, battened Rogallo wing with form filled leading edges.

The Trike unit itself has a bungee shock cord suspended rear swing-axle, and spring steel suspended steerable nosewheel. The main wheels are 21 inch for operation from unprepared fields.

The wing is strengthened over a standard hang glider in order to carry the extra loads imposed by the trike. The powerplant is the twin-cylinder Kawasaki 440 fan cooled engine with CD ignition and recoil start direct drive.

Optional accessories include: Javelin 208 wing, floats, skis, airboat package, brakes, flight instruments and electric start.

The following is a pilot report by Dan Johnson, Publisher of *Whole Air* magazine, as published in the March/April 1982 issue.

Transitioning from hang gliders to the Flight Designs ATV (trike) is an experience of mixed emotions.

Excitement is present on either side of the fence. A new world is awaiting that first flight. Even true for pilots with other ultralight air time, you can expect the trike concept to be quite different. If you are a proponent of weight shift, you will love triking. If achieving soaring flight (on a motorized system) is important to you, the trike idea holds excellent promise.

Frankly though, do not concern yourself with soaring on the first flight. Not, mind you, that it cannot be accomplished; you simply ought to get the fundamentals down first. It will not even consume a whole day.

On the "darker" side of the fence is *fear*. One of the earlier transitioning flyers observed was a deeply experienced ultralight pilot. An airman whose credentials can make for endless "war stories," came in visibly shaken from his first encounter. He was also smiling so widely, that it seemed his face could crack in the cold morning air.

The mixed bag of emotions is extremely positive, overall; the mention of the fear is only to suggest that, indeed, this is a very different specie of flying animal.

In the case of the Jet Wing ATV (All Terrain Vehicle), the animal is a tiger, and on lift-off, you feel as though you have an especially fleet cat by the proverbial tail. But this is getting out of sequence — let us start nearer the beginning, and follow a sample transition through the steps. Since witnessing ten such transition experiences first-hand, a pattern for success has been discovered.

After extensive conversation on *exactly* how to proceed, and after getting nods of agreement on each step, the wise sequence of which seemed undeniable, two early transitions (let us call them Dave and Scotty) blasted off the runway in a crescendo of decibels, two-cycle smoke, fear and

Fig. 1-37. Flight Designs Jetwing ATV marries a Rogallo wing to a trike unit.

apprehension, seeking the safety of being airborne.

In both cases, perfect flights were achieved, and apologies were offered for so badly violating the careful steps each had planned and agreed to follow. Funny thing. The most important consideration, however, brought them back safely, as both are accomplished pilots who stayed with the flight till its satisfactory conclusion back on the tarmac. A novice would have been in big trouble. But a novice might have followed directions. Etch this into your mind before your initial trike experience arrives.

Beginning

Locate a good strip (probably your Flight Designs dealer has one), the kind usually sought for ultralight training. Hard surface assures smoothness, but a smooth grass strip will do just fine. A thousand feet or more is highly advised, with no significant obstacles/hazards in a surrounding perimeter of another thousand feet. Use *calm* winds only . . . zero is absolutely best.

Get used to the overall system by ground handling. Force yourself (or your friend) to spend at least twenty minutes doing nothing but taxiing and feeling out the throttle, specifically articulation of the throttle and the acceleration produced by various settings. [As yet the Flight Designs throttle does not hold its position so your hand must stay on it.] In *NO* event should the nosewheel lift off the ground during this part of preparation. Be careful. Use an airspeed indicator and keep the speed *below* 25 mph.

Next, go to "high speed" taxiing. It is possible, though tricky, to raise *just* the nosewheel. As the Jet Wing is balanced lightly over the nosewheel, and as acceleration is fast, the nose comes up *very* subtly, and in the aforementioned cases of Dave and Scotty, once the nose wheel was raised, the rest followed very rapidly. So advising another twenty minute session of "high speed" taxi has a specific point. The idea is to slowly, smoothly increase the speed to *nearly* 30 mph. (rotation or lift-off speed), then back off the throttle to about one-third to one-half. *NOT* all the way, however. At this time, while good forward motion is present, push the bar forward several times, pausing, relaxing, then pushing out again, each such time a little farther. [During the acceleration, hold the bar at trim, which is approximately above the knees.] When the energy dies down, slowing you to say, 15 mph., start the cycle again, by accelerating back to nearly, but not quite, 30 mph. In the initial push-outs, you may raise the nosewheel. This is why you reduce the throttle first, so as not to get airborne . . . not yet. But it will impart some extremely valuable information on pitch control, authority, and the sensation of how the trike carriage wants to swing underneath you. The importance of this is difficult to over-stress. When you feel you have gotten it down, do it a couple more times. You will be *so* glad you did.

Crow-hopping is a customary technique for training in ultralights. A new student should not get too high till more knowledge is gained. Crow-hopping in the Jet Wing is darn near impossible. Maybe it is not even advisable. Recall here, though, that this transition training method is *NOT* for beginners. Hang III, Intermediate skills are strongly recommended first. All this is to explain why the "high speed" taxi session is very important and should not be cut short. The next step will put you in the air and climbing at 700 fpm.

Blast Off

"Blast-off" may sound overly dramatic, but judge its accuracy *after* you have experienced it. Basically, once you are 100 feet in the air and climbing fast, you can relax. Until then, "alert" is the key word. It, and "lateral control." You tow pilots may comprehend this phrase very well, as the same instructions apply to a pop-start launch. Do not worry about a stall. At full power, you *cannot* stall the Jet Wing. And since forward speed is good (30 mph.), lateral response will be good, too. Use it! Stay all over that bar till you have stabilized in straight ahead, climbing flight. But again, this is out of sequence. Let us go back to the start of the runway, approach end, it is called.

Clear the traffic area first. The last thing you need is a distraction like a twin engine Baron zooming just overhead because you began your take-off run just as he was on final. It is also darn impolite, not to say dangerous.

Then smoothly add power to ¾ or more. That amount is not terribly critical. Move the bar forward to approximately full arm extension, and hold it there. The rolloff is surprisingly long. Remember, a wing like the Demon needs some airspeed to begin lifting, especially with the 115 pound Jet Wing package attached. Plan on 100-200 feet. A small (36 inch) propeller and prop air flow blockage are probably other factors, as is the need of the Kawasaki to wind up before max thrust is obtained.

So now, you are rolling down the runway, accelerating. As 30 mph. is approached, the nose will lift (distinctly but very smoothly) and when it does, the trike carriage will begin to move directly under the Center of Gravity. Now the nosewheel will be straight in front of you, the angle of attack very high (like towing, almost). When the carriage moves forward, you should relax your pushout, returning the bar to trim, above your knees, where trim remains regardless of power settings. If you have not already done so, add the rest of the throttle for sustained climb to 100 feet, and maintain lateral control precisely, correcting all course deviations as quickly as they can be recognized.

Do *NOT* release the throttle! This cannot be over-emphasized. Think about this all the while you are leading up to actual lift-off. The *most* common error of new ultralight students is releasing the throttle exactly at lift-off, as they are surprised by the rapid rotation and initial climb attitude. If this occurs without pull-in (body forward) a nose-in becomes very likely. This will do you and the Jet Wing no good at all.

Here is an iron-clad rule to commit to memory regarding powered craft. "The *throttle* controls the altitude; the *control bar* (or stick) *movement* controls the *speed.*"

Once at 100 feet or so, retard the throttle somewhat to help prolong engine life and aid cooling, and continue climbing. Keep a sharp eye for any other traffic. Maintain even power using your sense of sound; it is quite accurate. Relax. At least, try.

Maneuvers

At a thousand feet or so, you should quit gazing around and prepare to practice some maneuvers. Do some basic turns, right and left, at about 1/3 to 1/2 throttle. Then again, with steeper turns. After that, try a series of reversals, linked 180's or 360's. Do these shallow first, then steeper. If you have plenty of altitude, reduce the throttle to what is called "idle thrust," and repeat all the above.

This will cut your altitude, so climb back up. Clear both sides, plus front and rear of other traffic, then begin stall practice. Start at half throttle. Expecting only a mellow nose-over, stall and recover twice, then clear the area again. Always use whatever bar movement seems necessary to maintain lateral control throughout the stall. Do an accelerated stall (stall from 45° bank) experiencing stall at a much higher airspeed.

Now, repeat the above under full power. Expect a mush only, but extreme angle of attack. This will elevate you so that you can now do a third full repeat, but at idle thrust. Here you can expect a breaking nose-over. Clear the engine periodically by revving it, to assure the power will come on when you want it. Two-cycle engines "load up" at idle speeds.

Landings

Your last maneuver in this check-out flight should be a simulated landing. Imagine a runway at a thousand feet. An altimeter is handy for this, but references to a ridge (if available) will work. Pretend you are doing the real thing. One comforting thought about now is that the landing is one of the easiest maneuvers to do.

Line up with your "runway" once again maintaining precise lateral control. Control your approach altitude with power till the "field" is positively made. Make all throttle movements as smooth as possible. When you are sure that a steep glide will get you to the field, *slowly* release the throttle to idle thrust.

Start this while high. The sink rate as the propeller idles is 400 fpm. or so, and about 300 fpm. engine off. The glide will vary with atmospheric conditions but will not drop below 5:1, and can stay at 8:1. Adjust to these factors of your power-off descent rate. Keep a good airspeed, even as the ground rises up to you at a rapid closure rate, flare to "touchdown."

The touchdown will be much slower than the take-off roll, but is still rapid. A 25 mph. approach speed is recommended. Also, it may be useful to "pump" the bar, once the ground is close. This transmits a *feel* for pitch authority, and slows your forward speed incrementally, which in turn will continue your descent. Plan to finally use full arm extension in the flare out. Do *not* add power except to execute a go-around, and even a "little power to smoothen things out . . ." will more likely confuse the effort than aid it. Try it both ways later on, and decide for yourself. But now power has been preferred by all transition-ees to date.

Since this was a simulated landing, you should repeat the maneuver at least once before actualizing a real landing. Once on the runway again, you can finally relax, for real, then discuss your relative success with a knowledgeable friend or your instructor. Finally repeat the take-off and landing phases till you are quite comfortable. Twenty-five such repetitions are not unreasonable before you operate out of small fields or land out on a cross-country flight.

Evaluation

After my first experience with the Jet Wing ATV (but *not* my first trike experience), I had one word to sum up the feeling . . . S M O O T H.

The Jet Wing ATV operates powerfully yet more gracefully than *any* other ultralight I have flown. Of course, I am partial to modern hang gliders, enjoy the simplicity of weight shift, and prefer neutral stability (hence quick banking and light pitch pressure). It took some time before I would fly ten feet off the ground with confidence — a maneuver I enjoy in the Quicksilver. But thermalling the Jet Wing ATV was vastly more pleasurable.

I can do 360's *inside* a Quicksilver turning at a normal rate; can climb with the best of them; cruising with the faster craft; and can land easier than most other ultralights. Still, this is no beginner ship. Training a novice *can* be done, but should be approached with extreme trepidation!

But I can go soaring with just the wing, even including triking to the soaring site, disconnecting the carriage, and powering back home when the thermals die away. I can car-top the entire rig with ease in my little Datsun pick-up. I can set it up by myself in 15-20 minutes (though not the first times). And "cross-country" in the Jet Wing takes on a whole new significance.

The entire Jet Wing ATV sells for $4350, ready to fly. Since it is competitive in performance, and can still be just a glider too, it has no peers in my opinion, though this will be best realized by an intermediate or better pilot. The package is unique in the *entire* industry as it carries Product Liability Insurance [no one else has been able to afford this], and as such, dictates no trike-only sales at this time. But even this is under development, so by Spring of '82, you will probably be able to purchase just the trike carriage for your present wing, for about $2450. Once you have seen the system, first hand, I doubt you will quibble over the cost. The finish is exceptional (see *Whole Air*, Nov/Dec 1981).

And if you do not have a state-of-the-art wing, you ought to "jet" down to your Flight Designs dealer. A whole new world of flying awaits you.

Specifications

Wingspan	33 ft. 6 in.
Length	12 ft.
Height	12 ft.
Wing Area	175 sq. ft.
Engine Make, Model, HP	Kawasaki TA440A, 30 hp.
Prop Diameter/Pitch	N.A.
Reduction Ratio	N.A.
Fuel Capacity/Consumption	5 gal./1.25 gph.
Gross Weight	480 lbs.
Empty Weight	217 lbs.
Useful Load	235 lbs.
Wing Loading	2.74 psf.
Power Loading	16 lb/hp.
Design Load Factors	+4, -2
Construction Time	8 man-hrs.
Field Assembly Time	15 min.
Pricing	$3,600.

Flight Performance

Velocity Never Exceed	52 mph.
Top Level Speed	47 mph.
Cruise Speed	40 mph.
Stall Speed (in free air)	22 mph.
Sea Level Climb Rate	400 fpm. @ 37 mph.
Takeoff Run	50 ft.
Dist. Req'd. to clear 50 ft.	N.A.
Landing Roll	75 ft.
Service Ceiling (100 fpm climb)	10,000 ft.
Range at Cruise	160 mi.
L/D (Glide Ratio)	7-to-1 @ 25 mph.
Minimum Sink Rate	350 fpm. @ 23 mph.

Jetwing ATV
Flight Designs, Inc.
P.O. Box 1503
Salinas, CA 93902
(408) 758-6896
Matt O'Gwynn

Gemini International — Prospector

The Prospector is a twin engined, cable braced, high wing monoplane with upright V-tail, tricycle landing gear, and three-axis aerodynamic controls. Rudder pedals control the rudder, while a center mounted stick actuates the elevator and ailerons. The control system uses ball bearing pulleys.

The airframe features heavy duty 6061-T6 aluminum tubing and aircraft type fittings and cable. All assemblies are jig-built for accuracy and ease of manufacture. The wing is a basic ladder type frame with kingpost supported upper rigging, and lower rigging anchored to the undercarriage.

The flying surfaces are all pre-sewn dacron sailcloth envelopes that slip on over the frames. A fabric fairing envelope is also available for the fuselage tubes to completely enclose the pilot for comfort. The pilot sits on a canvas type seat below the wing.

The standard powerplants consist of two wing leading edge mounted 18 hp. solo engines with direct drives, featuring recoil starting. The landing gear includes 10 inch wheels, and a steerable nosewheel and optional brake.

The flying characteristics are docile with no surprises. An airspeed indicator is standard.

Fig. 1-38. Hummingbird Prospector with optional fuselage fairing covers.

Optional accessories include: flight instruments, cover bags, floats, propellers, 16 inch wheels, skis and custom color fabric.

The aircraft is car-toppable and each one is built and test flown before delivery. Contact Gemini International for further information.

Specifications

Wingspan	34 ft.
Length	21 ft.
Height	8 ft.
Wing Area	163 sq. ft.
Engine Make, Model, HP	2 solo 210s, 18 hp. each
Prop Diameter/Pitch	36 in/24 in.
Reduction Ratio	Direct drive
Fuel Capacity/Consumption	4.4 gal./1.5 gph.
Gross Weight	527 lbs.
Empty Weight	207 lbs.
Useful Load	320 lbs.
Wing Loading	3.23 psf.
Power Loading	14.64 lb/hp.
Design Load Factors	+4.5, -3.5
Construction Time	Factory built
Field Assembly Time	35 min.
Pricing	$6,995.

Flight Performance

Velocity Never Exceed	65 mph.
Top Level Speed	55 mph.

Cruise Speed	35-40 mph.
Stall Speed (in free air)	21 mph.
Sea Level Climb Rate	850 fpm. @ 27 mph.
Takeoff Run	100 ft.
Dist. Req'd. to clear 50 ft.	N.A.
Landing Roll	75 ft.
Service Ceiling (100 fpm. climb)	15,000 ft.
Range at Cruise	100 mi.
L/D (Glide Ratio)	10-to-1
Minimum Sink Rate	300 fpm. @ 27 mph.

Prospector
Gemini International, Inc.
1080 Linda Way, #2
Sparks, NV 89431
(702) 331-3638
Ed Sweeney

Gemini International — Model 103

Fig. 1-39. Hummingbird model 103 was designed to provide the maximum performance allowable under FAR 103.

The Model 103 is similar in appearance and construction to the Prospector, except that the wing is strut braced. It offers slightly improved performance, and a greatly reduced field assembly time. It is available as both a kit and in factory-built form. Various options are available for customizing purposes.

Specifications

Wingspan	36 ft.
Length	21 ft.
Height	4 ft. 6 in.
Wing Area	163 sq. ft.
Engine Make, Model, HP	2 solo 210s, 18 hp. each
Prop Diameter/Pitch	36 in/24 in.
Reduction Ratio	Direct drive
Fuel Capacity/Consumption	4.5 gal.
Gross Weight	527 lbs.
Empty Weight	240 lbs.
Useful Load	287 lbs.
Wing Loading	3.23 psf.
Power Loading	14.64 lb/hp.
Design Load Factors	+4.5, -3.5

Construction Time	N.A.
Field Assembly Time	15 min.
Pricing	$5,495.

Flight Performance

Velocity Never Exceed	70 mph.
Top Level Speed	60 mph.
Cruise Speed	45-50 mph.
Stall Speed (in free air)	20 mph.
Sea Level Climb Rate	900 fpm. @30 mph.
Takeoff Run	N.A.
Dist. Req'd. to clear 50 ft.	N.A.
Landing Roll	N.A.
Service Ceiling (100 fpm. climb)	N.A.
Range at Cruise	N.A.
L/D (Glide Ratio)	11-to-1
Minimum Sink Rate	N.A.

Hummingbird Model 103
Gemini International, Inc.
1080 Linda Way, #2
Sparks, NV 89431
(702) 331-3638
Ed Sweeney

Golden Age Aircraft — *Waco II*

The Waco II is an open cockpit taildragger biplane with tractor engine. It features three-axis aerodynamic controls via stick and rudder pedals. It is sold factory built.

The ultralight is constructed with a fuselage of welded 4130 steel tubing. The wings use stamped aluminum ribs and built up aluminum spars. "N" struts connect the two wings, which are wire braced to the fuselage and cabane struts. The cockpit features a wood grained instrument panel, and all necessary controls. The entire airframe is covered with 2.8 oz. Ceconite and doped.

Power is supplied by the Global 35 hp. four stroker, which runs on either auto gas or avgas. It features aircraft grade castings, crossflow combustion, an integrated fuel intake system, and a counterbalanced forged steel crankshaft. Fuel consumption is approximately 1.8 gph.

The Waco II Super Deluxe version includes these items as standard: brakes, custom prop, seat and shoulder belts, 150 mph. airspeed indicator, tuned exhaust, wheel pants, circular engine cowling, altimeter, compass, electric tach, electric clock, CHT, EGT, electric Hobbs hour meter, 720 channel VHF radio, molded wing tips, and wing fairing.

The air vehicle is available in three different versions and prices: the Standard for $6,995., the Deluxe for $8,695., and the Super Deluxe for $9,987. Factory options include: 10 channel radio, 720 channel radio, 200

Fig. 1-40. Golden Age Aircraft's Waco II, recalls a bygone era of flight.

channel navigation system, floats, chair parachute, cockpit enclosure, 52 hp. engine, and a trailer.

Specifications

Wingspan	26 ft. 0 in.
Length	18 ft. 6 in.
Height	6 ft. 3 in.
Wing Area	168 sq. ft.
Engine Make, Model, HP	Global 900cc, 35 hp.
Prop Diameter/Pitch	58 in/27 in.
Fuel Capacity/Consumption	5 gal./1.8 gph.
Gross Weight	536 lbs.
Empty Weight	248 lbs.
Useful Load	288 lbs.
Wing Loading	3.19 psf.
Power Loading	15.31 lb/hp.
Design Load Factors	+6, -4
Construction	Factory Built
Field Assembly Time	30 min.
Pricing	$6,995.

Flight Performance

Velocity Never Exceed	110 mph.
Top Level Speed	63 mph.
Cruise Speed	60 mph. @ 60% power
Stall Speed (in free air)	26 mph.
Sea Level Climb Rate	650 fpm. @ 50 mph.
Takeoff Run	150 ft.
Dist. Req'd. to clear 50 ft.	225 ft.
Landing Roll	100 ft.
Service Ceiling (100 fpm. climb)	16,000 ft. (Est.)
Range at Cruise	180 mi.
L/D (Glide Ratio)	13-to-1 @ 43 mph.
Minimum Sink Rate	150 fpm. @ 38 mph.

Waco II
Golden Age Aircraft Co.
P.O. Box 846
Worthington, Ohio 43085
(614) 431-1277
Gene Eubanks

Goldwing — UL

Fig. 1-41. Goldwing UL is a foam and fiberglass composite designed for those who want something different.

The Goldwing UL is an ultralight aircraft of the canard configuration. Conventional three-axis controls are incorporated into this all molded sandwich construction, foam-fiberglass-carbon graphite and Kevlar composite air vehicle. Handling is described as straightforward and docile with very forgiving characteristics. It is sold only in a completely ready-to-fly condition.

The nose-mounted canard not only provides lift, but also pitch stability and control. Winglets provide directional stability while increasing the effective aspect ratio, without a sacrifice in handling. Split rudders produce yaw while maintaining the winglet advantage. Spoilers and ailerons are used simultaneously for roll control at all speeds. The fully independent three-axis control system enables the Goldwing to handle crosswind takeoffs and landings.

The "UL" is a total re-design of the standard Goldwing homebuilt version, featuring: a refined squared-off fuselage, new lighter and wider landing gear, a windshield, upholstered seat, light power package and graphite cantilevered spar structure. Other standard features include: built-in tie downs, airspeed indicator, and seat belt and shoulder harness. The base powerplant is the 25 hp. Zenoah single cylinder two-stroke, and the 37 hp. Kawasaki is optional. A low const trailer is also available.

Performance with the Zenoah engine is something like this. Full throttle at sea level gives a climb of over 500 fpm. at 45 mph. At the economy cruise

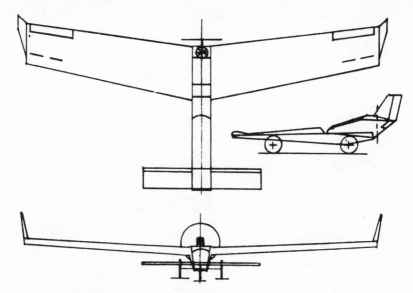

Fig. 1-42. Three-view drawing of the Goldwing UL canard.

setting of 50% throttle, the airspeed should be around 48 mph., while fuel consumption drops to one gallon per hour. The top level speed is 63 mph. per FAR 103, and Vne is 70 mph.

During stall and spin testing, the original Goldwing prototype was capable of being flown with full aft stick at an indicated 27 mph, while maintaining full control at all power settings. The canard would not stall unless forced into an accelerated stall. In that case, the canard would rise above the horizon, make a gentle break at 24 mph., and then rise back up to the horizon where it would remain, with the stick full aft.

Spins were attempted repeatedly by forcing an accelerated stall, then kicking in full rudder. The nose dropped down to the horizon, while the wingtip dropped into a 30 degree bank, resulting in a slow speed turn. The Goldwing appears to be very spin resistant.

Specifications

Wingspan	30 ft.
Length	12 ft.
Height	5 ft. 6 in. (winglets)
Wing Area	140 sq. ft.
Engine Make, Model, HP	Zenoah, 25 hp
Prop Diameter/Pitch	N.A.
Reduction Ratio	2.25-to-1
Fuel Capacity/Consumption	3 gal./1 gph.
Gross Weight	540 lbs.
Empty Weight	250 lbs.
Useful Load	290 lbs.
Wing Loading	4.22 psf.

Power Loading	21.6 lb/hp.
Design Load Factors	+3.8, -1.8
Construction Time	Factory built
Field Assembly Time	15 min.
Pricing	$7,595.

Flight Performance

Velocity Never Exceed	70 mph.
Top Level Speed	63 mph.
Cruise Speed	55 mph. @ 75% power
Stall Speed (in free air)	26 mph. (canard)
Sea Level Climb Rate	500 fpm. @ 45 mph.
Takeoff Run	150 ft.
Dist. Req'd. to clear 50 ft.	N.A.
Landing Roll	200 ft.
Service Ceiling (100 fpm. climb)	N.A.
Range at Cruise	125 mi.
L/D (Glide Ratio)	16-to-1 @ 42 mph
Minimum Sink Rate	325 fpm. @ 35 mph.

Goldwing "UL"
Goldwing, Ltd.
Amador County Airport
PO Box 1123
Jackson, CA 95642
(209) 223-0384

Greenwood Aircraft — *Witch*

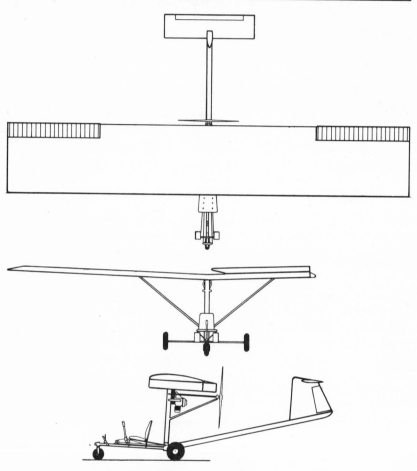

Fig. 1-43. Three-view drawing of the Greenwood Aircraft Witch.

The Witch is a single engine pusher monoplane with a T-tail and three-axis aerodynamic controls. Its landing gear is designed to facilitate over the road towing.

The ultralight is constructed of metal and wood. The fuselage is 4130 steel, while the tail and tail boom are aluminum. The wings are made of foam ribs capped with mahogany plywood cap strips.

The prototype featured a wing that folded and rotated to facilitate towing and storage, while all controls remained connected. Since the prototype was made however, several modifications have been made, the wing attachment system being one of them. Contact Greenwood Aircraft for further details.

Specifications

Wingspan	31 ft. 6 in.
Length	18 ft. 5 in.
Height	5 ft. 1 in.
Wing Area	140 sq. ft.
Engine Make, Model, HP	Zenoah G25B, 23 hp.
Prop Diameter/Pitch	60 in.
Reduction Ratio	N.A.
Fuel Capacity/Consumption	2½ gal./1 gph.
Gross Weight	435 lbs.
Empty Weight	220 lbs.
Useful Load	215 lbs.
Wing Loading	3.11 psf.
Power Loading	21.75 lb/hp.
Design Load Factors	N.A.
Construction Time	N.A.
Field Assembly Time	10 min.
Pricing	$5,800.

Flight Performance

Velocity Never Exceed	100 mph.
Top Level Speed	50 mph.
Cruise Speed	45 mph. @ 75% power
Stall Speed (in free air)	27 mph.
Sea Level Climb Rate	810 fpm.
Takeoff Run	200 ft.
Dist. Req'd. to clear 50 ft.	N.A.
Landing Roll	250 ft.
Service Ceiling (100 fpm. climb)	14,000 ft.
Range at Cruise	90 mi.
L/D (Glide Ratio)	N.A.
Minimum Sink Rate	N.A.

Witch
Greenwood Aircraft, Inc.
P.O. Box 401
Alexandria, MN 56308
(612) 762-2020
John Hall

HighCraft — *Bucaneer*

The Bucaneer is a cable braced, high wing monoplane with pusher propeller. It features three-axis aerodynamic controls, and a cruciform tail.

The air vehicle is constructed by the classic ultralight methods using aluminum tubing frames braced with a kingpost and cables. Three different models are available, all with a double surfaced wing. (1) The standard model is an open frame type, universal to the industry. (2) By attaching an optional pod/windscreen assembly, the standard becomes the deluxe streamlined version. (3) This version is an amphibian, featuring retractable main gear and tail wheel, along with a fiberglass reinforced hull. Flotation stability is achieved by a sponson mounted near each wing's outboard compression strut.

All versions are sold as pre-drilled, bolt-together kits. Optional features include side screens and a heater for high altitude and/or winter flying.

Specifications

Wingspan   35 ft. 0 in.
Length   N.A.

Fig. 1-44. Highcraft Bucaneer is an amphibious design in a conventional configuration.

Height	N.A.
Wing Area	147 sq. ft.
Engine Make, Model, HP	Rotax 277, 28 hp.
Prop Diameter/Pitch	60 in/42 in.
Reduction Ratio	3-to-1
Fuel Capacity/Consumption	5 gal./1.5 gph.
Gross Weight	453 lbs.
Empty Weight	228 lbs.
Useful Load	225 lbs.
Wing Loading	3.26 psf.
Power Loading	16.18 lb/hp.
Design Load Factors	N.A.
Construction Time	N.A.
Field Assembly Time	N.A.
Pricing	N.A.

Flight Performance

Velocity Never Exceed	75 mph.
Top Level Speed	50 mph.
Cruise Speed	45 mph. @ 75% power
Stall Speed (in free air)	18 mph.
Sea Level Climb Rate	600 fpm.
Takeoff Run	100 ft.
Dist. Req'd. to clear 50 ft.	N.A.
Landing Roll	75 ft.

Service Ceiling (100 fpm. climb)	N.A.
Range at Cruise	N.A.
L/D (Glide Ratio)	N.A.
Minimum Sink Rate	N.A.

Buccaneer
HighCraft Corporation
P.O. Box 899
Longwood, FL 32750
(305) 831-6688

Hoverair — Drifter

The Drifter is an ultralight hot air balloon. It first flew in England in 1979, where it is manufactured by Colt Balloons, Ltd. It uses the same aircraft grade components as the larger balloons.

The envelope is made of ripstop nylon and is available in a variety of colors. A Nomex mouth is included to help protect against burn damage while inflating. Stainless steel aircraft grade cables and four quick disconnect links attach the envelope to the backpack unit. Deflation is accomplished through a direct action parachute top, rigged with an all Kevlar cord system. The Drifter is normally supplied with a 20,000 cu. ft. envelope, but a 16,000 cu. ft. model is available on special order.

The Drifter back pack disassembles into three main units: 1) burner swivel and support structure, 2) LPG tank, and 3) harness and shoulder bracket.

The burner unit was developed specifically for the Drifter because the demand on a small burner is different from the larger models. It produces a sharp pencil-like flame to ease inflation and avoid burner damage around the mouth. It also has fast and complete combustion so as not to overheat the envelope crown. The unit has a high power to weight ratio.

The swivel consists of a hard aluminum load ring running on three sealed ball bearings. This minimizes friction and allows easy repositioning of the pilot. The load from the swivel ring is transferred through a steel tube to the heater tank collar.

Fig. 1-45. Hoverair Drifter is a one-man, hot air balloon designed for ultralight flyers. It collapses into a rather small package.

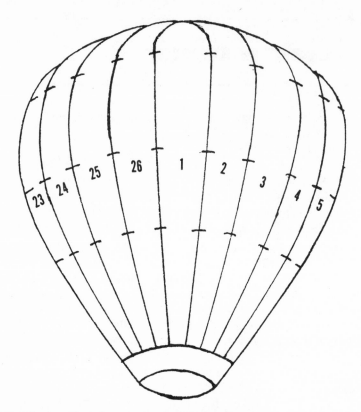

Fig. 1-46. A drawing of the balloon envelop depicting the various gores.

The LPG heater tank is a 10 gallon aluminum version, to which the shoulder brackets are attached. Space is also provided for the electronic lighter and the fuel level warning system. The pilot light can be lit instantly by operating the ignition button on the right hand shoulder bracket. The spark generator is the piezoelectric type requiring no batteries or maintenance. The fuel tank sends a signal at a present level to a buzzer inside the left hand shoulder bracket. This unit uses a 9 volt dry battery for power and is deactivated with an exterior toggle switch. A pyrometer for measuring temperature, is located in the envelope crown and completes the list of standard instrumentation.

The pilot's harness was quite time consuming to design, according to the factory. It had to be just so to provide maximum comfort. All parts are stressed to a minimum of 2000 pounds, and most actually have a 5000 pound proof. The harness webbing itself has a breaking strength of 6000 pounds. Also provided for is the quick disconnect system which attaches with two Capewell locks, and the optional emergency parachute.

When not in use, the Drifter folds down into two carrying bags. One is the size of a duffel bag, while the other is the size of a large suitcase. The Drifter can be carried aboard commercial airlines as check-on baggage.

An instruction course developed by an FAA Designated Balloon Flight Examiner is included in the purchase price. Even though a license is not required by the FAA, special knowledge is definitely needed to operate the balloon. The course consists of a Balloon Pilot's Manual, videotape instructions from set-up to deflation, and an examination to test your knowledge of the skills you'll need to have aloft.

Seating

One person up to 300 pounds in weight, including harness.

Weights

Empty — 95 lbs.
With propane — 137 lbs.

Envelope

26 gore rip stop nylon with parachute top and Kevlar cord for quick deflation. Choice of over a dozen colors.

Burner

Stainless steel tube construction, producing seven million BTU/HR. Propane fueled, piezoelectric ignition.

Tank

Ten gallon aluminum tank with quick disconnect couplings and low propane level warning buzzer.

Standard Instrumentation

1. Low fuel level warning buzzer.
2. Piezoelectric flame igniter.
3. Pyrometer for measuring envelope temperature.

Carrying Bags

Two cordura bags with velcro closures contain the complete Drifter when deflated.

Drifter
Hoverair, Ltd.
1385 Fairfax Dr. Unit B
San Francisco, CA 94124
(415) 756-0330
Stan Swansby

Hovey — *Delta Bird*

The Delta Bird is a tractor biplane with taildragger landing gear and three-axis aerodynamic controls. It is marketed by the designer in plan form only, however all materials are available from Ken Knowles Sport Aircraft, Inc. Construction is simple, and the designer claims the air vehicle can be built by one man working alone with no special tools or skills.

The fuselage is basically an "A"-frame with an added keel structure to carry the engine and landing gear loads. 6061-T6 aluminum tubing is used throughout. Tube stubs at four points on each side are used for wing spar attachments. The fuel tank is mounted overhead and fills the gap between the upper wing panels.

The tail boom is a three inch aluminum tube, the structure being attached to the fuselage frame by two lower and one upper bolt so that it may be disassembled for storage and transport. The engine is mounted on four rubber shock mounts that tie onto a $\frac{1}{8}''$ aluminum plate supported by three fuselage tubes.

The wing structure is a ladder frame with compression members and diagonals forming a Warren Truss, to carry wing bending as well as drag/anti-drag loads. The ribs are $\frac{1}{2}''$ diameter aluminum tubes hand formed to an airfoil curve. Full span ailerons are used on the upper wing panels only.

Fig. 1-47. Hovey Delta Bird captures the romance of the biplane era. It's constructed of typical ultralight materials.

A set of three eye bolt and clevis hinges tie the one inch diameter aileron spar to the wing aft spar. Aileron ribs and trailing edges are also ½" diameter aluminum tubing. Aluminum sheet gussets and pop rivets are used at all joints.

The empennage (tail group) is fabricated from one inch diameter tubes. All tube bends are made with a common electricians conduit bender. Sheet metal gussets and pop rivets are used at all joints. The horizontal tail is removeable for transport. Three pairs of eye bolts are used for the elevator hinges, while two pairs are used for the rudder hinge. All flying surfaces are covered with 1.8 oz. heat shrink dacron, glued to the airframe with "Fab-Tac" cement.

The landing gear consists of aluminum tubing pop riveted to steel tube end fittings, which simplify alignment and rigging. Bungee cords at the centerline provide shock absorption. The main wheels are the five inch diameter go-kart type. The steerable tailwheel is a prefabricatd unit that hooks to the rudder cables. Three aluminum leaf springs provide shock absorption.

The control system consists of a center mounted control stick for pitch and roll, while rudder pedals control yaw. A quadrant type throttle control is positioned for left hand operation. The tail controls are moved via 3/32-inch cables, which the ailerons are pushrod operated. Torsional springs at the rudder pedal pivot points provide cable tensioning and pedal positioning. Turnbuckles provide stick positioning and cable tension.

The plans are completely detailed to-scale, presented on ten 17 x 22 sheets of lithographic prints. Conventional aircraft drafting practice is used with the inch decimal system of dimensioning. Sections and views are taken where needed. Each part is identified by a dash number of the drawing it is shown on. Wing rib tubes and airfoil shapes are shown full scale. A ½-inch plywood tool for hand bending ribs is also detailed on the prints.

An instruction book is also included with the plans to assist the builder in constructing and assembling the Delta Bird. Aligning, rigging, weight and balance checking as well as flight operations are included. Step by step construction sequences are described with do's and don't's suggested. Initial flight test and flight check out procedures with flight limitations are included. All plan sets are serialized and follow-up notices are sent out for critical revisions as necessary.

The wide track landing gear and steerable tailwheel are said to provide excellent directional control through speeds where rudder control is effective. Elevator control becomes effective immediately upon application of power. There is no reported tendency to groundloop or nose over. There is no provision for brakes, however Ken Brock Mfg., Inc. has a set of miniature hydraulic brakes designed specifically for their five-inch diameter wheels which are under development.

The designer claims responsiveness in pitch, roll and yaw is positive but not sensitive in all modes of flight. There is no noticeable pitch trim change with addition or reduction of power and engine torque is not felt. Some adverse roll/yaw coupling may be noticed with uncoordinated control inputs, however, the rudder is very effective in handling this. It is virtually impossible to stall the Delta Bird. As the stall is approached, a mush or sink develops at 26 mph. with no significant change in attitude. If the stick is held back, the sink will continue until the stick is moved forward for recovery. Power may be used to reduce the sink rate.

No sudden break or loss of control will occur even at bank angles of 45°. Due to the limited speed range, high speed stalls in pull-ups or steep turns are not encountered. A violent pitch-up manuever at high speed to extreme pitch angles will produce a true stall. However, doing this is really aerobatic, and the Delta Bird is not rated for aerobatics.

Spin tests have not been conducted because the designer feels spins cannot be inadvertently encountered in the Delta Bird. Stability is positive about all three axis, with no hunting or flutter.

Takeoffs are done in a normal manner with no tricky rudder action required. Acceleration is rapid and rotation is made at 30-35 mph. Climb angles are accordingly steep. The high drag of the Biplane configuration results in an L/D of 6 to 1. Power off landings retain full control through the flare.

Normal landings can be full stall (three point) or wheel type. There is no tendency to porpoise or groundloop. Both takeoff and landing require less than 250 feet of ground roll.

Specifications

Wingspan	24 ft. 0 in.
Length	15 ft. 0 in.
Height	6 ft. 0 in.
Wing Area	152 sq. ft.
Engine Make, Model, HP	Cuyuna 430R, 30 hp.
Prop. Diameter/Pitch	54 in/27 in.
Reduction Ratio	2-to-1
Fuel Capacity/Consumption	3.5 gal./2.5 gph.
Gross Weight	420 lbs.
Empty Weight	218 lbs.
Useful Load	202 lbs.
Wing Loading	2.76 psf.
Power Loading	14 lb/hp.
Design Load Factors	+3, -3
Construction Time	N.A.
Field Assembly Time	30 min.
Pricing	N.A. (The ultralight is plans-built.)

Flight Performance

Velocity Never Exceed	60 mph.
Top Level Speed	60 mph.
Cruise Speed	45 mph. @ 42% power
Stall Speed (in free air)	26 mph.
Sea Level Climb Rate	400 fpm.
Takeoff Run	250 ft.

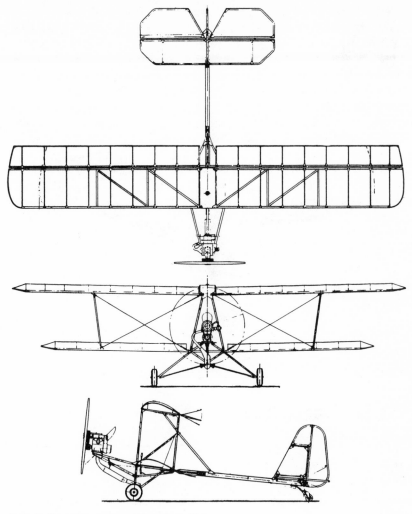

Fig. 1-48. Three-view drawing of Hovey Delta Bird.

Dist. Req'd. to clear 50 ft.	N.A.
Landing Roll	250 ft.
Service Ceiling (100 fpm. climb)	N.A.
Range at Cruise	50 mi.
L/D (Glide Ratio)	6-to-1
Minimum Sink Rate	N.A.

Delta Bird
Aircraft Specialties
Box 1074
Canyon Country, CA 91251
(805) 252-4054
Bob Hovey

K

Kolb Company — *Flyer*

Fig. 1-49. The Kolb Flyer traces its beginnings back to the late 1960s. Features a strut-braced wing and twin-engines.

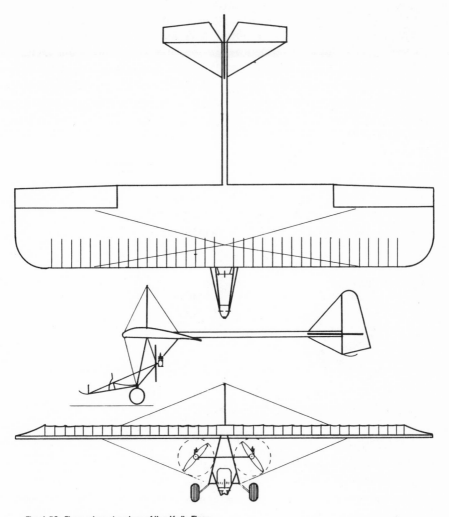

Fig. 1-50. Three-view drawing of the Kolb Flyer.

The Kolb Flyer is a conventionally controlled high wing monoplane with twin engines and tail dragger landing gear.

Interestingly, the Flyer's heritage goes back to 1970, when the original prototype was first flown. At that time it was a "just-for-fun" project, which was flown, then shelved until 1980. At that time, it was restored and displayed at Oshkosh, where much interest was received. The original direct drive McCullochs were replaced by geared Stihl chain saw engines which worked well, but were thought too expensive.

After being shown at Tullahoma 1980, a new Flyer was built with wire-braced wings, instead of struts, for greater strength with less weight, while allowing a shorter set-up and take-down time. Other small modifications were incorporated such as different wheels, more comfortable seating and a slightly more compact structure. The engines are now direct drive 16 hp. Solos.

The aircraft is capable of being flown on one engine, with no yaw difficulty from an engine out, since the thrust lines are so close to the fuselage centerline. The long tail arm provides for large tail volumes and good stability. According to the designer, the Flyer is possessed of docile and forgiving flight characteristics.

Plans and raw materials kits are available from Kolb Co., Inc.

Specifications

Wingspan	29 ft.
Length	20 ft.
Height	4 ft. 3 in.
Wing Area	160 sq. ft.
Engine Make, Model, HP	2 Solos, 13 hp. each
Prop. Diameter/Pitch	34 in/10 in.
Reduction Ratio	Direct drive
Fuel Capacity/Consumption	1.7 gal./1 gph.
Gross Weight	420 lbs.
Empty Weight	185 lbs.
Useful Load	235 lbs.
Wing Loading	2.63 psf.
Power Loading	16.15 lb/hp.
Design Load Factors	+4, -2
Construction Time	300 man-hrs.
Field Assembly Time	20 min.
Pricing	$2,995.

Flight Performance

Velocity Never Exceed	65 mph.
Top Level Speed	50 mph.
Cruise Speed	35 mph.
Stall Speed (in free air)	18 mph.
Sea Level Climb Rate	300 fpm. @ 29 mph.
Takeoff Run	150 ft.
Dist. Req'd. to clear 50 ft.	N.A.
Landing Roll	75
Service Celing (100 fpm. climb)	N.A.
Range at Cruise	50 mi.
L/D (Glide Ratio)	10.8-to-1 @ 27 mph.
Minimum Sink Rate	N.A.

Flyer
Kolb Company, Inc.
R.D. 3, Box 38
Phoenixville, PA 19460
(215) 948-4136
Dennis Souter

Kolb Company — *Ultrastar*

The Ultrastar is a state of the art high wing monoplane taildragger with a conventional tail group, and steerable tailwheel. The pilot sits up front and the engine, in pusher configuration, is right behind. A side mounted stick and rudder pedals actuate the three axis aerodynamic controls.

The airframe is built up of both aluminum and steel, and covered with dacron and doped. The wings, struts and tail surfaces are framed of aluminum, as is the tail boom which is connected to the center of the wing. The fuselage (pilot and engine support structure) is made as a weldment of chromoly steel. It picks up the aluminum tube wing struts and landing gear as well. The pilot is seated in a padded fiberglass seat and restrained by a lap belt.

The air vehicle can be bought in three stages of kits, consisting of: airframe materials, covering, and accessories. Or, all kits can be purchased at once, for a savings. The various kits include the following items:

Airframe Materials Kit: Plans and construction manual, all steel and aluminum tubing and plate; bolts, nuts, and washers; rivets; cable; turnbuckles; rod and bearings and inserts for rod end bearings; nicopress sleeves and thimbles; clevis and clevis pins; pulleys; hinges; sheet metal stampings for wing spars; front, main and rear; machined tubes for aileron and elevator horns; welding rod; safety pins, and safety wire.

Covering Materials Kit: Dacron fabric and tape; fabric cement and dope; cleaner-solvent; and, gap seal materials.

Fig. 1-51. The Kolb Ultrastar features a welded steel tubing "fuselage", and conventional three axis controls with full span ailerons. Craft is quite maneuverable.

Fig. 1-52. Ultrastar's wings fold in ten minutes for transport and storage.

Accessory kit: Cuyuna UL II-02 engine with muffler, carburetor and fuel pump; poly V-belt reduction system; laminated hardwood propeller; load shock mounts for engine and muffler; rigid seat and seat cover; wheels and tires; 2 gas tanks of 1.75 gal. each), fuel line and clamps; and, springs for muffler mounting.

In flight, the Ultrastar provides its pilot with superb maneuverability. Its generous control surfaces allow excellent low speed control. Its long tail moment arm yields large tail volumes, and superb stability and control. The air vehicle is very steady. The relatively low aspect ratio, short span wings, coupled with full span ailerons, add up to a nice roll response. Then too, the larger chord makes for a larger Reynolds Number and greater aerodynamic efficiency.

No dihedral is needed in the wing, and makes for enhanced aileron response and excellent crosswind capability. The low slung engine, as well as the pilot's position, aid roll stability, and concentrate the greatest masses near the center of gravity - a formula that spells overall enhanced maneuverability.

Stalls are straight forward with no tendency to drop a wing. The Ultrastar offers no surprises, and can be considered as easy to handle and forgiving. In general, it can be said to possess nice handling qualities.

In the future, the factory plans to offer kits with the fuselage assembly pre-welded. This, in addition to the now available rib kit, should cut construction time to below 50 man-hours.

Specifications

Wingspan	27 ft. 6 in.
Length	20 ft.
Height	6 ft.
Wing Area	150 sq. ft.

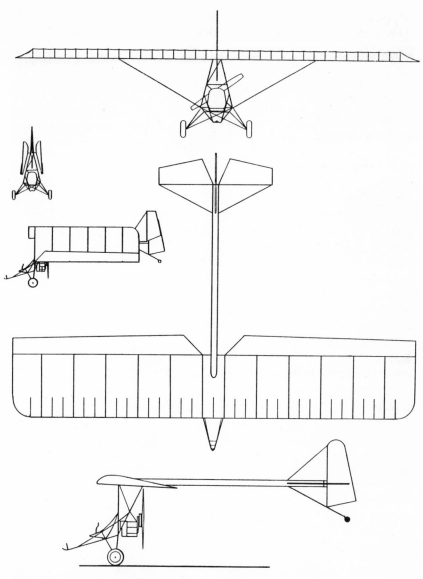

Fig. 1-53. Three-view drawing of Kolb Ultrastar, along with two views of it folded.

Engine Make, Model, HP	Cuyuna UL II-02, 35 hp.
Prop. Diameter/Pitch	50 in/30 in.
Reduction Ratio	1.96-to-1
Fuel Capacity/Consumption	3.4 gal.
Gross Weight	515 lbs.
Empty Weight	250 lbs.
Useful Load	265 lbs.
Wing Loading	3.43 psf.
Power Loading	14.71 lb/hp.

Design Load Factors	+4, -2
Construction Time	300 man-hrs. (raw materials kit)
Field Assembly Time	5 min.
Pricing	$3,595.

Flight Performance

Velocity Never Exceed	70 mph.
Top Level Speed	62 mph.
Cruise Speed	56 mph. @ 75% power
Stall Speed (in free air)	25 mph.
Sea Level Climb Rate	800 fpm. @ 32 mph.
Takeoff Run	75 ft.
Dist. Req'd. to clear 50 ft.	N.A.
Landing Roll	100 ft.
Service Ceiling (100 fpm. climb)	N.A.
Range at Cruise	150 mi.
L/D (Glide Ratio)	N.A.
Minimum Sink Rate	N.A.

Ultrastar
Kolb Company, Inc.
R.D. 3, Box 38
Phoenixville, PA 19460
(215) 948-4136
Dennis Souter

Manta Products — *Fledge III/Foxbat*

The Foxbat is a Fledge III hang glider with a trike unit installed. The tricycle landing gear features a rear axle, 20 inch main wheels and a steerable nose wheel. The engine is located aft the pilot and can drive the propeller either directly or via a reduction unit.

The aircraft is controlled by tip rudders activated by control bar sliders, and weight shift for pitch. It can be flown either as a hang glider or powered ultralight.

The Foxbat is available only as a factory prefabricated assembly kit and requires simple bolt-together assembly. It is available separately as a trike or with the Fledge hang glider wing from Manta Products. It should be noted that the Fledge hang glider is strengthened so it can take the additional weight of the Foxbat Trike.

Specifications

Wingspan	33 ft. 6 in.
Length	10 ft.
Height	6 ft.

Fig. 1-53a. Manta's Foxbat features a trike unit attached to a Fledgling III hang glider wing.

Wing Area	157 sq. ft.
Engine Make, Model, HP	Kawasaki 440, 38 hp.
Prop. Diameter/Pitch	52 in/30 in.
Reduction Ratio	2-to-1
Fuel Capacity/Consumption	5 gal./2 gph.
Gross Weight	475 lbs.
Empty Weight	220 lbs.
Useful Load	255 lbs.
Wing Loading	3.02 psf.
Power Loading	12.5 lb/hp.
Design Load Factors	=4.57, -3
Construction Time	6-8 man-hrs.
Field Assembly Time	30 min.
Pricing	$5,402.

Flight Performance

Velocity Never Exceed	63 mph.
Top Level Speed	63 mph.
Cruise Speed	45 mph. @ 65% power
Stall Speed (in free air)	23 mph.
Sea Level Climb Rate	500 fpm. @ 30 mph. (At gross weight, standard conditions)

Takeoff Run	75 ft.
Dist. Req'd. to clear 50 ft.	200 ft.
Landing Roll	50-75 ft.
Service Ceiling (100 fpm. climb)	unknown, but above 15,000 msl
Range at Cruise	110 mi.
L/D (Glide Ratio)	8-to-1 @ 34 mph. (estimated)
Minimum Sink Rate	300 fpm. @ 30 mph. (estimated)

Manta Fledge III /Foxbat
Manta Products Inc.
1647 East 14th St.
Oakland, CA 94606
(415) 536-1500
William J. Armour

Maxair Sports — Hummer

The Hummer is a high wing monoplane with conventional landing gear, a V-tail and pusher engine. It is a "from-the-ground-up" design which incorporates both hang glider and conventional aircraft construction techniques. The pilot sits up front and controls flight by a joystick connected to the tail via mixer. Construction features a non-welded, pop-riveted and bolted together, wire braced airframe of aluminum tubing.

The most obvious part of the Hummer's airframe is its irrigation pipe "fuselage", which serves as a backbone or keel, and supports the wing, with the engine further aft. Up front is bolted a bucket seat, instrument panel and control stick assembly. Immediately behind the seat a trio of triangles mount the landing gear and transmit landing loads to the fuselage. Directly below the engine, you'll find the tailwheel, which steers via the stick. Bringing up the rear is the V-tail and ruddervators, ala Beechcraft Bonanza. The wing tops it all off, and is wire braced to the fuselage.

The flying surfaces are covered by pre-sewn envelopes of dacron sailcloth, which slide on over the appropriate framework. No doping or gluing is required, as various blots and velcro centers secure the fabric in place. The wing features "ribs" made of airfoil shaped aluminum tubing sewn into the upper surface of the envelope. The under surface bottoms-out on the wing frame's compression struts, but "cambers-up" between them, giving the wing a net undercamber.

Fig. 1-54. Maxair Sports Hummer is a traildragger with pusher engine, and rudder and elevator controlled by the stick.

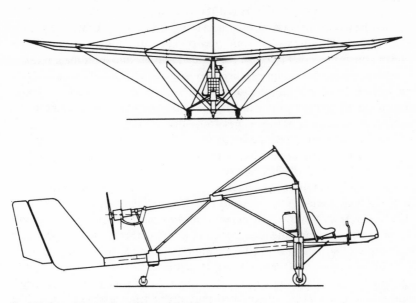

Fig. 1-55. Two-view drawing of Hummer prototype.

The kit comes from the factory with all shaped, machined or otherwise difficult parts prefabricated. The instruction manual/plans are well done and easy to follow, being separated into various sub-assemblies such as: control stick, fuselage/landing gear, king post, tailwheel, tail, etc. Flying and landing wires are pre-swaged, insuring proper rigging of the wing.

The Hummer gets its go from a 250cc Zenoah engine which, due to its location and muffler, is quite quiet. A fuel line runs from the translucent plastic tank located just behind the pilot, and includes a pressure bulb for easy priming. The tank is its own fuel gauge! Starting is accomplished by a pull from the "T"-handle positioned next to the instrument console, which connects to the recoil starter via cable. Choke and throttle levers (bicycle type) are mounted on the stick for each adjustment.

Flying the Hummer is simplicity itself, at least for rated pilots — the Hummer wants to fly. After it's assembled and rigged, a preflight is made, consisting of a walk-around inspection of every nut, bolt, cable and fabric — an easy task since everything is exposed.

Getting seated is quite easy. Simply sit down, lift one leg over the console and rest both feet on the bar. Fasten your seatbelt, prime the engine, set the choke and crack the throttle. After yelling "clear" flip the ignition switch on and give a good healthy yank of the "T" handle. If she doesn't catch, do it again. As soon as she fires, kill the choke and set the throttle at about 2,000 rpm and let her warm-up for several minutes.

Now you're ready to taxi. Go slow, at first, and get accustomed to steering with the stick. As time progresses, gradually increase rpm and airspeed. Above 12 mph, get the stick forward to raise the tail and steer with the rudder. Practice until you're sure of your ability. As you slow from a tail high taxi condition, you'll find improved response by bringing the stick back so the tailwheel gets a firm footing to do its thing. Be aware of the wind direction and velocity. Turning away from a crosswind could lift the outside wing, causing the other panel to strike the ground and ground loop the aircraft.

Confident of your taxiing ability, accelerate to stall speed and get "light-on-your-feet", by relaxing the forward stick. The Hummer wants to fly, so throttle back and then resume tail high taxiing. Accelerate and unstick again, skimming the ground at just inches above it.

Practice unsticking and landing, gradually increasing the length of flight as well as the height. Before too long, you'll be ready to fly. Open the throttle to 5,800 rpm and go into a high speed, stick forward, taxi. Accelerate to about 30 mph and let the stick come back — you'll be flying. Continue climbing at around 30 mph and do the pattern. Two hundred feet above the field is all you need. Hold power, about 4,000 rpm for cruise, cutting back to 3,000 when halfway through the base leg. Once on final, throttle back to 2,000 or so, keeping the stick forward to maintain 30-35 mph, depending on wind conditions. Check your descent and fly it onto the field — touching it at around 30 mph. (If it's a long final, be sure to clear the engine every half minute.) In other words, do a wheel landing, and not a three pointer. The Hummer may bounce, depending on your descent speed, but just let it go, it'll recover all by itself. If you try to stop the bounce, you'll only over-control it and bounce again.

Always bear in mind that the Hummer is a power glider, with the emphasis on the word glider. It's a good idea to make it a habit of doing the landing pattern as if it were a glider. That 2-cycle engine could quit at any time and shouldn't be relied on too heavily.

In flight, the Hummer is, in a word, docile. In winds under 5 mph you won't realize it hasn't got any ailerons. The turns are coordinated, but should be led with a little forward stick for more responsive handling. When taking off in a 5 mph crosswind, she'll weathercock immediately after liftoff and require into-the-crosswind stick. Landing in that same crosswind can be hazardous. Be certain the Hummer is on a straight and level glide path. The side slip "roll" which occurs due to a corrective yaw control imput, can drift the ship sideways, away from the intended landing spot. Only a little sideways ground motion can be tolerated. The plane will handle just about that much. As soon as you touchdown, track directly into the wind, as shown by the windsock.

Stalls are straight forward, with no tendency to drop a wing, thanks to that generous washout at the tips. The stall itself is more a mush than anything else, with little altitude lost in recovery. Power on, it will not stall at all, but just mush along.

Needless to say, the visibility from the front "office" is unrestricted, so much so that flight in the Hummer makes the pilot feel almost as though he were flying without the aid of an airplane.

The Hummer is available in both A and B models. The B is capable of hauling the heavier pilots, which is basically a weight and balance, "wing-shoved-forward-to-accommodate" situation. (reduction drive opt.) A pilot fairing is also available.

Specifications

Wingspan	34 ft.
Length	18 ft.
Height	8 ft.
Wing Area	128 sq. ft.
Engine Make, Model, HP	Zenoah G25B — 250cc — 22 hp.
Prop. Diameter/Pitch	52 in/32 in.
Reduction Ratio	2¼-to-1
Fuel Capacity/Consumption	5 gal./1½ gph.
Gross Weight	440 lbs.
Empty Weight	185 lbs.
Useful Load	250 lbs.
Wing Loading	2.5-3.0 psf.
Power Loading	19.77 lb/hp.
Design Load Factors	=4, -3
Construction Time	85 man-hrs.
Field Assembly Time	11 min.
Pricing	$4,550. Including instruments!

Flight Performance

Velocity Never Exceed	65 mph.
Top Level Speed	55 mph.
Cruise Speed	30-45 mph. @ 50-75% Power
Stall Speed (in free air)	22-24 mph.
Sea Level Climb Rate	600+ fpm. @ 45 mph.
Takeoff Run	100 ft/150 ft. grass
Dist. Req'd. to clear 50 ft.	
Landing Roll	150 ft/60 ft. grass
Service Ceiling (100 fpm. climb)	10,000 ft.
Range at Cruise	100 mi.
L/D (Glide Ratio)	9-to-1 @ 30 mph.
Minimum Sink Rate	225 fpm. @ 30 mph.

The HUMMER
Maxair Sports, Inc.
32 Water Street
Glen Rock, PA 17327
(717) 235-2107
Bill Hanson

Maxair Sports — Drifter

The Drifter is a cable-braced, high wing monoplane pusher with cruciform tail and full span ailerons. It features construction similar to the Hummer, from where it evolved.

The Drifter was designed primarily with the conventional aircraft pilot in mind. The elevator and ailerons are stick controlled, while the tail wheel and rudder are actuated by rudder pedals. The main wheels roll on ball bearings with grease fittings, and are fitted with pneumatic tires. The landing gear legs are tubular steel with a wide track and inherent spring. Brakes are an option.

Power is provided by the 40 hp. Kawasaki, complete with reduction drive, generator and recoil starter (electric start is optional). The wing is double surfaced and capable of sustaining status loads of 6 G's positive and 4.5 G's negative, without yielding. The Drifter is not designed for aerobatics, however, the load carrying capacity was incorporated to insure structural integrity when confronted with turbulence and its induced loads.

Specifications

Wingspan	30 ft.
Length	19 ft.
Height	8 ft.
Wing Area	160 sq. ft.
Engine Make, Model, HP	Kawasaki 440 cc 40 hp., 2-cycle, twin cylinder
Prop. Diameter/Pitch	58 in/27 in.
Reduction Ratio	2.25-to-1
Fuel Capacity/Consumption	5 gal./2 gph.
Gross Weight	500 lbs.
Empty Weight	240 lbs.
Useful Load	240 lbs.
Wing Loading	2.5-3.25 psf.
Power Loading	12.5 lb/hp.
Design Load Factors	=6, -5
Construction Time	45 man-hrs.
Field Assembly Time	8 min.
Pricing	$5,500.

Flight Performance

Velocity Never Exceed	80 mph.
Top Level Speed	60 mph.
Cruise Speed	30-50 mph. @ 50-75% power
Stall Speed (in free air)	25 mph.

Fig. 1-56. Maxair Sports Drifter evolved from Hummer, but features cruciform tail and full span ailerons.

Sea Level Climb Rate	1200 fpm. @ 50 mph.
Takeoff Run	75 ft. surfaced/100 ft. grass
Dist. Req'd. to clear 50 ft.	
Landing Roll	150 ft. surfaced/60 ft. of grass
Service Ceiling (100 fpm. climb)	10,000 ft.
Range at Cruise	200 mi.
L/D (Glide Ratio)	8-to-1 @ 30 mph.
Minimum Sink Rate	225 fpm. @ 30 mph.

The DRIFTER
Maxair Sports, Inc.
32 Water Street
Glen Rock, PA 17327
(717) 235-2107
Bill Hanson

(Mighty) Little Aircraft Co. — *Pintail*

The Pintail is a high wing canard pusher controlled by a unique, all moving canard. It is similar in appearance to the earlier Tomcat, except that it is now strut-braced instead of relying on cables.

The unswept, dihedral-less main wing is supported by two dihedral wings swept back 13°. These so-called dihedral wings are the major lateral stabilizing surfaces, being effective as a fin by providing side area aft the CG. They also tie the roll and yaw reactions of the air vehicle together, producing a single coordinated roll/yaw reponse to a control input or gust. Unlike the Tomcat though, roll is controlled directly by ailerons.

The canard wing, while providing inherent longitudinal stability, also controls pitch and yaw. Its angle of attack controls pitch, while sideways tilts affect yaw.

The powerplant selected for the Pintail is the Kawasaki 440 of 37 hp, turning a 54 inch propeller via a reduction drive. A recoil pull starter enables the pilot to start the engine from his seat. The engine is rubber shock mounted, and its thrustline is such that no trim changes occur from power-on to power-off. A T-handled throttle control is positioned for left hand operation.

The fuselage is a single 4½ diameter aluminum tube to which dihedral wings, engine mount, canard, seat and landing gear are fastened. Control lonkages are run inside the boom.

The undercarriage is of light tubular construction with integral rubber shock absorbers. The three wheels are nylon hubbed, ball bearing mounted

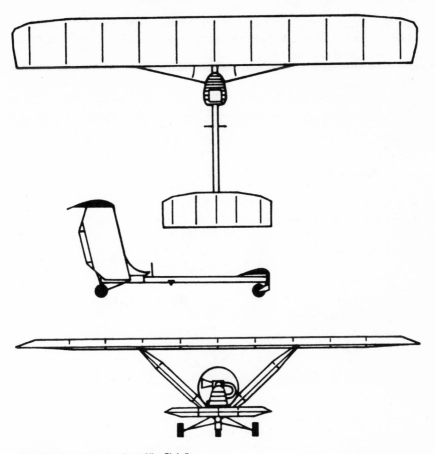

Fig. 1-58. Three-view drawing of the Pintail.

and fitted with light weight pneumatic tires and tubes. The nosewheel is connected to the control system for steering, and is sprung mounted.

The Pintail's wings are double surfaced and are reported to remain clean and quiet throughout the speed range of the aircraft. They are unique in that they are mylar reinforced.

The engine, seat, fuel tank, kevlar reinforced landing gear and all control linkages remain intact as the fuselage module. The Pintail folds to a trailerable package in about 15 minutes, and can be reassembled in about 20 minutes.

The overall flying characteristics belie the aircraft's radical appearance. The factory claims the Pintail possesses solid, responsive handling. Control pressures are light but positive. Roll response should be superior to that of the earlier Tomcat.

The kit comes complete with pre-sewen dacron wing coverings, cut and drilled tubing, cable, cable adjusters, formed parts, bent tube and sheet, and preformed brackets and fittings. All welding, brazing, milling and other specialized machine work is completed. All hardware, the engine, propeller, fiberglass bucket seat, plans and instruction books, as well as a flight training manual and log book are included. Even hydraulic disk brakes and basic instrumentation are standard.

Specifications

Wingspan	30 ft. 0 in.
Length	13 ft. 9 in.
Height	5 ft. 11 in.
Wing Area	185 sq. ft.
Engine Make, Model, HP	Kawasaki 440, 37 hp.
Prop Diameter/Pitch	54 in/28 in.
Reduction Ratio	2-to-1
Fuel Capacity/Consumption	5 gal./2 gph.
Gross Weight	530 lbs.
Empty Weight	250 lbs.
Useful Load	280 lbs.
Wing Loading	2.86 psf.
Power Loading	14.32 lb/hp.
Design Load Factors	+5, -3
Construction Time	50 man-hrs.
Field Assembly Time	20 min.
Pricing	$6,500.

Flight Performance

Velocity Never Exceed	75 mph.
Top Level Speed	63 mph.
Cruise Speed	55 mph. @ 80% power
Stall Speed (in free air)	26 mph.
Sea Level Climb Rate	NA
Takeoff Run	NA
Dist. Req'd. to clear 50 ft.	NA
Landing Roll	NA
Service Ceiling (100 fpm. climb)	NA
Range at Cruise	NA
L/D (Glide Ratio)	NA
Minimum Sink Rate	NA

Pintail
The Little Aircraft Co.
P.O. Box 255843
Sacramento, CA 95865
Phone (916) 424-2413
Tim Clark

Mitchell Aircraft — B-10

The B-10 is an all wooden construction, medium performance flying wing with three-axis aerodynamic controls. It can be scratch built from plans or purchased as a complete kit.

Seemingly in defiance of conventional aircraft logic, the B-10 is nonetheless a relatively stable flyer. The "secret" to its success lies in the successful use of a good wing section and tip mounted stabilators. The NACA 23015 airfoil combines good lift characteristics with a zero pitching moment. The center section of the wing is flat, and swept back at 12 °, while the two outboard panels are set at 6° dihedral. It is the sweep-back and dihedral, along with tip rudders that give the aircraft good directional stability.

To prevent a flying wing from pitching nose down and tucking under, the trailing edge must be reflexed, and the tips washed-out. The B-10 incorporates separate control surfaces called stabilators, to perform this function, the main wing itself having neither reflex nor washout. The stabilators are actually small movable wings mounted upside down below and aft the trailing edge, which immerses them in the high pressure air under the wing — enabling them to be effective, even though the upper wing surface may have stalled. They can be rotated up simultaneously for elevator effect, or differentially to serve as ailerons, via an overhead joystick and mixer in the wing itself. Only up movements of from 2° to 36° are possible, insuring positive pitch stability.

Fig. 1-59. The Mitchell B-10 is a flying wing of wooden construction. Photos shows one in mock military dress.

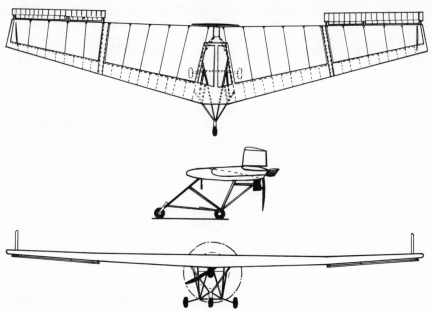

Fig. 1-60. Three-view drawing of the B-10.

A rudder is located at each wing tip and actuated by a foot bar. The rudders are cable connected to the bar.

The B-10's wing is built-up in a proven "D" section spar of birch plywood skin formed over foam ribs spaced every 4½". The ribs aft the spar are conventional wooden trusses, with extra heavy ribs in the center, carrying the rear spar and power cage. The entire wing is covered with ceconite and doped. It's a basic, simple, strong, yet light design with the more critical parts (e.g., the "D" section leading edge spar) prefabricated. All brackets, plates and fittings are aircraft specification.

The pilot and engine are carried in a chromoly 4130 cage hanging from the wing's center section. The pusher powerplants can vary from two-stroke go-kart types to snowmobile units, swinging a 44", hand carved wooden propeller via a 3:1 reduction V-belt drive. The fuel cell holds two gallons of fuel-oil mix, and under normal climb-cruise conditions, duration is more than an hour with reserve. Shutting down the engine to soar, of course, extends flight time to whatever. Air restarts are routine, simply requiring a pull on the rope.

The power cage is easily detached from the wing via four Quick-Pins, and the entire disassembly process requires less than 10 minutes. The outer wing panels are folded in over the center section, which makes for a fairly compact arrangement for transport by auto rooftop.

Assembling the B-10 is also a relatively simple matter, which can be accomplished in under 10 minutes. Lower the wing onto the power cage and install four Quick-Pins (Q-Pin). Remove the six Q-Pins holding the folded outer wing panels and re-insert the Q-Pins. Plug in the rudders and secure

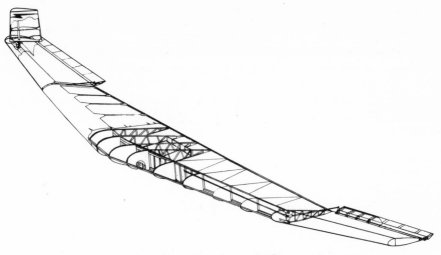

Fig. 1-61. Cutaway of the B-10s cantilevered wooden construction.

with a Q-Pin on each. The joystick is then inserted into its socket and secured by another Q-Pin. Gas-oil mixture is put into the tank and you're ready for your pre-flight inspection.

Getting into the power cage takes some maneuvering, but after a few attempts it becomes second nature. After you're settled into the padded seat and back support and fasten your seatbelt, you are fairly comfortable. All controls are within easy reach, with the joystick positioned for a comfortable right hand grip, while the throttle lever is located on the power cage's left diagonal for easy left hand actuation. A small console located on the floor between the pilot's legs contains rpm and CHT gauges and ignition on-off switch. An airspeed indicator is located on the right front diagonal.

After the engine is primed and ignition switched on, a pull on the starting rope located above the left shoulder jolts the engine to life. It doesn't take much to get the plane moving, and takeoffs are accomplished in under 200 feet. Rotation occurs almost at once, and then lift off. Landing roll is less than 100 feet.

In flight, the Mitchell's control response is brisk, but not over sensitive, though it can be over-controlled until the proper "feel" is developed. Remember, this aircraft has no tail! Climb rate exceeds 900 fpm while top speed is well over 60 mph. The aircraft has a very straightforward stall, with no break and no tendency to drop a wing. The center-section always stalls first, while the outer panel and all controls remain effective. Little altitude is lost during stall recovery, which is quite positive.

In keeping with the motorglider concept, the B-10 can indeed be soared — it's 16-to-1 glide ratio will allow both thermal and ridge soaring whenever conditions permit. When the lift runs out, all you do is restart the engine and fly on without having to land out, preventing a lot of grief and aggravation.

The B-10 is available in several basic packages: 1) Ready-to-fly, which includes everything. 2) An economy kit, excluding engine, instruments and undercarriage. 3) A homebuilder's special, including all hardware and raw materials only. 4) An engine package which includes the complete propulsion system. 5) The undercarriage. 6) Plans only. Several options are also available including: flight instruments, brakes, bush landing gear parachute and harness, podule, XF-10 package and floats. Contact Mitchell Aircraft Corporation for more information.

Specifications

Wingspan	34 ft.
Length	9 ft.
Height	6 ft. at rudders
Wing Area	136 sq. ft.
Engine Make, Model, HP	Zenoah G25-B, 23 hp.
Prop. Diameter/Pitch	N.A.
Reduction Ratio	N.A.
Fuel Capacity/Consumption	3 gal./1 gph.
Gross Weight	525 lbs.
Empty Weight	180 lbs.
Useful Load	345 lbs.
Wing Loading	3.86 psf.
Power Loading	22.83 lb/hp.
Design Load Factors	=4.8, -4.8
Construction Time	200 man-hrs.
Field Assembly Time	5 min.
Pricing	$4,195. (kit), $6,995 (fly away)

Flight Performance

Velocity Never Exceed	N.A.
Top Level Speed	63 mph.
Cruise Speed	55 mph. @ 75% power
Stall Speed (in free air)	25 mph.
Sea Level Climb Rate	900 fpm.
Takeoff Run	175 ft.
Dist. Req'd. to clear 50 ft.	N.A.
Landing Roll	175 ft.
Service Ceiling (100 fpm. climb)	12,000 ft.
Range at Cruise	135 mi.
L/D (Glide Ratio)	14-to-1 (16-to-1 w/podule)
Minimum Sink Rate	225 fpm. @ 35 mph.

B-10
Mitchell Aircraft Corp.
1900 S. Newcomb
Porterville, CA 93257
(209) 781-8100
Tom Sawyer

Mitchell Aircraft — A-10 Silver Eagle

The Silver Eagle is similar to the original B-10 version, but with several improvements, along with being factory built. Major among the changes is the fact that the wing and vertical stabilizers are all aluminum.

The fully cantilevered wing employs the traditional "D" cell construction, with a shear web and upper and lower spar caps. The NACA 23015 airfoil is formed by a new process based on honeycomb, using injected SP502 foam developed by NASA for the space shuttle program. All skins are 2024-T3 alclad sheet aluminum, and all fuselage tubing and spar caps are 6061-T6 aluminum. Aerodynamic fairings are pre-molded light-weight fiberglass, and are standard equipment.

The landing gear is a cantilevered torque-tube system providing independent suspension with a minimum of parts. The wheel base has been lengthened over the B-10's, eliminating tip back of the unoccupied air vehicle. The nosewheel is steerable and includes a brake as standard equipment.

The A-10 is controlled by stabilators and tip rudders just like the B-10. However, the stick is floor mounted, with pitch and roll controlled through a ball bearing mixer to the stabilators.

The NASA Witcomb Winglets (vertical stabilizers) double as drag rudders for directional control. They are operated independently by rudder pedals, making it possible to deploy both simultaneously for glide path control. For transport, the rudders fold down by removing a single hinge pin.

The Silver Eagle is powered by the Zenoah 242cc engine. It drives a 50 inch

Fig. 1-62. Mitchell A-10 is aluminum version of B-10. It's sold only as a factory built air vehicle.

laminated hardwood prop via a Manta Poly V-reduction drive system. A Mikuni pumper carburetor and Fischer QHP exhaust system, enable the engine to develop good power with low noise, and yet be fuel efficient as well.

Despite its long wingspan, the A-10 has a nice roll rate, when side stick is coordinated with rudder. Crosswind capabilities are said to be outstanding and, since there are no tail surfaces, there is no tendency for the air vehicle to weathercock. Stalls are straight forward, and the controls can be trimmed for hands-off flying. The Silver Eagle can also be soared engine off, thanks to a 16-to-1 glide ratio and a minimum sink rate of 240 fpm.

Field assembly time is no more than 5 minutes, and the wings fold for trailer transport.

Specifications

Wingspan	34 ft 4 in.
Length	10 ft.
Height	7 ft. (at rudders)
Wing Area	156 sq. ft.
Engine Make, Model, HP	Zenoah 242cc, 23 hp.
Prop. Diameter/Pitch	50 in.
Reduction Ratio	N.A.
Fuel Capacity/Consumption	3 gal./1.25 gph.
Gross Weight	553 lbs.
Empty Weight	250 lbs.
Useful Load	303 lbs.
Wing Loading	3.54 psf.
Power Loading	24 lb/hp.
Design Load Factors	+6, -5
Construction Time	Factory Built
Field Assembly Time	5 min.
Pricing	$5,995.

Flight Performance

Velocity Never Exceed	N.A.
Top Level Speed	63 mph.
Cruise Speed	58 mph. @ 75% power
Stall Speed (in free air)	27 mph.
Sea Level Climb Rate	650 fpm.
Takeoff Run	225 ft.
Dist. Req'd. to clear 50 ft.	535 ft.
Landing Roll	200 ft.
Service Ceiling (100 fpm. climb)	12,000 ft.
Range at Cruise	1512 mi. (no reserve)
L/D (Glide Ratio)	16-to-1
Minimum Sink Rate	240 fpm.

A-10 Silver Eagle
Mitchell Aircraft Corp.
1900 S. Newcomb, Porterville, CA 93257, (209) 781-8100, Tom Sawyer

P

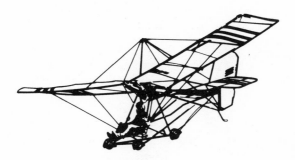

ParaPlane Corp. — *ParaPlane*

Fig. 1-63. The unique paraplane requires very little skill to fly. It's actually a parachute powered by two engines and contrarotating props.

The ParaPlane is a ram-air inflated gliding parachute, with engine and cockpit suspended below. It features two engines driving countrarotating propellers and is advertised as non-stallable.

The airframe is constructed of aluminum and contains the seat and engines. Two metal rings surround the propellers. The pilot is seatbelted and shoulder harnessed in place. Controls consist of throttle for climbing and descending, and foot bars for turning and flaring. Press one foot bar, and that's the direction you turn. Press both foot bars simultaneously for your landing flare.

The unit is quite compact, and will fit inside the trunk of many cars. If one engine quits, the ParaPlane will descend with a glide ratio of 6-to-1.

Specifications

Wingspan	30 ft. 6 in. (36 ft. for "Extraspan" model)
Length	5 ft. 8 in.
Height	5 ft. 7 in.
Wing Area	375 sq. ft. (450 sq. ft. for "Extraspan" model
Engine Make, Model, HP	2-Solo 210cc, 15 hp. each
Prop. Diameter/Pitch	50 in. contrarotating
Reduction Ratio	
Fuel Capacity/Consumption	4.5 gal./3 gph.
Gross Weight	355 lbs.
Empty Weight	139 lbs.
Useful Load	185 lbs.
Wing Loading	95 psf.
Power Loading	11.83 lb/hp.
Design Load Factors	N.A.
Construction Time	Ready-to-fly
Field Assembly Time	15 min.
Pricing	$3,750.

Flight Performance

Velocity Never Exceed	30 mph.
Top Level Speed	26 mph.
Cruise Speed	26 mph.
Stall Speed (in free air)	will not stall
Sea Level Climb Rate	300 fpm. @ 26 mph.
Takeoff Run	N.A.
Dist. Req'd. to clear 50 ft.	N.A.
Landing Roll	N.A.
Service Ceiling (100 fpm. climb)	N.A.
Range at Cruise	35 mi.
L/D (Glide Ratio)	3-to-1 @ 26 mph.
Minimum Sink Rate	N.A.

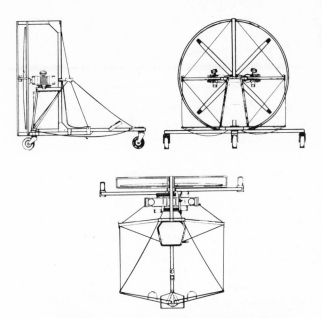

Fig. 1-64. Three-view drawing of the Paraplane's power package and fuselage.

ParaPlane
ParaPlane Corporation
5801 Magnolia Avenue
Pennsauken, NJ 08109
(609) 663-2234
Joe Shively

Phase Three — *Eclipse*

The Eclipse is a high wing monoplane with tricycle landing gear, an inverted V-tail, and pusher engine. This cantilevered, elliptically winged air vehicle employs some incredibly unique structural and control concepts, that are quite different from all other ultralights.

The wing is certainly the heart of this design. First of all, it is elliptical in planform, which is the most efficient shape, aerodynamically. Structurally, the wing is made up of a girder-like spar and truss type ribs. The ribs are positioned both chordwise and diagonally to the chord for torsional rigidity. The rib sections ahead of the spar are covered with a mylar stiffening sheet to maintain airfoil shape. The entire wing is covered with a pre-sewn envelope of stabilized dacron sailcloth.

The wing also has no separate control surfaces — roll is achieved by wing warping. Push rods running behind the spar, transmit roll control inputs to an appropriate mechanism which twists the outer portion of the wing aft the spar. It is aerodynamically clean and seems to work satisfactorily.

The tail is an inverted V of elliptical planform. It is also theoretically very efficient and is warped to provide yaw and pitch control.

A series of aluminum tubing triangles make up the fuselage and a spring and shock absorber suspended tricycle undercarriage. The engine is mounted

Fig. 1-65. Phase Three Eclipse features unusual eliptical cantilevered wing and tail surfaces. All surfaces are warped for control.

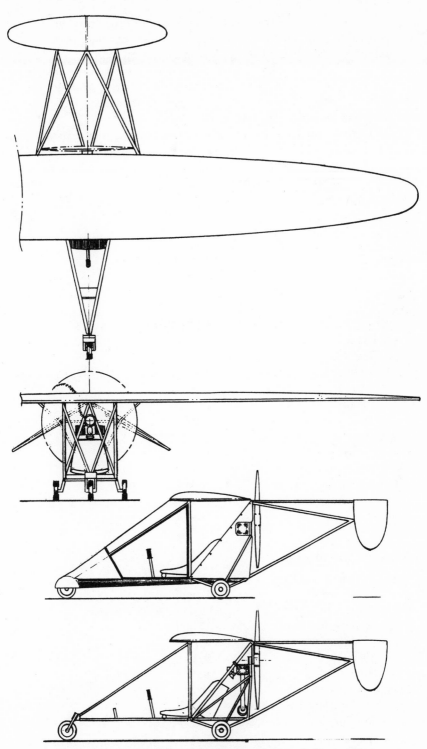

Fig. 1-66. Four-view drawing of the Eclipse. Side view depicts it with and without a fairing.

behind the pilot and turns a reduction drive propeller between the tail support tubes. The pilot sits below the wing near the center of gravity. A steerable nosewheel handles the ground maneuvering chores.

The Eclipse has a smaller wing and higher wing loading than most ultralights, which should make it more tolerant of gusts. And, despite the higher wing loading, it still manages a 25 mph stall, thanks to the efficiency of the wing and, of course, the low empty weight.

The factory claims the air vehicle is very stable, and it appears to be so, based on observed flight demonstrations. With a 170 pound payload, the Eclipse is capable of handlig 6 G's, positive and negative. The ultralight is controlled via stick and rudder pedals, which function in conventional aircraft fashion.

Specifications

Wingspan	32 ft. 2 in.
Length	14 ft.
Height	5 ft.
Wing Area	114 sq. ft.
Engine Make, Model, HP	KFM 107ER, 25 hp.
Prop. Diameter/Pitch	54 in/23 in.
Reduction Ratio	2.1-to-1
Fuel Capacity/Consumption	5 gal./1.3 gph.
Gross Weight	395 lbs.
Empty Weight	165 lbs.
Useful Load	230 lbs.
Wing Loading	3.46 psf.
Power Loading	15.8 lb/hp.
Design Load Factors	+6, -6
Construction Time	N.A.
Field Assembly Time	30 min.
Pricing	$5,495.

Flight Performance

Velocity Never Exceed	N.A.
Top Level Speed	63 mph.
Cruise Speed	55 mph. @ 75% power
Stall Speed (in free air)	25 mph.
Sea Level Climb Rate	N.A.
Takeoff Run	50 ft.
Dist. Req'd. to clear 50 ft.	N.A.
Landing Roll	70 ft.
Service Ceiling (100 fpm. climb)	N.A.
Range at Cruise	150 mi.
L/D (Glide Ratio)	N.A.
Minimum Sink Rate	N.A.

Eclipse

Phase Three, Inc.
1334 Lutheran Church Road
Dayton, OH 45427
(513) 854-5266
Douglas C. Lyons

Pioneer International Aircraft — *Flightstar*

The Flightstar is a strut-braced, high wing tractor monoplane with three axis aerodynamic controls. The pilot sits in a cage at the air vehicle's center of gravity, behind a nose fairing and windshield. The bungee cord suspended chromemoly undercarriage is tricycle, with a steerable nosewheel. The air vehicle is state of the art.

The wing is a basic ladder frame with tubular leading edge, rear spar, compression members, and ribs. It is supported by a V-strut assembly bolted to the bottom of the pilot cage near the rear landing gear leg. Full span ailerons are hinged to the rear spar.

The pilot cage consists of parallel bars on either side of the pilot, connected to the tail boom via a trio of tubular triangles. The engine and reduction drive are mounted over the front of the tail boom, which goes through the wing center section and on back to the tail group. The pilot is restrained by a seat belt and shoulder harness system. The fuel tank is positioned behind the seat.

The Flightstar is possessed of excellent flying qualities, and should feel comfortable to licensed pilots and ultralight pilots with experience. Response in all three axis is very good, and stick pressures are light and proportional. Ground handling is also excellent. The ailerons do create a bit of adverse yaw, which is happily corrected for with appropriate application of rudder.

Fig. 1-67. Pioneer Flightstar is strut-braced tri-geared ultralight with cruciform tail, tractor engine and full span ailerons.

134

Fig. 1-68. Flightstar features an optional ballistic parachute that will lower both the airframe and pilot in case of mishap.

Pioneer offers a rather unique safety device as an option — a ballistic parachute system mounted immediately behind the engine. It explosively launches a 29-foot canopy, pressure packed in a deployment bag, via an aerospace quality pyrotechnic charge. Deployment occurs rises first, following by suspension lines and finally the canopy itself, in 1.5 seconds. The engineering design criteria was to affect a safe recovery of both aircraft and pilot from as low as 200 feet above the ground. The unit is hermetically sealed, and the activation is completely mechanical, employing no electronics. It is available to manufacturers of all ultralight aircraft as a factory option on new aircraft, as well.

Specifications

Wingspan	30 ft. 0 in.
Length	16 ft. 6 in.
Height	7 ft. 5 in.
Wing Area	144 sq. ft.
Engine Make, Model, HP	Kawasaki TA440A, 35 HP @ 5,500 rpm.
Prop. Diameter/Pitch	58 in/27 in.
Reduction Ratio	2-to-1
Fuel Capacity/Consumption	5 gal./1.8 gph. @ 65% power
Gross Weight	500 lbs.
Empty Weight	250 lbs.
Useful Load	220 lbs. with full fuel (30 lbs.)
Wing Loading	2.6-3.5 psf.
Power Loading	132 lb/hp.

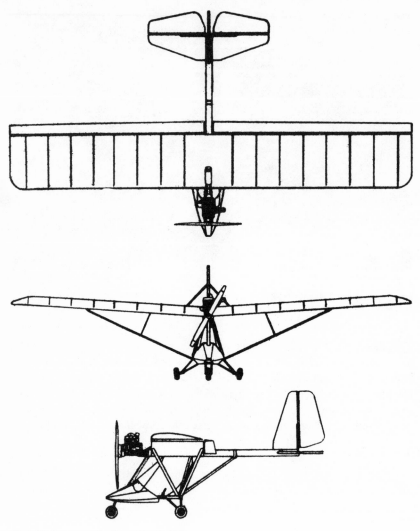

Fig. 1-69. Three-view drawing of the Flightstar.

Design Load Factors	+6, -4
Construction Time	16-20 man-hrs.
Field Assembly Time	20-30 min.
Pricing	$7,495. retail

Flight Performance

Velocity Never Exceed	70 mph.
Top Level Speed	63 mph.
Cruise Speed	50 mph. @ 65% power
Stall Speed (in free air)	25 mph.
Sea Level Climb Rate	850 fpm. @ 35 mph.
Takeoff Run	100 ft.

Dist. Req'd. to clear 50 ft.	300 ft.
Landing Roll	200 ft. pavement, 100 ft. grass
Service Ceiling (100 fpm. climb)	12,000 ft. (estimated)
Range at Cruise	150 mi.
L/D (Glide Ratio)	7-to-1 @ 35 mph.
Minimum Sink Rate	350 fpm. @ 35 mph.

Flightstar
Pioneer International Aircraft, Inc.
Pioneer Industrial Park
Manchester, CT 06040
(203) 644-1581
Sales Manager

Pterodactyl — Pterodactyl Series and Light Flyer

The Pterodactyl stable of ultralights consists of the tailless Pfledge, the canard elevatored Ptraveler, Ascender II, Ascender II+, and the Light Flyer. The first four models are based on the Fledge IIB hang glider wing, while the latter craft is a biplane with a biplane canard elevator and vertical tail.

Let's begin our description with the first four models. Their wings are a basic ladder type frame of bolted together aluminum tubing, wire braced to an underslung pilot cage. The dual spar wing allows for a rigid airfoil to be maintained in conjunction with reflexed, removeable ribs. Dihedral and washout all defined by the flying wires, precluding incorrect rigging. The wing's unique construction allows it to be broken down for car top transport, as well. Stabilized dacron sailcloth covers the wings, while the elevators are covered with doped dacron.

The 16 inch nosewheel of all five models features a shockcord suspension. The 20 inch mains feature a fiberglass springrod suspension.

All five models have power supplied by the 30 hp, twin cylinder Cuyuna 430. The Pfledge and Ptraveler feature a direct drive propeller, while the two Ascenders and the Light Flyer employ reduction drives.

The Pfledge is controlled by a combination of weight shift for pitch, with tip rudders for yaw/roll. The tip rudders are activated by two independent twist grips, one for each hand. Individual rudder deflection results in a yaw/roll and turn, while simultaneous deflections control both glidepath and pitch trim.

The Ptraveler, the two Ascenders and the Light Flyer are controlled solely by aerodynamic means, with no weight shifting involved. Pitch is controlled

Fig. 1-70. The original Pterodactyl Fledgling.

Fig. 1-71. The Pterodactyl Ascender is really a Pterodactyl with a front elevator, eliminating the need to shift weight for pitch control.

by a forward elevator, while yaw/roll is controlled by tip rudders. The controls are stick actuated.

The Light Flyer is quite different from the other four models, not only in appearance, but in construction as well. The wing panels are ladder frames alright, but they incorporate stamped aluminum ribs and doped dacron coverings. The upper and lower planes are supported in typical biplane fashion, with aluminum tubing interplane struts cross-braced with stainless steel cables. The air vehicle cannot be broken-down for car top transport. Whereas the Ptraveler and the Ascenders have their tip rudders actuated by sideways stick movements, the Light Flyer has pedal operated rudders.

A factory pilot aptly describes the takeoff and landing technique of an early Pfledge. "The landing gear holds the aircraft at a positive angle of attack, so all the pilot has to do is accelerate the aircraft to flying speed and keep aimed down the runway. Low speed steering is done by turning the nosewheel, but from 10 mph on rudders must be used. At approximately 20 mph (about 25 mph today), the Pfledge leaves the ground — it takes roughly 250 feet (125 feet today) of ground run in no wind. Once off, the pilot moves forward slightly trimming to an airspeed of 30 mph (about 35 today) for best R.O.C.

On final approach, maintain 25 mph (about 31 today) minimum flying speed. Flying too slow puts the aircraft close to the stall and reduces the rudder effectiveness for glidepath control. On final, both rudders should be slightly out. The glide can then be extended or shortened by reducing or increasing the amount of simultaneous rudder deflection. To flare, both rudders are fully deflected. The increased drag above the CG lifts the nose, increasing the angle of attack. Touchdown on the mains first. Use rudders then nosewheel during rollout.

Fig. 1-72. The Light Flyer is a biplane canard inspired by the original Wright Brothers Kitty Hawk Flyer.

After a brief interview with Jack McCormack (President of Pterodactyl), following his historic flight from Monterey to Oshkosh, which was flown in formation with Keith Nicely, the author felt the following:

"Small town America is simply enamored and enthralled at the sight of an ultralight. It's almost as if the airplane was just recently invented. And, in a sense, it has been re-invented — at least on a scale where common folk can relate to and understand them. Barnstorming is alive and well and growing in strength. Soon, people everywhere will be flying."

Furthermore, in the words of Jack McCormack, after flying Donner Pass, "The beauty of the mountains in the morning is awesome . . . Ultralights are the only way to fly. I would not have traded places with anyone in the world at that moment."

The other four models are controlled solely by aerodynamic means, while the pilot is seated in either a hammock style or rigid seat. All models are sold as bolt-together assembly kits. Contact Pterodactyl for further details.

Pfledge
Specifications

Wingspan	33 ft. 0 in.
Length	10 ft. 0 in.
Height	11 ft. 0 in.
Wing Area	162 sq. ft.
Engine Make, Model, HP	Cuyuna 430-D, 30 hp.
Prop. Diameter/Pitch	36 in/16 in.
Reduction Ratio	Direct drive
Fuel Capacity/Consumption	5 gal./1.5 gph.
Gross Weight	420 lbs.
Empty Weight	185 lbs.

Useful Load	235 lbs.
Wing Loading	2.6 psf.
Power Loading	14 lb/hp.
Design Load Factors	+4.4, -3.3
Construction Time	50 man-hrs.
Field Assembly Time	40 min.
Pricing	$4,320.

Flight Performance

Velocity Never Exceed	N.A.
Top Level Speed	55 mph.
Cruise Speed	35-45 mph.
Stall Speed (in free air)	23 mph.
Sea Level Climb Rate	400 fpm.
Takeoff Run	125 ft.
Dist. Req'd. to clear 50 ft.	N.A.
Landing Roll	100 ft.
Service Ceiling (100 fpm. climb)	15,000 ft.
Range at Cruise	100 mi.
L/D (Glide Ratio)	9-to-1
Minimum Sink Rate	400 fpm.

Ptraveler

Specifications

Wingspan	33 ft. 0 in.
Length	N.A.
Height	N.A.
Wing Area	173 sq. ft.
Engine Make, Model, HP	Cuyuna 430-D, 30 hp.
Prop. Diameter/Pitch	36 in/16 in.
Reduction Ratio	Direct drive
Fuel Capacity/Consumption	5 gal./1.5 gph.
Gross Weight	450 lbs.
Empty Weight	200 lbs.
Useful Load	250 lbs.
Wing Loading	2.6 psf.
Power Loading	15 lb/hp.
Design Load Factors	N.A.
Construction Time	55 man-hrs.
Field Assembly Time	45 min.
Pricing	$4,680.

Flight Performance

Velocity Never Exceed	N.A.
Top Level Speed	55 mph.

Cruise Speed	35-45 mph.
Stall Speed (in free air)	25 mph.
Sea Level Climb Rate	400 fpm.
Takeoff Run	125 ft.
Dist. Req'd. to clear 50 ft.	N.A.
Landing Roll	100 ft.
Service Ceiling (100 fpm. climb)	15,000 ft.
Range at Cruise	100 mi.
L/D (Glide Ratio)	9-to-1
Minimum Sink Rate	425 fpm.

Ascender II
Specifications

Wingspan	33 ft. 0 in.
Length	16 ft. 10 in.
Height	9 ft. 1 in.
Wing Area	173 sq. ft.
Engine Make, Model, HP	Cuyuna 430-R, 30 hp.
Prop. Diameter/Pitch	54 in/27 in.
Reduction Ratio	N.A.
Fuel Capacity/Consumption	5 gal./1.5 gph.
Gross Weight	465 lbs.
Empty Weight	215 lbs.
Useful Load	250 lbs.
Wing Loading	2.68 psf.
Power Loading	15.5 lb/hp.
Design Load Factors	N.A.
Construction Time	80 man-hrs.
Field Assembly Time	45 min.
Pricing	$4,980.

Flight Performance

Velocity Never Exceed	N.A.
Top Level Speed	55 mph.
Cruise Speed	40-50 mph.
Stall Speed (in free air)	25 mph.
Sea Level Climb Rate	1000 fpm.
Takeoff Run	80 ft.
Dist. Req'd. to clear 50 ft.	N.A.
Landing Roll	50 ft.
Service Ceiling (100 fpm. climb)	18,000 ft.
Range at Cruise	100 mi.
L/D (Glide Ratio)	8-to-1
Minimum Sink Rate	450 fpm.

Ascender II+
Specifications

Wingspan	33 ft. 0 in.
Length	16 ft. 10 in.
Height	9 ft. 1 in.
Wing Area	173 sq. ft.
Engine Make, Model, HP	Cuyuna 430-R, 30 hp.
Prop. Diameter/Pitch	54 in/27 in.
Reduction Ratio	N.A.
Fuel Capacity/Consumption	5 gal./2 gph.
Gross Weight	535 lbs.
Empty Weight	235 lbs.
Useful Load	300 lbs.
Wing Loading	3.09 psf.
Power Loading	17.83 lb/hp.
Design Load Factors	N.A.
Construction Time	75 man-hrs.
Field Assembly Time	45 min.
Pricing	$5,260.

Flight Performance

Velocity Never Exceed	N.A.
Top Level Speed	60 mph.
Cruise Speed	40-50 mph.
Stall Speed (in free air)	
Sea Level Climb Rate	400 fpm.
Takeoff Run	90 ft.
Dist. Req'd. to clear 50 ft.	N.A.
Landing Roll	50 ft.
Service Ceiling (100 fpm. climb)	20,000 ft.
Range at Cruise	100 mi.
L/D (Glide Ratio)	8-to-1
Minimum Sink Rate	475 fpm.

Light Flyer
Specifications

Wingspan	26 ft. 0 in.
Length	15 ft. 8 in.
Height	7 ft. 0 in.
Wing Area	174 sq. ft.
Engine Make, Model, HP	Cuyuna 430R, 30 hp.
Prop Diameter/Pitch	
Reduction Ratio	2-to-1
Fuel Capacity/Consumption	5 gal./1.5 gph.
Gross Weight	500 lbs.

Empty Weight	240 lbs.
Useful Load	260 lbs.
Wing Loading	2.87 psf.
Power Loading	16.67 lb/hp.
Design Load Factors	
Construction Time	
Field Assembly Time	15 min.
Pricing	$5,420.

Flight Performance

Velocity Never Exceed	55 mph.
Top Level Speed	55 mph.
Cruise Speed	35-45 mph.
Stall Speed (in free air)	24 mph.
Sea Level Climb Rate	800 fpm.
Takeoff Run	110 ft.
Dist. Req'd. to clear 50 ft.	N.A.
Landing Roll	50 ft.
Service Ceiling (100 fpm. climb)	18,000 ft.
Range at Cruise	100 mi.
L/D (Glide Ratio)	
Minimum Sink Rate	

Light Flyer
Pterodactyl, Ltd.
Box 191
Watsonville, CA 95076
(408) 724-2233
Toni James

Quad City Ultralights — Challenger

Fig. 1-73. The Challenger uses the KFM horizontally opposed twin cylinder engine as a pusher.

The Challenger is a strut-braced high wing "cabin" monoplane with pusher engine and tricycle landing gear. It features conventional three axis controls, a cruciform tail, and steerable nosewheel. Rudder and nosewheel are controlled by pedals, while elevator and aileron chores are handled by a center-mounted stick.

Specifications

Wingspan	32 ft.
Length	18 ft. 9 in.
Height	6 ft.
Wing Area	128 sq. ft.
Engine Make, Model, HP	KFM 107ER, 25 hp.
Prop. Diameter/Pitch	54 in/24 in.
Reduction Ratio	2-to-1
Fuel Capacity/Consumption	5 gal.
Gross Weight	530 lbs.
Empty Weight	242 lbs.
Useful Load	288 lbs.
Wing Loading	4.14 psf.
Power Loading	21.2 lb/hp.
Design Load Factors	N.A.
Construction Time	50 man-hrs.
Field Assembly Time	10 min.
Pricing	$5,495.

Flight Performance

Velocity Never Exceed	70 mph.
Top Level Speed	63 mph.
Cruise Speed	60 mph. @ 86% power
Stall Speed (in free air)	25 mph.
Sea Level Climb Rate	700 fpm. @ 50 mph.
Takeoff Run	N.A.
Dist. Req'd. to clear 50 ft.	N.A.
Landing Roll	N.A.
Service Ceiling (100 fpm. climb)	10,000 ft.
Range at Cruise	200 mi.
L/D (Glide Ratio)	11-to-1
Minimum Sink Rate	N.A.

Challenger
Quad City Ultralights
425 E. 59th Street
Davenport, IA 52807
(319) 386-3578
Sales Manager

Raven Industries — *Orbiter MG-300*

Fig. 1-74. The Orbiter is a balloon that uses helium for lift.

MG-300 Pattern Sheet

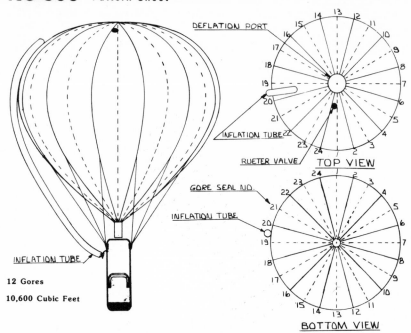

Fig. 1-75. Three-view drawing of the Raven Orbiter ultralight balloon.

The Orbiter is a helium filled ultralight balloon. The new balloon is designed to comply with FAR Part 103, while still meeting with the factory's safety factors and quality of this type certificated models.

The Orbiter has an envelope 28.8 feet in diameter, 27 feet in height, and weighs about 115 pounds. With a volume of 10,600 cubic feet of helium, the balloon falls under the AA-3 category. The naturally shaped envelope has 12 gores and is equipped with a Rueter gas valve and a replaceable rip panel module.

The basket is 30 inches long by 38 inches high and weighs around 38 pounds. It's aluminum frame has a molded high impact base liner and fabric sides. Instrumentation includes an altimeter, rate-of-climb meter, and ten 30 pound ballast bags.

The manufacturer warns that any manned balloon requires some degree of skill to operate. Raven Industries and its dealers will sell the Orbiter only to persons with a private hot air balloon pilot license. If you do not have a license, training for it may be taken at your local Raven dealership.

Specifications

Envelope

Volume	300 cubic meters (10,600 cu. ft.)
Diameter	28.8 ft.
Height	27 ft.

Weight	115 lbs.
Gross Lift	698 lbs. (helium only)
Gores	12
Shape	Natural
Gas Valve	Rueter
Rip Panel	Replaceable factory fabricated module

Note: Horizontal or diagonal gores, artwork, and special designs are extra cost options.

Basket

Size	30 in. x 30 in. x 38 in. high
Weight	38 lbs.
Materials	Aluminum frame, molded high impact base liner, fabric sides
Ballast Bags	10, 30 lb. bags
Instruments	Altimeter, rate-of-climb
Features	Resting Hammock
Pricing	$7,995.

Orbiter Ultralight MG300
Raven Industries, Inc.
Box 1007
Sioux Falls, SD 57117
(605) 335-0199
Larry Manderscheid

R. D. Aircraft — *Skycycle*

The Skycycle is a cable braced, high wing tractor monoplane with tail-dragger landing gear.

The airframe is of mixed construction. The fuselage is constructed of 4130 steel tubing welded in a triangular truss. The wing is of the twin spar type with leading and trailing edges. The spars are made from one inch thick Douglas Fir "stair stock", available at your local lumber yard. The tail surfaces are made from wood and foam. A steel tubing type tail is optional.

The aircraft is controlled by a center mounted joystick which activates rudder and elevator. A three-axis control system, with ailerons and rudder pedals, is also available. In flight, the aircraft offers no surprises and is described as being docile and forgiving.

Plans, raw materials and kits are available from R. D. Aircraft.

Specifications

Wingspan	32 ft.
Length	19 ft.
Height	6 ft. 4 in.
Wing Area	153 sq. ft.
Engine Make, Model, HP	Any 20-30 hp. ultralight engine
Prop. Diameter/Pitch	54 in/22 in.
Reduction Ratio	N.A.
Fuel Capacity/Consumption	5 gal./1 gph.

Fig. 1-76. The Skycycle features a welded steel tubing fuselage and wooden wings.

Fig. 1-77. The Skycycle is a fairly conventional high wing tractor monoplane, reminiscent of the Aeronca C-3 of the 1930s.

Gross Weight	500 lbs.
Empty Weight	239 lbs.
Useful Load	261 lbs.
Wing Loading	3.27 psf.
Power Loading	25-16.67 lb/hp.
Design Load Factors	+3.5, -2.0
Construction Time	200 man-hrs.
Field Assembly Time	20 min.
Pricing	$3,995. (complete materials kit)
	$4,895. (factory built)

Flight Performance

Velocity Never Exceed	55 mph.
Top Level Speed	55 mph.
Cruise Speed	45 mph.
Stall Speed (in free air)	25 mph.
Sea Level Climb Rate	250 fpm.
Takeoff Run	150 ft.
Dist. Req'd. to clear 50 ft.	N.A.
Landing Roll	150 ft.
Service Ceiling (100 fpm. climb)	N.A.
Range at Cruise	200 mi.
L/D (Glide Ratio)	N.A.
Minimum Sink Rate	N.A.

Skycycle
R. D. Aircraft
P.O. Box 211, Dart Airport
Mayville, NY 14757
(716) 753-2113
Bob Dart

Robertson Aircraft — B1-RD

The B1-RD is a cable braced, aluminum and dacron, high wing monoplane with taildragger landing gear. It features a conventional independent three-axis control system actuated by a center mounted joystick and rudder pedals.

The main gear consists of 16 inch wheels with bungee cord suspension and a steerable tail wheel. The pilot sits on the center of gravity and is restrained by a seatbelt and shoulder harness. The aircraft is powered by a Cuyuna 430R driving a tractor propeller via a reduction drive.

All parts are anodized, plated or painted, pre-drilled and pre-bent. All cables are cut to exact length with the fittings swaged in place. The flying surfaces are presewn and all nuts and bolts are packaged and labeled. A complete construction manual accompanies each kit. It is car-toppable.

Options include: custom sails, remote starter and choke kit, 20-inch wheels, windscreen, chrome fenders and hardware, chromed axle, tow hook with quick release, strobe light, double-surface wing, electric start, flight instruments, floats, parachute and storage bags.

Complete kits are available from Robertson Aircraft Corporation.

Specifications

Wingspan	32 ft. 6 in.
Length	19 ft. 0 in.
Height	7 ft. 0 in.

Fig. 1-78. The Robertson 81-RD features free flying ailerons, tractor engine.

Wing Area	162 sq. ft.
Engine Make, Model, HP	Cuyuna 430-R, 30 hp.
Prop. Diameter/Pitch	72 in/36 in.
Reduction Ratio	3-to-1
Fuel Capacity/Consumption	5 gal./1.5 gph.
Gross Weight	530 lbs.
Empty Weight	250 lbs.
Useful Load	270 lbs.
Wing Loading	3.27 psf.
Power Loading	17.67 lb/hp.
Design Load Factors	+3, -2
Construction Time	50 man-hrs.
Field Assembly Time	60 min.
Pricing	$5,995.

Flight Performance

Velocity Never Exceed	55 mph.
Top Level Speed	50 mph.
Cruise Speed	38 mph.
Stall Speed (in free air)	15 mph.
Sea Level Climb Rate	850 fpm. @ 20 mph.
Takeoff Run	50 ft.
Dist. Req'd. to clear 50 ft.	N.A.
Landing Roll	30 ft.
Service Ceiling (100 fpm. climb)	12,000 ft.
Range at Cruise	125 mi.
L/D (Glide Ratio)	8.5-to-1
Minimum Sink Rate	300 fpm. @ 22 mph.

"B1-RD"
Robertson Aircraft Corp.
Snohomish County Airport
Everett, WA 98204
(206) 355-8702
Larry White

Ritz Aircraft — Standard Model A

The Standard is a strut-braced, parasol wing pusher with taildragger landing gear and it is constructed mainly of wood, and features an independent, three-axis aerodynamic control system. It is sold as a kit for $1,995.

The airframe construction revolves around a unique "in-the-slot" technique, coupled with geodetic structures. Fuselage longerons and cross members, and wing spar caps and rib caps are pre-slotted at the factory. The homebuilder simply applies glue to the interconnecting pieces, and inserts them into the slots at the appropriate locations. This method is quite fast, allowing a rib to be assembled in three or four minutes. In fact, the designer claims all the ribs can be assembled in a single evening. The spars are said to require another evening, and the wing assembly a weekend. The detail work, such as small attachments, cutting the aileron etc., require more time. The landing gear is pre-molded, shaped and sanded, and gets bolted to the fuselage. All metal parts, like the motor mount-wing support, struts and control system parts, are welded and drilled at the factory — the builder bolts or epoxy laminates them in place. The ultralight can be built with the basic handtools found around most households.

The prototype was reportedly very easy and pleasant to fly.

Specifications

Wingspan	36 ft.
Length	18 ft.
Height	5 ft.
Wing Area	140 sq. ft.
Engine Make, Model, HP	Solo 210, 16 hp.
Prop. Diameter/Pitch	50 in./24 in.
Reduction Ratio	2.9-to-1
Fuel Capacity/Consumption	5 gal./1 gph.
Gross Weight	370 lbs.
Empty Weight	170 lbs.

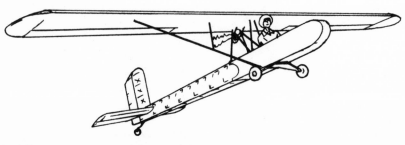

Fig. 1-79. An artist's sketch of the Ritz standard.

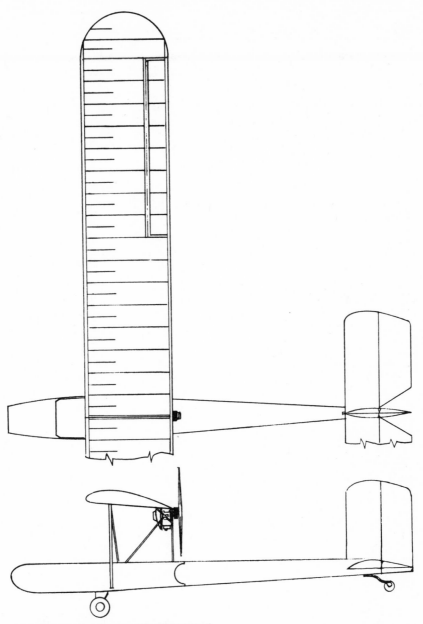

Fig. 1-80. A two-view drawing of the Ritz standard.

Useful Load	200 lbs.
Wing Loading	2.64 psf.
Power Loading	23.13 lb/hp.
Design Load Factors	+4, -2
Construction Time	250 man-hrs.
Field Assembly Time	10 min.
Pricing	$1,995.

Flight Performance

Velocity Never Exceed	75 mph.
Top Level Speed	60 mph.
Cruise Speed	45 mph. @ 60% power
Stall Speed (in free air)	20 mph.
Sea Level Climb Rate	N.A.
Takeoff Run	120 ft.
Dist. Req'd. to clear 50 ft.	N.A.
Landing Roll	N.A.
Service Ceiling (100 fpm. climb)	N.A.
Range at Cruise	240 mi.
L/D (Glide Ratio)	12-to-1 @ 40 mph.
Minimum Sink Rate	N.A.

Ritz Standard Model "A"
Ritz Aircraft Co.
Shipmans Creek Rd.
Wartrace, TN 37183
(615) 857-3419
Jerry Ritz - Mark Gonzalez

Rotec — Rally 2B

The Rally 2B is a high wing, cabled braced monoplane with three-axis controls and conventional landing gear. It is equipped with a pusher engine, above mounted control stick, and rudder pedals. Both kits and factory-built units are available.

The airframe construction is basically hang glider, consisting primarily of anodized aluminum tubing braced with cable. The wing is a basic ladder type frame with pre-formed aluminum tubing ribs inserted into pockets in the fabric, which is pre-sewn, stabilized dacron sailcloth. Assembly is by bolts only — there is no welding involved.

The powerplant is a 2-cycle, twin cylinder engine with fan cooling and recoil starter, and includes an alternator as well. It is rated at 38 hp., which is transmitted to a 52 inch diameter laminated maple propeller via a shaft and reduction drive.

The landing gear is shock absorbing with 20 inch mains for operation from unimproved fields. The double tail wheel is full swiveling, permitting small radius turns.

William Adaska, Rotec president and aeronautical engineer, has this to say about the Rally.

"Aerodynamic feedback forces give the pilot control position information. All controls exhibit self-centering forces in flight. A simple artificial force field system was tested, but considered unnecessary. All control inputs are positive

Fig. 1-81. The Rotec Rally 2-B uses a basic wire-braced aluminum airframe, covered with dacron sailcloth.

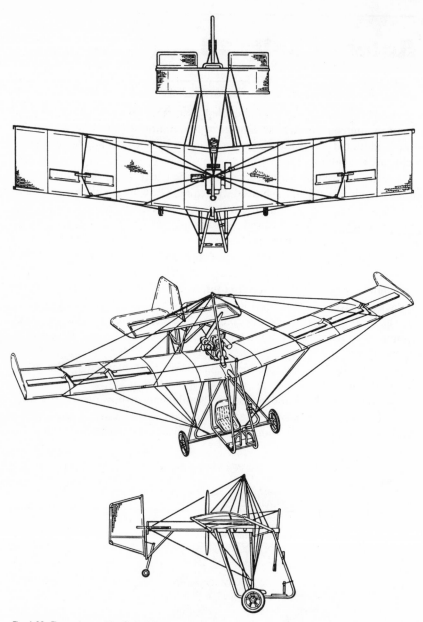

Fig. 1-82. Three-views of the Rally 2-B.

and in the standard direction (forward stick for nosedown, etc.) except during tail slides. Such intentional aerobatics are prohibited by the manufacturer.

The stick forces increase slightly with airspeed to achieve the same pitch, roll or yaw rates. The aircraft becomes more stable above all axes with increasing airspeed. At low speeds, larger control inputs are needed to obtain the same pitch, roll and yaw rates, but control forces are light. Control power is high, allowing maneuverability even below stall. The ailerons are effective during taxi in higher winds. The elevator and rudder are "blown" by the propeller, giving them good control power during critical takeoff periods in gusty winds. The rudder, sweep and dihedral combine to allow coordinated turns with rudder only. During the powered flight, the rudder's control over roll is stronger than the ailerons.

Control harmony designed into the Rally 2B results from matching control surface size to the low flying speeds. The lightest control force is pitch. The aileron input forces are next lowest. The rudder requires the highest forces, but they're easily handled by the pilot's legs. The airplane can be slipped for losing altitude and during crosswind landings."

Mr. Adaska goes on to evaluate flying the Rally 2B.

"Set stick mounted ignition "on". Pull engine compression release line and pull starter rope overhead, starting engine. Buckle-up into bucket seat and place feet on pedals. Excessive taxiing and idling is permissable because of the fan cooled engine. Turn "on" position lights and strobe.

Control taxi using rudder. The tail wheel may be lifted with full power and forward stick, allowing a quick turn. The airplane can't nose over because of the forward cockpit structure. Check gauges in front of pilot. Twist throttle at base of control stick, adding full power. At about 5 mph, push stick forward raising tail. Hold about four seconds, accelerating to takeoff speed, (20 mph), and rotate into the air.

Inherent stability is provided by the high wing and large tail. The pitch rate due to fore and aft stick inputs is about twice the roll rate with no noticeable delay.

Turns can be made using either the rudder or ailerons or both for coordination. Shallow aileron turns are "self-coordinated", requiring no rudder input. The rudder automatically "washes-out" slightly in a roll due to its weight.

Turns around a point are easily made by lining up the leading edge tip with the point. Little actual force is needed to hold the Rally in the turns. Once placed, one finger will be all that's needed. High banked turns over 30° greatly slow the aircraft and are best initiated at higher airspeeds, depending on the stall speed at that angle.

The aircraft exhibits positive longitudinal stability throughout its speed range. Push the stick forward to go faster. Cruise speed is about 35 mph. with 45 mph. maximum.

The propeller delivers very little thrust at 45 mph., therefore acting as a speed brake.

Landing approaches are normally made power on, unless too high. The aircraft tends to float in ground effect (below 15 feet) which can help smooth the touchdown."

Specifications

Wingspan	31 ft.
Length	16 ft. 10 in.
Height	10 ft. 4 in.
Wing Area	155 sq. ft.

Engine Make, Model, HP	Rotax 377, 38 hp.
Prop. Diameter/Pitch	52 in/34 in.
Reduction Ratio	2.18-to-1
Fuel Capacity/Consumption	3.5 gal./1.7 gph.
Gross Weight	452 lbs.
Empty Weight	220 lbs.
Useful Load	232 lbs.
Wing Loading	2.92 psf.
Power Loading	11.89 lb/hp.
Design Load Factors	+3, -1.5
Construction Time	50 man-hrs.
Field Assembly Time	45 min.
Pricing	$4,800.

Flight Performance

Velocity Never Exceed	50 mph.
Top Level Speed	50 mph.
Cruise Speed	45 mph. @ 75% power
Stall Speed (in free air)	18 mph.
Sea level Climb Rate	500 fpm. @ 30 mph.
Takeoff Run	75 ft.
Dist. Req'd. to clear 50 ft.	N.A.
Landing Roll	50 ft.
Service Ceiling (100 fpm. climb)	10,000 ft.
Range at Cruise	90 mi.
L/D (Glide Ratio)	7-to-1
Minimum Sink Rate	N.A.

Rally 2B
Rotec Engineering, Inc.
P.O. Box 220
Duncanville, TX 75116
(214) 298-2505
David Dutson

Rotec — *Rally Sport*

The Rally Sport is basically a beefed-up, clipped wing Rally 2B. The wingspan has been reduced to 27 feet, heavier cables were added, as were heavier compression struts, leading and trailing edges. The tail booms were also modified to handle increased torsional loads. With all this, the factory claims the ultralight is capable of loops, rolls, spins, hammerhead stalls, chandelles and the split-S.

The air vehicle is powered by a 48 hp Rotax driving a 60 inch pusher prop through a CPS reduction drive, enabling a climb rate of 1200 fpm. It is available in both kit form and ready-to-fly.

The author would like to caution anyone anticipating aerobatics to first get proper instruction from a qualified aerobatic instructor. This type of flying can put great stresses on both the pilot and airframe, which can be aggravated by improper technique. Aerobatics are not to be taken lightly, for they can easily lead to disaster. Aerobatics in this type of air vehicle is questionable.

Specifications

Wingspan	27 ft.
Length	10 ft. 4 in.
Height	16 ft. 7 in.

Fig. 1-83. The Rally Sport caught during a loop.

Wing Area	135 sq. ft.
Engine Make, Model, HP	Rotax 503, 48 hp.
Prop. Diameter/Pitch	60 in/28 in.
Reduction Ratio	2.25-to-1
Fuel Capacity/Consumption	3.5 gal./2 gph.
Gross Weight	470 lbs.
Empty Weight	248 lbs.
Useful Load	220 lbs.
Wing Loading	3.48 psf.
Power Loading	9.79 lb/hp.
Design Load Factors	+6, -3
Construction Time	50 man-hrs.
Field Assembly Time	30 min.
Pricing	$5,600.

Flight Performance

Velocity Never Exceed	60 mph.
Top Level Speed	60 mph.
Cruise Speed	50 mph. @ 60% power
Stall Speed (in free air)	23 mph.
Sea Level Climb Rate	1200 fpm. @ 32 mph.
Takeoff Run	70 ft.
Dist. Req'd. to clear 50 ft.	N.A.
Landing Roll	75 ft.
Service Ceiling (100 fpm. climb)	10,000 ft.
Range at Cruise	75 mi. (3.5 gal. tank)
L/D (Glide Ratio)	6.8-to-1 @ 30 mph.
Minimum Sink Rate	N.A.

Rally Sport
Rotec Engineering, Inc.
P.O. Box 220
Duncanville, TX 75116
(214) 298-2505
David Dutson

S

Skyhigh Ultralights — *Skybaby*

Fig. 1-84. The Skybaby is designed to be built from plans. It's constructed mostly of wood.

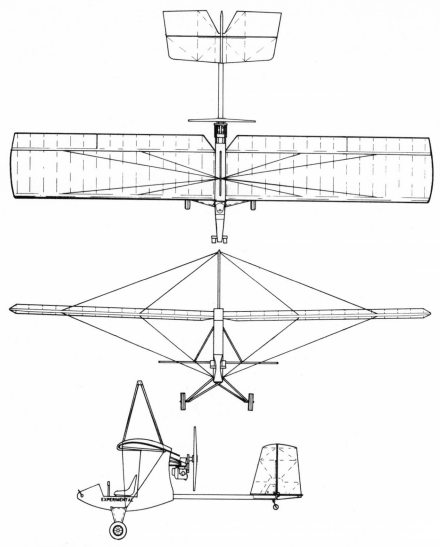

Fig. 1-85. Three-view drawing of the Skybaby reveals a somewhat conventional high wing monoplane layout.

The Skybaby is a high wing, cable braced monoplane with independent, three-axis controls. It is constructed of aircraft plywood, aluminum and steel tubing, with Douglas Fir spars. The pilot sits up front for unrestricted visibility.

The aircraft is designed for homebuilding, while meeting a 155 pound, 3 pounds per square foot criteria. It can be powered by either the Mc101 or Yamaha KT100 go-kart engines, but the KT100 is recommended for heavier pilots and high density altitudes. The plans are presented on ten 24 x 36 inch fully detailed sheets. A step-by-step manual is provided to minimize first-time builder problems. Many parts and assemblies including: welded landing gear assemblies, control assemblies, reduction drive, seats, ribs, bushings, bearings, etc., are available from the designer on request.

The Skybaby is responsive and easy to fly and should offer no surprises. Ground handling is good due to a steerable tailwheel and bungee sprung main gear. Plans are available from Skyhigh Ultralights.

Specifications

Wingspan	32 ft.
Length	17 ft.
Height	6 ft.
Wing Area	132 sq. ft.
Engine Make, Model, HP	Cuyuna 215 - 20 hp.
Prop. Diameter/Pitch	54 in/24 in.
Reduction Ratio	2.5-to-1
Fuel Capacity/Consumption	1.5 gal.
Gross Weight	400 lbs.
Empty Weight	190 lbs.
Useful Load	210 lbs.
Wing Loading	3.1 psf.
Power Loading	20 lb/hp.
Design Load Factors	+5, -3
Construction Time	200 man-hrs.
Field Assembly Time	20 min.
Pricing	Plans $55.00

Flight Performance

Velocity Never Exceed	50 mph.
Top Level Speed	45 mph.
Cruise Speed	30-35 mph.
Stall Speed (in free air)	22-24 mph.
Sea Level Climb Rate	500 fpm. @ 28 mph. 20 hp. Cuyuna
Takeoff Run	150 ft.
Dist. Req'd. to clear 50 ft.	750 ft.
Landing Roll	200 ft.
Service Ceiling (100 fpm. climb)	10,000 ft.
Range at Cruise	70 mi.
L/D (Glide Ratio)	9-to-1 @ 32 mph.
Minimum Sink Rate	300 fpm @ 32 mph.

Skybaby
Skyhigh Ultralights Inc.
P.O. Box 64
Langhorne, PA 19047
(215) 752-3581 after 6 p.m.
Paul Rokowski

Sorrell — SNS-8 Hiperlight

The Hiperlight is a negatively staggered, taildragger biplane with a completely enclosed cabin. It features conventional three-axis aerodynamic controls, and a mixture of steel and aluminum construction.

The wings are built up of sheet aluminum components, including a D-section leading edge, shear web, and stamped ribs. The interplane struts are aluminum tubing. Only the lower wing has control surfaces — full span flaperons. The wings are of constant chord and equal span, and have a somewhat undercambered airfoil. They are braced with stainless steel cable.

The nose and cabin areas of the fuselage are of welded 4130 chromemoly steel tubing. This is where the pilot is seated and where the wings attach. The aft portion of the fuselage is made up of heliarced aluminum tubing, as are the tail feathers. The front of the fuselage picks up a Rotax 277 with reduction drive. A neat cowling shrouds the powerplant almost totally, except for the carburetor and exhaust.

The main landing gear consists of garden variety tractor wheels and tires, mounted at the end of spring steel rod gear legs. The tailwheel is solid soft rubber, mounted at the end of a spring steel rod, and it steers with the rudder. This undercarriage arrangement helps smooth out mildly rough ground, and makes three point landings the order of the day.

The entire airframe is covered with zero porosity, rip stop, heat shrinkable dacron that needs no doping. This should facilitate the homebuilder when

Fig. 1-86. The Sorrell Hiperlight flies well on only 28 HP. Handles much like an airplane.

and if kits are offered. The windshield, cabin sides opposite the pilot's head and the nose area below the windshield are lexan, offering good visibility, especially for a biplane. The windshield is hinged on the right, therefore the pilot enters from the left, facing aft. He then must do a 180 before taking his seat and strapping in.

Those who have flown the Hiperlite say that it flies like an airplane. Stick pressures are, of course, light, but also harmonious, and they become heavier with airspeed, as they should. The flaperon system adds to this feeling because when the stick is pulled past neutral, both ailerons are drooped somewhat, adding to the lift with little change in pitch. This helps bring the stalling speed within FAR 103 guidelines, while adding to the nice feel of the air vehicle. The prototype's somewhat smallish vertical fin left a little to be desired in the yaw stability department, but production versions will see that changed. The rudder however, is quite powerful.

At the start of the takeoff run, the tail will easily come up, and the Hiperlight will accelerate briskly. On grass, she's off in 175 feet. Visibility over the nose is excellent, even in the three point attitude, but especially with the tail up. Climbout is done at around 38 mph, and the rate should be over 600 fpm.

The overall in-flight behavior is nimble, and stalls are gentle and straight forward. The ship may be said to possess nice handling qualities. The approach is surprisingly glider-like, thanks to the little bibe's 10-to-1 glide ratio. It isn't until the final flare that drag builds up — thanks to the broad expanse of the bottom of the fuselage, causing the ultralight to land. After touchdown, the rollout takes 175 on grass. A hard-surfaced runway landing would require more, making brakes a good idea.

At present, only ready-to-fly versions are being sold however, kits are being considered.

Specifications (Prototype)

Wingspan	21 ft.
Length	15 ft. 6 in.
Height	5 ft. 1½ in.
Wing Area	132 sq. ft.
Engine Make, Model, HP	Rotax 277, 28 hp.
Prop. Diameter/Pitch	50 in/28 in.
Reduction Ratio	2-to-1
Fuel Capacity/Consumption	5 gal./1 gph.
Gross Weight	500 lbs.
Empty Weight	243 lbs.
Useful Load	257 lbs.
Wing Loading	3.79 psf.
Power Loading	17.9 lb/hp.
Design Load Factors	+6, -4
Construction Time	50 man-hrs.
Field Assembly Time	10 min.
Pricing	$8,500. (estimated)

Flight Performance (Prototype)

Velocity Never Exceed	95 mph.
Top Level Speed	75 mph.
Cruise Speed	60 mph. @ 50% power
Stall Speed (in free air)	28 mph.
Sea Level Climb Rate	600 fpm. @ 38 mph.
Takeoff Run	175 ft. on grass
Dist. Req'd. to clear 50 ft.	420 ft. on grass
Landing Roll	175 ft. on grass
Service Ceiling (100 fpm. climb)	N.A.
Range at Cruise	300 mi.
L/D (Glide Ratio)	10-to-1 @ 40 mph.
Minimum Sink Rate	375 fpm @ 40 mph.

SNS-8 "Hiperlight"
Sorrell Aviation
16525 Tilley Rd. So.
Tenino, WA 98589
(206) 264-2866
Mark or Tim Sorrell

Spectrum Aircraft — *Beaver*

The Beaver is a strut-braced, high wing monoplane with pusher engine and tricycle landing gear. It features three axis aerodynamic controls actuated by a side mounted stick and rudder pedals.

The airframe is constructed primarily of aluminum tubing in a bolt-together fashion. The wing is a basic ladder frame with internal drag and anti-drag bracing. It is supported by a pair of struts per panel, including jury struts. The airfoil is formed by preformed aluminum tubing ribs that slip into the presewn dacron wing envelope. The trailing edge carries ailerons of 67% span.

The pilot sits atop a large diameter keel tube that runs below the propeller and rearward to where it picks up the empennage. The tail surfaces are framed of aluminum tubing, and covered by envelopes of dacron sailcloth. A large rudder and elevator handle yaw and pitch control. The elevator is activated via cables and pulleys from the stick. Rudder pedals control the rudder through cables run inside the keel tube.

According to the factory, the Beaver's most outstanding feature is the responsive roll control attained with the large ten foot ailerons. This allows for light stick pressures and high maneuverability in the air or on the ground in crosswind conditions. The trailing edge of the airfoil is lowered two inches providing a slight under camber. This makes for a shorter takeoff roll and a slower stall speed.

Fig. 1-87. The Spectrum Beaver uses typical ultralight constructional features.

The stall characteristics are said to be excellent with no tendency to drop a wing, while recovery is smooth with very little loss in altitude. The control surfaces remain responsive even at the stall.

Optional items include: a nose fairing, full enclosure, amphibious floats, skis, and instruments.

Specifications (with 175 lb. pilot)

Wingspan	33 ft.
Length	N.A.
Height	N.A.
Wing Area	158 sq. ft.
Engine Make, Model, HP	Rotax 277, 28 hp (35 hp. optional)
Prop. Diameter/Pitch	58 in/28 in.
Reduction Ratio	2-to-1
Fuel Capacity/Consumption	4.6 gal./1.25 gph.
Gross Weight	426 lbs.
Empty Weight	232 lbs.
Useful Load	N.A.
Wing Loading	2.7 psf.
Power Loading	15.2 lb/hp.
Design Load Factors	N.A.
Construction Time	30 man-hrs.
Field Assembly Time	N.A.
Pricing	$5,950.

Flight Performance

Velocity Never Exceed	62 mph.
Top Level Speed	62 mph.
Cruise Speed	30-55 mph.
Stall Speed (in free air)	24 mph.
Sea Level Climb Rate	600 fpm.
Takeoff Run	100 ft.
Dist. Req'd. to clear 50 ft.	320 ft.
Landing Roll	125 ft.
Service Ceiling (100 fpm. climb)	N.A.
Range at Cruise	160 mi.
L/D (Glide Ratio)	11-to-1
Minimum Sink Rate	N.A.

Beaver
Spectrum Aircraft, Inc.
#3-9531-192nd Street
Surrey, BC V3T 4W2 CANADA
(604) 888-2055
Sales Manager

Sport Flight Engineering — Sky Pup

The Sky Pup is a high wing cabin monoplane with a tractor engine and taildragger landing gear. It is constructed primarily of foam and wood and is designed for the homebuilder.

The wing consists of a D-section leading edge made-up of foam nose ribs, wooden leading edge nose, and birch plywood skin. The spar has a foam shear web, capped by wooden strips. The ribs are also foam with wooden cap strips. The trailing edge is wood. The wing is constructed in three sections: a flat center section, and two dihedral panels. Each joint is made of aircraft grade steel attach fittings, and requires only three bolts to fasten together. The center section is made a permanent part of the fuselage, the wing panels being removed for transport or storage.

The fuselage is framed in wooden longerons, with sides, bottom and top of foam. Plywood is used in the nose and wing areas, as well as for gussets in higher stress areas. The tail feathers are framed in wood.

A single, tapered piece of maple makes up the landing gear legs, giving a natural springiness. A short axle is bolted on to the end of each leg to pick up the standard 20″ wheels. A triangular piece of wood makes up the tail skid.

The entire air vehicle is covered in fabric by the so-called "blanket" method, requiring no seams or doping. The fabric is sealed and protected by a glossy polyurethane finish at the mill.

Fig. 1-88. The Sky Pup is a cantilevered tractor monoplane of wooden construction, designed to be built from plans.

171

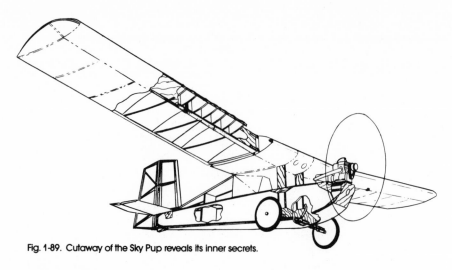

Fig. 1-89. Cutaway of the Sky Pup reveals its inner secrets.

The ultralight is controlled by a stick actuating the elevator and rudder pedals wagging the rudder. The designer claims this two-control system, coupled with a large dihedral, allows for adequate roll control. Ground maneuvering is accomplished by a blast from the prop down elevator to lift the tail, and rudder to turn while the tail is off the ground. In flight, the Sky Pup is gentle and forgiving, and offers no surprises.

The Sky Pup can be powered by any engine of from 15 to 20 hp. The designer further claims the entire airframe, less engine and prop, can be built for less than $1000. To achieve this, many materials can be bought locally in standard sizes. For materials not obtainable locally, the designer lists the suppliers in the instructions.

The ultralight is sold only as a set of plans, direct from Sport Flight.

Specifications

Wingspan	31 ft.
Length	15 ft. 11 in.
Height	4 ft. 4 in.
Wing Area	130 sq. ft.
Engine Make, Model, HP	Cuyuna 215 RR, 20 hp.
Prop. Diameter/Pitch	58 in/24 in.
Reduction Ratio	2.25-to-1
Fuel Capacity/Consumption	2 gal./1 gph.
Gross Weight	400 lbs.
Empty Weight	195 lbs.
Useful Load	205 lbs.
Wing Loading	3.08 psf.
Power Loading	20 lb/hp.
Design Load Factors	+6, -3
Construction Time	N.A.
Field Assembly Time	15 min.
Pricing	Plans $50.

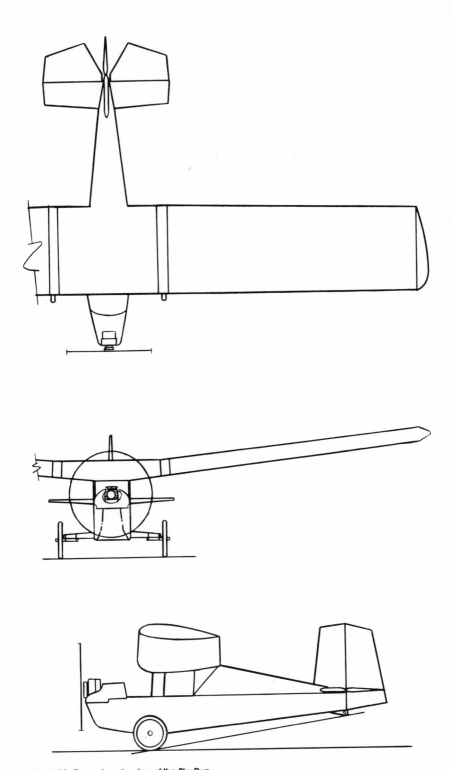

Fig. 1-90. Three-view drawing of the Sky Pup.

Flight Performance

Velocity Never Exceed	69 mph.
Top Level Speed	63 mph.
Cruise Speed	55 mph.
Stall Speed (in free air)	26 mph.
Sea Level Climb Rate	450 fpm.
Takeoff Run	200 ft.
Dist. Req'd. to clear 50 ft.	N.A.
Landing Roll	N.A.
Service Ceiling (100 fpm. climb)	N.A.
Range at Cruise	N.A.
L/D (Glide Ratio)	12-to-1
Minimum Sink Rate	260 fpm.

Sky Pup

Sport Flight Engineering, Inc.

P.O. Box 2164

Grand Junction, CO 81502

(303) 245-3899

Sales Manager

SR-1 Enterprises — *Hornet*

The Hornet is a strut and cable braced biplane with taildragger landing gear and cruciform tail. It is controlled by a conventional three-axis system with a side stick activating elevator and ailerons, and foot bar deflecting the rudder.

The airframe is constructed primarily of aluminum and steel tubing. The wings are basic ladder frames with drag and anti-drag diagonal cables inside the airfoil. The fuselage incorporates three longerons supporting the tail and pilot cage forward of the lower wing. The pilot sits out front in a swingseat, feet resting on the rudder bar which is attached to an anti-noseover skid. The 20 inch main wheels are bungee shock cord suspended for unprepared field operations, while a steel rudder post supports a tail skid.

In flight, the Hornet is stable, gentle and forgiving, offering no surprises. The ailerons are quite large and of the anti-adverse yaw type minimizing use of rudder to coordinate turns. The tails surfaces are also large and effective.

The Hornet is powered by a Cuyuna UL II-02, mounted to a steel truss behind the pilot, between the two wings. The Kawasaki engines may be used, as well.

Optional items include whatever the purchaser desires and the aircraft may be custom built to suit. Complete kits are available from SR-1 Enterprises.

Specifications

Wingspan	32 ft. 10 in.
Length	18 ft. 0 in.
Height	6 ft. 10 in.
Wing Area	216 sq. ft.
Engine Make, Model, HP	Llyod-23 hp. Cuyuna UL II-02-35 hp. Kawasaki 37 hp. and 62 hp.

Fig. 1-91. The Hornet brings back the flavor of the biplane era with ultralight construction.

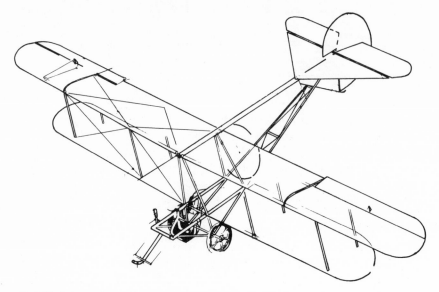

Fig. 1-92. Cutaway shows major structural components of the Hornet.

Prop. Diameter/Pitch	N.A. three-blade std.
Reduction Ratio	2-to-1
Fuel Capacity/Consumption	5 gal./1.8 gph.
Gross Weight	675 lbs.
Empty Weight	252 lbs.
Useful Load	425 lbs.
Wing Loading	3.125 psf.
Power Loading	
Design Load Factors	+8.8, -7.6
Construction Time	80 man-hrs.
Field Assembly Time	22 min.
Pricing	$4,990. Kit

Flight Performance

Velocity Never Exceed	80 mph.
Top Level Speed	65 mph.
Cruise Speed	55 mph. @ 75% power, Cuyuna (45% 62 hp. Kawasaki)
Stall Speed (in free air)	19 mph.
Sea Level Climb Rate	750 fpm. @ 33 mph., Cuyuna (1500 fpm. at 36 mph. 62 hp. Kawasaki)
Takeoff Run	70 ft.
Dist. Req'd. to clear 50 ft.	
Landing Roll	50 ft.
Service Ceiling (100 fpm. climb)	10,000 ft.
Range at Cruise	150 mi.

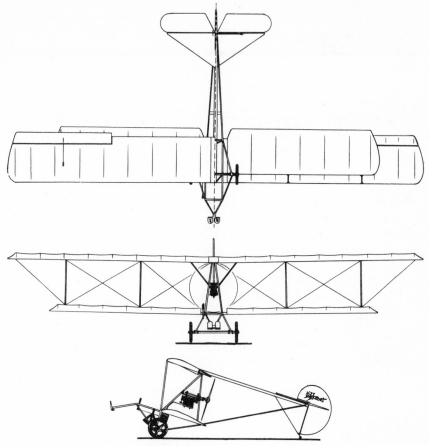

Fig. 1-93. Three-view drawing of the SR-1 Hornet.

L/D (Glide Ratio)	9.8-to-1 @ 35 mph.
Minimum Sink Rate	250 fpm. @ 24 mph.

Hornet
SR-1 Enterprises
2319 Endicott
St. Paul, MN 55114
(612) 646-3884
Keith Erickson

Starflight — TX-1000

The TX-1000 is a high wing pusher monoplane with conventional three-axis controls and tricycle landing gear. A side mounted stick control elevator and spoilers, while rudder pedals actuate the rudder and steerable nosewheel.

The airframe is constructed of bolted together aluminum tubing and interconnecting stainless steel cable. The wing is a basic ladder type frame, while the tail surfaces are frames of tubing. The engine is mounted beneath the wing center section, driving a pusher prop via a shaft and reduction drive. A pyramidal aluminum tubing frame contains the pilot's seat, with the landing gear at its base. A kingpost carries the landing cables supporting negative g-loads. The flying surfaces are covered in 5.3 oz. stabilized dacron sailcloth, the wings being doubled surfaced 30% back from the leading edge.

The TX-1000 has a 2-inch diameter leading edge, 1½-inch trailing edge and tail boom tubes, and 1-inch diameter, heavy wall compression struts. Stainless steel bushings and aluminum vibration insulators are used throughout, as are aircraft bolts, hardware and rigging. All exposed airframe tubing is coated with a bonded black epoxy, baked to a gloss finish.

The flight handling characteristics of the TX-1000 are described as responsive yet forgiving, by the factory. The wing has a 5° dihedral, and allows the air vehicle to be flown hands-off with an occasional touch of the rudder pedals.

Fig. 1-94. Starflight TX-1000 is a single surfaced ultralight with spoilers, rudder and elevator.

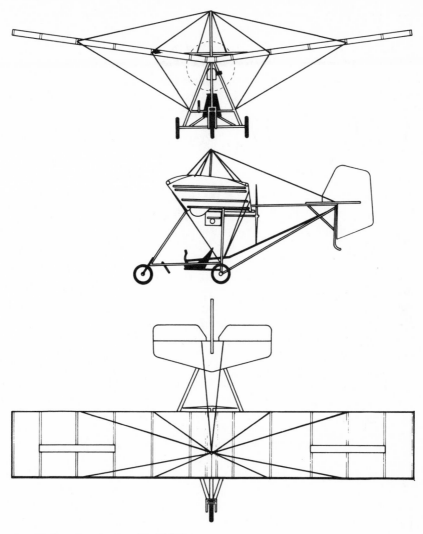

Fig. 1-95. Three-view drawing of the TX-1000.

Specifications

Wingspan	32 ft. 6 in.
Length	15 ft.
Height	9 ft.
Wing Area	160 sq. ft.
Engine Make, Model, HP	Rotax 377, 32 hp.
Prop. Diameter/Pitch	54 in/27 in.
Reduction Ratio	2.01-to-1
Fuel Capacity/Consumption	4.5 gal./1.5 gph.
Gross Weight	502 lbs.
Empty Weight	252 lbs.

Useful Load	250 lbs.
Wing Loading	3.14 psf.
Power Loading	15.69 lb/hp.
Design Load Factors	+5.8, -3.6
Construction Time	40 man-hrs.
Field Assembly Time	60 min.
Pricing	$5,195.

Flight Performance

Velocity Never Exceed	55 mph.
Top Level Speed	55 mph.
Cruise Speed	45 mph. @ 70% power
Stall Speed (in free air)	21 mph.
Sea Level Climb Rate	800 fpm. @ 38 mph.
Takeoff Run	175 ft.
Dist. Req'd. to clear 50 ft.	N.A.
Landing Roll	100 ft.
Service Ceiling (100 fpm. climb)	12,000 ft.
Range at Cruise	90 mi.
L/D (Glide Ratio)	7-to-1
Minimum Sink Rate	

TX-1000
Starflight Aircraft, Inc.
Liberty Landing Airport
Rt. 3, Box 197
Liberty, MO 64068
Dick Turner

St. Croix Ultralights — *Excelsior*

The Excelsior is a completely enclosed, strut braced, high wing monoplane with rudder, elevator and spoiler controls. Its most unique feature is a tail mounted pusher prop driven by a long shaft running back from the wing mounted engine through the main longeron.

The double tapered wings have a thick, high lift undercambered airfoil. The wingtips are fiberglass with a drooped conical camber, pop riveted to the D-section spar and tip rib. Ailerons provide roll control.

The cockpit features a semi-reclining seat and a lexan wind screen. A full enclosure is optional. A large instrument panel bulkhead allows space for gadgetry and gauges. All switches and controls are within easy reach of the pilot.

The tail mounted propeller is said to offer several advantages: it allows the best possible view; dispenses with the prop blast and allows for smaller tail controls because they see continuous airflow; does not compromise the fuselage shape; adds to the stability, and does not impart a twisting airflow over the fuselage, as a tractor arrangement would.

The low rudder is advantageous aerodynamically, in that it produces a rolling moment in the desired direction of turn. It also tends to pitch the nose up slightly in a turn.

The landing gear employs two bungee shock cushioned main wheels and a full castoring nosewheel. The main wheels ride on a 4130 steel welded frame assembly which forms the lower structural base of the fuselage. The nose

Fig. 1-96. St. Croix's Excelsior has its propeller behind the tail. It's driven by a long shaft and flexidyne drive.

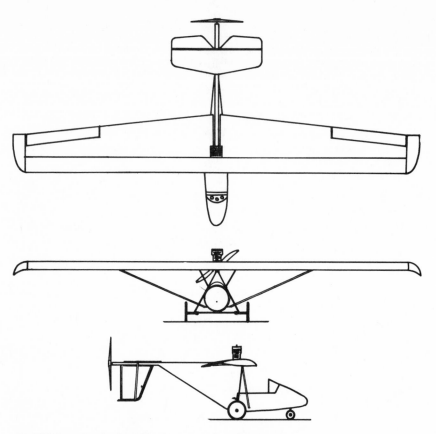

Fig. 1-97. Three-view drawing of Excelsior reveals its unique drive train.

wheel is mounted on the forward structural former which also carries the rudder bar. Both assemblies are factory jig welded and ready to pop rivet into position.

The fuselage is built of three aluminum tubes pop riveted to the main 3-inch diameter drive shaft housing/keel tube. An aluminum tube rudder is hinged to the aft section, and the horizontal tail assembly is mounted directly above. A pre-cut and lightened bulkhead is mounted to the down tubes behind the seat, while picking up the nose cone. A pre-bent aluminum seat is pop riveted to the nose tubes and forms a sturdy box structure around the pilot.

The wings are built-up using a D-section leading edge spar formed around foam ribs and pop riveted together. The entire D-tube assembly is factory jig built and virtually builds the wing. The builder must add the spoilerons which are preformed.

All 4130 steel parts are pre-welded and ready for installation. The completed airframe is covered with Stits Poly-Fiber Coatings — an aircraft grade dacron which glues to bare aluminum, is shrunk tight with an iron, and doped with Poly Brush and Poly Spray.

The power system is based on the Mott Taylor pioneered flexidyne coupling. It's a special type of clutch which effectively removes all potentially damaging vibration from a propeller drive shaft enabling the system to run smoothly without maintenance. This torsional resonance damper (flexidyne) is actually filled with thousands of tiny steel shot, and will transmit 100% of the power in the shaft, while dampening the power pulses of the engine. The power system comes completely prefabricated, and ready to install.

Complete kits are available from St. Croix Ultralights.

Specifications

Wingspan	34 ft. 7 in.
Length	17 ft. 6 in.
Height	6 ft. 1 in.
Wing Area	133 sq. ft.
Engine Make, Model, HP	Zenoah G25B, 20 hp. & WAM342
Prop. Diameter/Pitch	56 in/28 in.
Reduction Ratio	2.5-to-1
Fuel Capacity/Consumption	5 gal./1.25 gph.
Gross Weight	500 lbs.
Empty Weight	252 lbs.
Useful Load	240 lbs.
Wing Loading	3.38 psf.
Power Loading	22.5 lb/hp.
Design Load Factors	+4, -4
Construction Time	100 man-hrs.
Field Assembly Time	15 min.
Pricing	$5,800.

Flight Performance

Velocity Never Exceed	63 mph.
Top Level Speed	63 mph.
Cruise Speed	60 mph.
Stall Speed (in free air)	25 mph.
Sea Level Climb Rate	600 fpm. @ 50 mph.
Takeoff Run	200 ft.
Dist. Req'd. to clear 50 ft.	N.A.
Landing Roll	200 ft.
Service Ceiling (100 fpm. climb)	N.A.
Range at Cruise	200 mi.
L/D (Glide Ratio)	20-to-1 @ 35 mph.
Minimum Sink Rate	N.A.

Excelsior
St. Croix Ultralights
5957 Seville Street
Lake Oswego, OR 97034
(503) 636-4153
Chad Willie

Sun Aerospace — *Sun Ray*

The Sun Ray is an amphibious canard with pusher prop. The wing is a fully cantilevered, inverted gull type. It features three-axis aerodynamic controls. The pilot is seated in a central hull, which also contains a rear-mounted engine. Outrigger pontoons are located at the wing dihedral break.

The airframe is built primarily of DuPont Kevlar, a space age material that is stronger yet lighter than fiberglass. The advanced laminar flow airfoils are designed to be fully controllable down to a stall speed of 27 mph.

The aircraft is a prototype which had not flown at the time of this writing. Contact Sun Aerospace for further details.

Specifications

Wingspan	32 ft. 0 in.
Length	13 ft. 3 in.
Height	6 ft. 0 in.
Wing Area	130 sq. ft.
Engine Make, Model, HP	Kawasaki 35 hp.
Prop. Diameter/Pitch	56 in/30 in.
Reduction Ratio	2-to-1
Fuel Capacity/Consumption	2 gal./1.5 gph.
Gross Weight	520 lbs.
Empty Weight	250 lbs.

Fig. 1-98. The Sun Ray is a composite amphibian of unusual design.

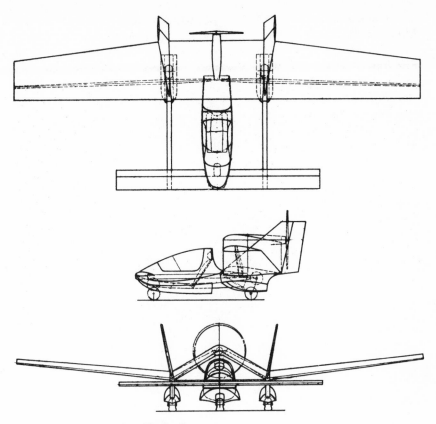

Fig. 1-99. Three-view drawing of the Sun Ray.

Useful Load	270 lbs.
Wing Loading	4 psf.
Power Loading	14.9 lb/hp.
Design Load Factors	+6, -6
Construction Time	150 man-hrs.
Field Assembly Time	Under 10 min.
Pricing	$7,595. suggested

Flight Performance

Velocity Never Exceed	85 mph.
Top Level Speed	63 mph.
Cruise Speed	55 mph. @ 60% power
Stall Speed (in free air)	27 mph.
Sea Level Climb Rate	600 fpm. @ 40 mph.
Takeoff Run	200 ft.
Dist. Req'd. to clear 50 ft.	300 ft.
Landing Roll	150 ft.
Service Ceiling (100 fpm. climb)	10,000 ft.
Range at Cruise	90 mi.

L/D (Glide Ratio)   14-to-1 @ 40 mph.
Minimum Sink Rate   250 fpm. @ 40 mph.

Sun Ray
Sun Aerospace Corp.
P.O. Box 317
Nappanee, Indiana 46550
(219) 773-3220
Mr. Russ McDonald

Swallow AeroPlane — Swallow A

The Swallow is a cable braced, high wing monoplane with three-axis, aerodynamic controls and a pusher propeller.

The airframe is constructed primarily of aluminum tubing and covered in presewn dacron. The fuselage consists of four aluminum tubing longerons supporting a cruciform tail, with the pilot's seat below the wing, surrounded by a pyramid of aluminum tubes. The main gear is sprung by fiberglass rods. The wing is a basic ladder frame of aluminum tubing, with diagonals for drag and anti-drag loads. All components are well-finished.

The Swallow incorporates aircraft hardware throughout, such as: pivoting cable pulleys and guards, die formed aluminum aileron ribs and AN bolts and fittings. The control system uses a 4130 chrome moly torque tube, pushrods and spherical bearing rod ends with teflon inserts at all pivot points.

Power is supplied by the Rotax 277, which puts out 28 hp. The engine is mounted at the nose of the air vehicle, and turns a pusher prop via a shaft extension and reduction drive at the trailing edge. This arrangement allows the pilot to sit at the center of gravity.

Ground handling is typical "airplane" — it goes in the direction of the depressed pedal. Crosswind handling is also "airplane", the Swallow having been operated in 23 mph. winds, 90° to the runway.

In flight, the Swallow also acts much like an airplane. It has the forgiving flying characteristics of most ultralights, but can handle more winds and turbulence than most.

The ailerons give a "medium" response until accompanied by an equal amount of rudder deflection, which produces a greatly improved roll rate.

Fig. 1-100. The Swallow incorporates many standard aircraft construction techniques. Has three-axis controls.

Slips are easily accomplished, thanks to the independent control system. As the nose comes up, drag rises dramatically above 6° or so, and serves as an effective glide path control. Stalls are straightforward, and the airplane offers no surprises. Normal approach speed is 45 mph. which allows for a good margin above stall, and added insurance against being knocked out of the air by a gust.

Complete kits are available from Aeroplane Marketing.

Specifications

Wingspan	34 ft. 5 in.
Length	18 ft. 1 in.
Height	8 ft. 11 in.
Wing Area	137.7 sq. ft.
Engine Make, Model, HP	Rotax 277 - 28 hp.
Prop. Diameter/Pitch	52 in/28 in.
Reduction Ratio	2-to-1
Fuel Capacity/Consumption	3.5 gal.
Gross Weight	
Empty Weight	252 lbs.
Useful Load	
Wing Loading	3.3 psf. (w/175 lb. pilot)
Power Loading	16 lb/hp.
Design Load Factors	+4, -3
Construction Time	100 man-hrs.
Field Assembly Time	45 min.
Pricing	$4,995.

Flight Performance

Velocity Never Exceed	70 mph.
Top Level Speed	60 mph.
Cruise Speed	45 mph. @ 75% power
Stall Speed (in free air)	26 mph. (175 lb. pilot)
Sea Level Climb Rate	550 fpm. @ 40 mph.
Takeoff Run	N.A.
Dist. Req'd. to clear 50 ft.	N.A.
Landing Roll	125 ft. (grass - no brakes)
Service Ceiling (100 fpm. climb)	N.A.
Range at Cruise	55 mi. (with 15 min. reserve)
L/D (Glide Ratio)	7-to-1 @ 40 mph.
Minimum Sink Rate	550 fpm. @ 40 mph.

Swallow A
Swallow Aeroplane Co., Inc.
Pistol Shop Road
Rockfall, CT 06481
(203) 347-9543
Sharon Wilcox

Teratorn Aircraft — TA

The Teratorn TA is a basic high wing pusher monoplane with taildragger landing gear. It features stick controlled spoilers and elevator, with a foot pedal actuated rudder. It is powered by the 38 hp Rotax 377.

Accessories include Kevlar floats, skis and flight instruments. The ultralight is sold as a bolt-together assembly kit.

Specifications

Wingspan	32 ft.
Length	18 ft.
Height	8 ft. 11 in.
Wing Area	160 sq. ft.
Engine Make, Model, HP	Rotax 377, 38 hp.
Prop Diameter/Pitch	58 in/32 in.
Reduction Ratio	2.6-to-1
Fuel Capacity/Consumption	4.4 gal./1 gph.
Gross Weight	500 lbs.
Empty Weight	237 lbs.

Fig. 1-101. The Teratorn TA features three-axis aerodynamic controls in a simple airframe.

Useful Load	
Wing Loading	3.12 psf.
Power Loading	14.70 lb/hp.
Design Load Factors	+4, -3
Construction Time	30 man-hrs.
Field Assembly Time	25 min.
Pricing	$4,595.

Flight Performance

Velocity Never Exceed	63 mph.
Top Level Speed	55 mph.
Cruise Speed	32 mph. @ 60% power
Stall Speed (in free air)	23 mph.
Sea Level Climb Rate	900 fpm. @ 28 mph.
Takeoff Run	50 ft.
Dist. Req'd. to clear 50 ft.	350 ft.
Landing Roll	50 ft.
Service Ceiling (100 fpm. climb)	N.A.
Range at Cruise	120 mi.
L/D (Glide Ratio)	8-to-1
Minimum Sink Rate	N.A.

Teratorn TA
Teratorn Aircraft Inc.

Teratorn Aircraft — Tierra

The Tierra is a high wing cabin monoplane with pusher engine and taildragger landing gear. It features all strut braced construction and conventional three-axis aerodynamic controls. It is sold as a bolt-together kit.

The airframe is constructed mostly of aluminum tubing. The wing is a basic ladder frame, strut braced to the rudimentary fuselage. The pilot sits in a padded seat, surrounded by a myriad of tubes. The tail group is supported by a trusswork of tubing that allows clearance for and enshrouds the propeller.

The engine is mounted above the wing center section and shaft drives the prop via a reduction drive and clutch. The clutch system is designed to reduce vibration and works in concert with the motor mounts which isolate the powerplant from the airframe.

The flying surfaces are covered with pre-sewn stabilized dacron sailcloth envelopes which slip on over the frames. The pilot enclosure is removeable via strategically placed zippers, for those who prefer open air flying. Flying with the enclosure is particularly useful during colder weather periods.

In flight, it appears to be stable and controllable about all axes and can handle a certain amount of crosswinds.

The Tierra can also be fitted with two seats and dual controls for flight training, but must then be registered as an amateur-built aircraft and flown by a licensed pilot.

Fig. 1-102. The Teratorn Tierra is a strut braced monoplane with space frame fuselage.

Specifications

Wingspan	31 ft. 6 in.
Length	18 ft. 6 in.
Height	1 ft. 6 in.
Wing Area	160 sq. ft.
Engine Make, Model, HP	377 Rotax
Prop Diameter/Pitch	60 in/30 in.
Reduction Ratio	
Fuel Capacity/Consumption	5 gal./1.5 gph.
Gross Weight	550 lbs.
Empty Weight	253 lbs.
Useful Load	297 lbs.
Wing Loading	3.43 psf.
Power Loading	15.27 lb/hp.
Design Load Factors	+6, -3
Construction Time	25 man-hrs.
Field Assembly Time	20 min.
Pricing	$5,595.

Flight Performance

Velocity Never Exceed	63 mph.
Top Level Speed	63 mph.
Cruise Speed	50 mph. @ 60% power
Stall Speed (in free air)	25 mph.
Sea Level Climb Rate	800 fpm. @ 38 mph.
Takeoff Run	50 ft.
Dist. Req'd. to clear 50 ft.	350 ft.
Landing Roll	75 ft.
Service Ceiling (100 fpm. climb)	N.A.
Range at Cruise	150 mi.
L/D (Glide Ratio)	10-to-1 @ 36 mph.
Minimum Sink Rate	N.A.

Tierra
Teratorn Aircraft Inc.
North Shore Dr.
Clearlake, IA
(515) 357-7161
Dale Kjellsen

U

Ultra Efficient Products — Invader Mk III-B

Fig. 1-103. The Invader is a shoulder wind cantilever monoplane with space frame fuselage.

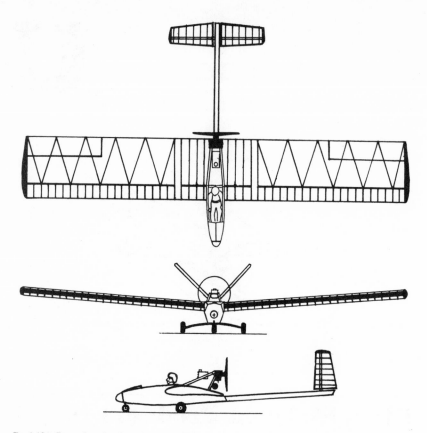

Fig. 1-104. Three-view drawing of the Invader.

Invader is a cantilevered shoulder wing monoplane with a pusher propeller. It features a three-axis control system in the form of stick activated, coupled ailerons and ruddervators. The pilot sits out front in a protective nose cowling with an open cockpit.

The wing and tail surfaces are constructed much like a large model airplane. The wing is built-up with two wooden spars and foam and wood ribs. Every other rib is positioned diagonally from the main spar to the trailing edge for torsional rigidity. The main spar, nose ribs and leading edge form a conventional D-section. The ruddervators are built up of wood and foam, with a single tubular aluminum spar. The ruddervators are free flying, i.e., the entire surface rotates about the spar. All flying surfaces are covered in clear mylar. The wing panels ae removable for transport and storage.

The fuselage pod is constructed of welded steel tubing, affording pilot protection. A single aluminum tube joins the pod structure under the pilot's seat and extends aft to support the ruddervators forming a long tail arm. Landing gear can be either tricycle with steerable nosewheel or taildragger with steerable tail wheel.

Motive power is supplied by a 28 hp. Rotax 277 in direct drive. The engine is mounted on a steel tubing truss behind the pilot and above the wing.

In flight the aircraft is gentle and forgiving and offers excellent control response. All turns are coordinated due to the coupled ailerons and ruddervators, so cross-controlling is not possible.

Plans are now available from Ultra Efficient Products. Contact the factory for kit availability.

Specifications

Wingspan	31 ft.
Length	17 ft.
Height	4 ft.
Wing Area	140 sq. ft.
Engine Make, Model, HP	Rotax 277, 28 hp.
Prop Diameter/Pitch	44 in/15 in.
Reduction Ratio	Direct drive
Fuel Capacity/Consumption	2.5 gal./1.25 gph.
Gross Weight	400 lbs.
Empty Weight	185 lbs.
Useful Load	225 lbs.
Wing Loading	2.86 psf.
Power Loading	14.29 lb/hp.
Design Load Factors	+3.5, -3.5
Construction Time	300 man-hrs.
Field Assembly Time	15 min.
Pricing	$60. (plans)

Flight Performance

Velocity Never Exceed	70 mph.
Top Level Speed	60 mph.
Cruise Speed	45 mph.
Stall Speed (in free air)	25 mph.
Sea Level Climb Rate	500 fpm.
Takeoff Run	100 ft.
Dist. Req'd. to clear 50 ft.	N.A.
Landing Roll	100 ft.
Service Ceiling (100 fpm. climb)	N.A.
Range at Cruise	100 mi.
L/D (Glide Ratio)	14-to-1
Minimum Sink Rate	N.A.

Invader Mk III-B
Ultra Efficient
1637 7th St.
Sarasota, FL 33577
(813) 955-0710
Nick Leichty

Ultraflight — *Lazair*

The Lazair is a twin-engined high wing monoplane with inverted V-tail, independent three-axis aerodynamic controls, and taildragger landing gear. It's a design that has been evolving since 1978, with successive changes leading to improvements in operation and flight performance.

The airframe is constructed primarily of aluminum — aluminum tubes for the struts, pre-formed pilot cage members, tail surfaces and tailboom. Aluminum is also used to form the "D"-cell leading edge and other structural components. The ribs are foam cores capped with aluminum strips.

The pilot sits in a high back padded seat with fabric back rest, and controls the ultralight with a center mounted stick pivoted from below, as well as rudder pedals. Two wide, 12-inch tires and wheels with brakes make up the main landing gear, allowing operation from unmowed grass fields. A full castering tailwheel protects the tip of each tail surface from side loads.

Constructing the air vehicle goes something like this. Support the leading edge "D"-cell with the front toward the floor. Set in the end ribs as indicated by the pre-drilled holes, add the rear spar and then the trailing edge ribs. Rivet on the aileron hinges and ailerons, the trailing edge and the wing tips —basically lining up, drilling and fastening.

The airframe is covered by DuPont Tedlar, which is a hybrid of teflon and mylar. It has all the strength and aerodynamic cleanliness of the former Mylar

Fig. 1-105. The Ultraflight Lazair in its latest garb, including: larger engines, wheel pants, center stick pivoted below the seat, and tail wheels.

Fig. 1-106. A close-up of the new Lazair, set up especially for licensed pilots.

covering, and also much greater resistance to ultraviolet rays. The coverings are attached to the airframe with an industrial grade double-sided tape, then heat shrunk with a hot air gun or hair dryer. Painting is not necessary, although it can be done according to taste.

The engine nacelles are riveted together and the propellers mounted. The wheels and control linkages are attached, and final adjustments made and checked for accuracy.

Assembly for flight requires two people about half an hour, from the time the ultralight is removed from its trailer. The fuselage and tail remain together as an assembly, while the wings and engines are separate. Ten bolts and nuts connect the wings and ailerons. The wing center section gap seal is put in place, as are the wing struts.

The engine assemblies are secured to blind nuts in the leading edges by four bolts. The gas tank is mounted behind the seat, actually forming a headrest, fuel lines are added and the throttles connected to complete the job. As always, a complete, walk-around pre-flight inspection is the final step before climbing aboard, strapping-in, and starting the engines.

In flight, the Lazair is docile and forgiving, yet responsive to the controls. Stalls are straight forward, with no tendency to drop a wing. Crosswinds can be dealt with thanks to the independent three-axis control system. Also, performance can be altered somewhat because of the ground adjustable pitch props.

Optional items include: the Orbit instrument package, skis, and floats. The Lazair may also be ordered with coupled ailerons and rudder for automatically coordinated turns.

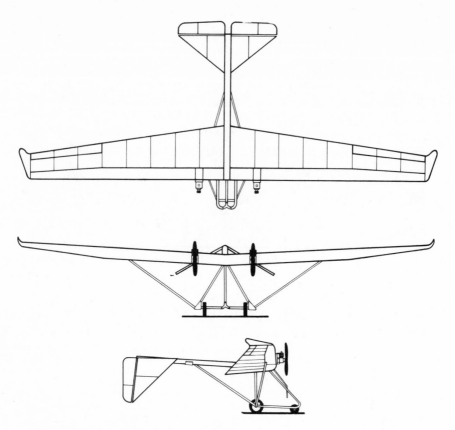

Fig. 1-107. Three-view drawing of the Lazair prototype.

Specifications

Wingspan	36 ft. 4 in.
Length	14 ft. 0 in.
Height	6 ft. 4 in.
Wing Area	142 sq. ft.
Engine Make, Model, HP	Two Rotax 185 cc — 9.5 hp. engines
Prop Diameter/Pitch	35 in. (Ground adjustable Pitch)
Reduction Ratio	N.A.
Fuel Capacity/Consumption	5 US gal./1.2 gph.
Gross Weight	530 lbs.
Empty Weight	210 lbs.
Useful Load	320 lbs.
Wing Loading - maximum	3.73 psf.
Power Loading - maximum	29.44 lb/hp.
Design Load Factors	+4, -2 (at 420 lbs.)
Construction Time	100-150 man-hrs.
Field Assembly Time	25 min.
Pricing	$5,400. U.S.

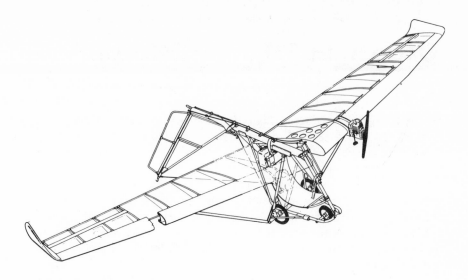

Fig. 1-108. Cutaway showing mani structural elements of the Lazair.

Flight Performance

Velocity Never Exceed	55 mph.
Top Level Speed	50 mph.
Cruise Speed	40 mph. @ 60% power
Stall Speed (in free air)	20 mph.
Sea Level Climb Rate	400 fpm. @ 25 mph.
Takeoff Run	100 ft.
Dist. Req'd. to clear 50 ft.	N.A.
Landing Roll	50 ft.
Service Ceiling (100 fpm climb)	N.A.
Range at Cruise	140 mi.
L/D (Glide Ratio)	
Minimum Sink Rate	

Lazair™ ultralight aircraft
Ultraflight Sales Ltd.
P.O. Box 370 (Nugent Road)
Port Colborne, Ontario, Canada L3K 1B7
(416) 735-8352
Linda M. Kramer, General Manager

Ultralight Flight — *Mirage*

The Mirage is a cable braced high wing monoplane with a double surfaced airfoil and drooped tips. It is controlled by a three-axis aerodynamic control system via joystick and rudder pedals. The pilot sits below the wing on a tricycle undercarriage.

The airframe consists primarily of aluminum tubing and steel fittings. The fuselage uses a four longeron tail support and "N"-strut pilot cage. The wing is a basic ladder type frame with internal diagonals for drag and anti-drag loads. The pilot sits supine on a sling type seat with high back. All flying surfaces are covered in pre-sewn dacron sailcloth envelopes. In general, the aircraft is well engineered and constructed.

Power is supplied by a Kawasaki TA-440A mounted in front of the wing, shaft driving a pusher propeller via a reduction drive.

In flight, the Mirage offers no surprises. It handles well and can do most anything an airplane can, thanks to the independent three-axis control system. The stick controls elevator and spoilers, while rudder pedals wag the tail.

Complete kits are available from Ultralight Flight, Inc.

Specifications

Wingspan	32 ft.
Length	18 ft.
Height	9 ft.

Fig. 1-109. The Mirage is a typical cable-braced aluminum airframe with dacron sailcloth covering.

Wing Area	144 sq. ft.
Engine Make, Model, HP	Kawasaka TA-440A, 35 hp.
Prop Diameter/Pitch	58 in/27 in.
Reduction Ratio	2-to-1
Fuel Capacity/Consumption	4 gal./1.8 gph.
Gross Weight	500 lbs.
Empty Weight	246 lbs.
Useful Load	254 lbs.
Wing Loading	3.47 psf.
Power Loading	14.29 lb/hp.
Design Load Factors	+5.8, -2.7
Construction Time	40 man-hrs.
Field Assembly Time	30 min.
Pricing	$4,795.

Flight Performance

Velocity Never Exceed	70 mph.
Top Level Speed	58 mph.
Cruise Speed	45 mph.
Stall Speed (in free air)	26 mph.
Sea Level Climb Rate	800 fpm. @ 30 mph.
Takeoff Run	100 ft.
Dist. Req'd. to clear 50 ft.	N.A.
Landing Roll	100 ft.
Service Ceiling (100 fpm. climb)	14,000 ft.
Range at Cruise	115 mi.
L/D (Glide Ratio)	7-to-1
Minimum Sink Rate	N.A.

Mirage
Ultralight Flight, Inc.
480 Hayden Station Road
Windsor, CT 06095
(203) 683-2760
Sales Manager

Ultralight Flight — *Phantom*

The Phantom is a high wing, single engine, cable braced monoplane with conventional three-axis aerodynamic controls. It features a distinctive pilot pod and tricycle undercarriage.

The airframe is constructed primarily of aluminum tubing and steel fittings. A cruciform tail is supported on a single boom. A pyramidal structure supports the pilot and undercarriage. The wing is a basic ladder type frame, supported by cables to the undercarriage and a king post. The landing gear is bungee cord suspended, and features a steerable nosewheel, as well as wheel pants over 10 inch wheels.

The powerplant is a Kawasaki 440-TA mounted in front of the wing, driving a tractor propeller via a reduction drive. It features dual electronic ignition and recoil starting, with electric starting optional.

Standard instruments include ASI and altimeter. Complete kits are available from Ultralight Flight Sales.

Specifications

Wingspan	28 ft. 6 in.
Length	16 ft. 6 in.
Height	7 ft. 3 in.
Wing Area	142 sq. ft.
Engine Make, Model, HP	Kawasaki TA-440A, 37 hp.
Prop Diameter/Pitch	58 in./27 in.
Reduction Ratio	2.3-to-1
Fuel Capacity/Consumption	3.8 gal./1.8 gph.
Gross Weight	510 lbs.

Fig. 1-110. Ultralight Flight's Phantom is more in tune with the state of the art: pilot pod, single tailboom, tractor engine, double surface wing, and full span ailerons.

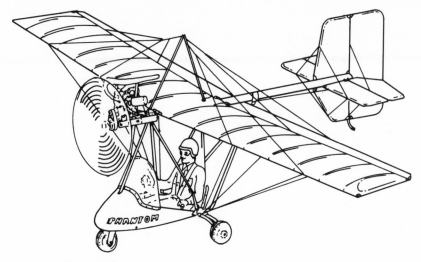

Fig. 1-111. Artist's sketch of the Phantom.

Empty Weight	250 lbs.
Useful Load	260 lbs.
Wing Loading	3.59 psf.
Power Loading	13.78 lb/hp.
Design Load Factors	+6.6, -4.4
Construction Time	70 man-hrs.
Field Assembly Time	30 min.
Pricing	$5,995.

Flight Performance

Velocity Never Exceed	100 mph.
Top Level Speed	61 mph.
Cruise Speed	55 mph. @ 65% power
Stall Speed (in free air)	26 mph.
Sea Level Climb Rate	800 fpm. @ 45 mph.
Takeoff Run	150 ft.
Dist. Req'd. to clear 50 ft.	N.A.
Landing Roll	100 ft.
Service Ceiling (100 fpm. climb)	14,500 ft.
Range at Cruise	105 mi.
L/D (Glide Ratio)	7-to-1
Minimum Sink Rate	490 fpm.

Phantom
Ultralight Flight, Inc.
480 Hayden Station Road
Windsor, CT 06095
(203) 683-2760
Sales Manager

Ultralight Soaring —
Wizard Series

Ultralite Soaring manufactures a series of high wing pushers with tricycle landing gear. They vary primarily by method of control and engine installation.

The airframes consist basically of cable braced aluminum tubing fastened together with AN hardware. They all feature engine mounts that allow an engine change with the removal of two bolts. The 16-inch wheeled undercarriage offers shock absorption, but the nosewheel does not steer. A blast from the prop with up elevator and appropriate rudder effectively steers them.

All flying surfaces are stabilized dacron sailcloth, pre-sewn as envelopes that slip on over the structural frames. The wing envelope contains pockets into which ribs are inserted. The first forty percent of the undersurface is also covered by the wing envelope, forming the leading edge.

There are four models in the Wizard stable, and they are all similar in appearance. The W-1 is the basic "weight-shift-coupled-to-rudder" version for beginners. The next model, the J-2, features spoilers and rudder coupled to a weight shift harness. Third is the full, three-axis control J-3 with fixed seat. Fourth is the T-38 two-seater trainer, which is not really an ultralight even though it looks like one. It must be registered as an amateur-built experimental aircraft and flown only by a licensed pilot. All models have engines driving a pusher propeller via a reduction drive.

Fig. 1-112. The Wizard J-3 is a single surfaced, cable-braced aluminum airframe with rudder, elevator and spoiler controls.

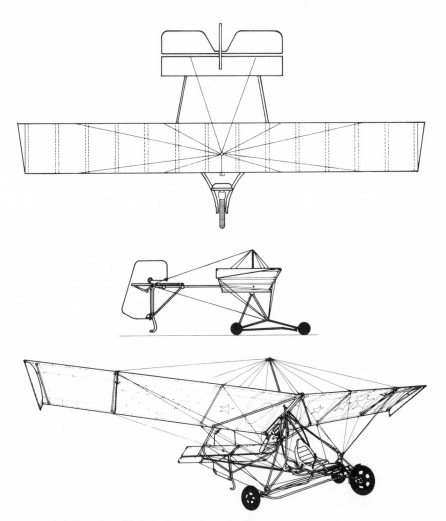

Fig. 1-113. Three-view of the Wizard reveal its construction.

All four versions are essentially bolt-together kits that breakdown for trailer transportation. Options include pontoons and custom sail work. All models come with several interchangeable power packages that have reduction drive, clutch and electric start. The seats are fully padded high backs, and feature quick release metal-to-metal seatbelts.

Specifications

Wingspan	32 ft. 4 in.
Length	17 ft.
Height	10 ft. 5 in.
Wing Area	161.5 sq. ft.
Engine Make, Model, HP	Yamaha KT-100S, 15 hp.
Prop Diameter/Pitch	48 in/20 in.
Reduction Ratio	3.6-to-1

Fuel Capacity/Consumption	4.25 gal./1 gph.
Gross Weight	450 lbs.
Empty Weight	210 lbs.
Useful Load	240 lbs.
Wing Loading	2.79 psf.
Power Loading	30 lb/hp.
Design Load Factors	N.A.
Construction Time	20 man-hrs.
Field Assembly Time	45 min.
Pricing	$3,495.

Flight Performance

Velocity Never Exceed	65 mph.
Top Level Speed	42 mph.
Cruise Speed	35 mph. @ 60% power
Stall Speed (in free air)	17 mph.
Sea Level Climb Rate	300 fpm. @ 35 mph.
Takeoff Run	100 ft.
Dist. Req'd. to clear 50 ft.	N.A.
Landing Roll	50 ft.
Service Ceiling (100 fpm. climb)	12,500 ft.
Range at Cruise	100 mi.
L/D (Glide Ratio)	9-to-1
Minimum Sink Rate	N.A.

Wizard W-1
Ultralite Soaring, Inc.

Specifications

Wingspan	32 ft. 4 in.
Length	17 ft.
Height	10 ft. 5 in.
Wing Area	161.5 sq. ft.
Engine Make, Model, HP	Rotax 277, 28 hp.
Prop Diameter/Pitch	N.A.
Reduction Ratio	2.4-to-1
Fuel Capacity/Consumption	4.25 gal./1.5 gph.
Gross Weight	450 lbs.
Empty Weight	175 lbs.
Useful Load	275 lbs.
Wing Loading	2.79 psf.
Power Loading	16.07 lb/hp.
Design Load Factors	N.A.
Construction Time	20 man-hrs.
Field Assembly Time	45 min.
Pricing	$3,895.

Flight Performance

Velocity Never Exceed	65 mph.
Top Level Speed	40 mph.
Cruise Speed	35 mph. @ 67% power
Stall Speed (in free air)	19 mph.
Sea Level Climb Rate	500 fpm. @ 35 mph.
Takeoff Run	80 ft.
Dist. Req'd. to clear 50 ft.	N.A.
Landing Roll	50 ft.
Service Ceiling (100 fpm. climb)	12,500 ft.
Range at Cruise	100 mi.
L/D (Glide Ratio)	9-to-1
Minimum Sink Rate	350 fpm.

Wizard J-2
Ultralite Soaring, Inc.

Specifications

Wingspan	32 ft. 4 in.
Length	17 ft.
Height	10 ft. 2 in.
Wing Area	161.5 sq. ft.
Engine Make, Model, HP	Kawasaki TA-440A, 36 hp.
Prop Diameter/Pitch	58 in/30 in.
Reduction Ratio	2.4-to-1
Fuel Capacity/Consumption	4.25 gal./1.8 gph.
Gross Weight	550 lbs.
Empty Weight	250 lbs.
Useful Load	300 lbs.
Wing Loading	3.41 psf.
Power Loading	15.28 lb/hp.
Design Load Factors	N.A.
Construction Time	20 hrs.
Field Assembly Time	45 min.
Pricing	$4,720.

Flight Performance

Velocity Never Exceed	65 mph.
Top Level Speed	50 mph.
Cruise Speed	40 mph. @ 51% power
Stall Speed (in free air)	20 mph.
Sea Level Climb Rate	900 fpm. @ 35 mph.
Takeoff Run	75 ft.
Dist. Req'd. to clear 50 ft.	N.A.
Landing Roll	50 ft.
Service Ceiling (100 fpm. climb)	12,500 ft.

Range at Cruise	75 mi.
L/D (Glide Ratio)	8-to-1
Minimum Sink Rate	600 fpm.

Wizard J-3
Ultralight Soaring, Inc.
3411 N.E. 6th Court
Pompano Beach, FL 33064
(305) 785-7853
Bill Waas

Ultravia — *Le Pelican*

The LePelican is a semi-enclosed, strut braced highwing monoplane with three-axis controls, and taildragger landing gear including steerable tail-wheel. It features a modified four cycle industrial engine, direct driving a tractor propeller. It is sold only as a kit.

Design and Construction

The airframe is constructed primarily of aluminum. The fuselage is basically a series of tubular triangles connected by a main rectangular longeron on top and two lesser tubular longerons on the bottom. Tubular-diagonals run on either side of the pilot, connecting the landing gear legs to the center of the top longeron. The engine mount itself is a pair of tubular triangles jutting forward of the pilot.

The tail surfaces are of tubular aluminum frames, including a triangular stabilizer with attached elevator. The vertical tail is all moving, the forward portion serving as an aerodynamic balance.

The wing is composed of an aluminum D-cell leading edge, with composite foam and aluminum ribs leading aft to a tubular aluminum trailing edge. A single strut ties the wing into the fuselage where the landing gear meets the lower longerons. Ailerons have replaced the original prototypes spoilers.

The entire structure is covered with dacron which is glued on, heat shrunk and doped.

Fig. 1-114. The Ultravia Le Pelican really looks like an Aeronca C-3. Flies like an airplane.

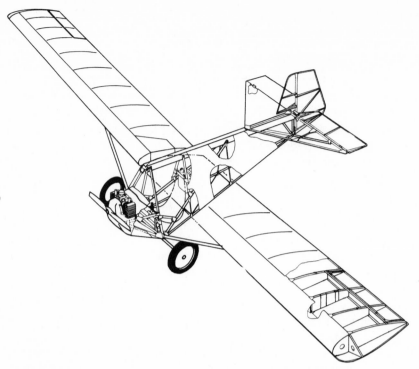

Fig. 1-115. Cutaway of Le Pelican shows mixed aluminum and wood construction.

The Engine

One of the most unique features of the LePelican is that it is one of the few ultralights powered by a four-cycle engine. Ultravia claims it is easier to start, much more reliable, economical, quieter and will outlast any two-cycle engine at least five times over. Of course, oil and gas are not mixed and the cruise rpm is very low, being only 2800 rpm. It burns a mere one gallon an hour at cruise.

Flying the Le Pelican

The sun is shining, it is warm out, and the wind is light and steady. You have just recently completed your dual flight instruction and can hardly wait to fly your first pattern. The safety belts are fastened, the engine is started and idles smoothly at 1200 rpm. The control surfaces respond as they should. After a final check of the instruments, you give the throttle a nudge and start moving towards the center of the runway. You check for aircraft in the pattern, then gradually increase power.

You push on the stick and the tail comes up. 15 mph, 20 mph. . . . the engine is turning 3500 rpm at full throttle. 25 mph, 30 mph. . . you gently ease back on the stick and the wheels leave the ground. You accelerate to 35 mph and begin climbing at 500 fpm.

Before the end of the 1500 foot runway, you have reached an altitude of 300 feet. You level out and maintain at 50 mph cruise at 2800 rpm. Crank in a shallow left bank for a short crosswind leg — a steep bank is not needed

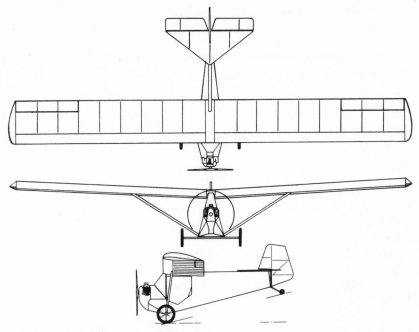

Fig. 1-116. Three-view drawing of Le Pelican.

because of the 5 knot wind. Left turn again for the downwind leg. Ground-speed is higher now, due to the tailwind.

Halfway up the runway you throttle back to begin your descent. Out past the end of the runway you make another left as you turn on to the base leg. Still another left puts you on final approach, as you establish a 40 mph descent. Opting for a wheel landing, you fly exactly over the center of the runway. Losing height, you gently touchdown at 32 mph. There wasn't a hint of a groundloop.

In general, the aircraft can be described as docile with a stall characterized by a gentle buffeting followed by a mushing sensation. It responds well to the controls. Trim is not affected by differing pilot weights, as the seat is located at the CG. It is also said by the factory that there are practically no trim changes with various throttle settings, thanks to the placement of the thrust line.

The Kit

The kit is broken down into five primary packages: fuselage, tail, wings, engine, and instruments and accessories. Optional items include 20 and 22 hp engines, brakes, doors and floats.

To assemble the aircraft you'll need a few basic hand tools, and some wood to build a rigging table. A complete instruction manual is included and there is no need to be proficient in reading plans, says the factory. Construction is said to require 150 man-hours.

The Le Pelican can be left assembled and tied down outside provided the surfaces are protected from sun and rain with wing and fuselage covers. Alternately, the flying surfaces can be detached from the fuselage by removing thirteen bolts, and the craft folded and kept on a trailer (Ultravia provides plans for modifying a standard trailer). Disassembly takes half an hour for two people. Contact Ultravia for further details.

Specifications

Wingspan	37 ft.
Length	14 ft.
Height	6 ft.
Wing Area	140 sq. ft.
Engine Make, Model, HP	Briggs and Stratton, 2 cylinder, 4 cycle, 18 hp at 3600 rpm
Prop Diameter/Pitch	43 in.
Reduction Ratio	N.A.
Fuel Capacity/Consumption	2.5 gal./1 gph. (at 50 mph)
Gross Weight	450 lbs.
Empty Weight	210 lbs.
Useful Load	240 lbs.
Wing Loading	2.87 psf.
Power Loading	22 lb/hp.
Design Load Factors	+4.4, -2.2 (- Safety factor of 1.5)
Construction Time	150 man-hrs.
Field Assembly Time	20 min.
Pricing	$5,895. (U.S.) in March 1983
Transport	Trailer

** direct drive

Flight Performance

Velocity Never Exceed	85 mph.
Top Level Speed	60 mph.
Cruise Speed	50 mph. @ 65% power
Stall Speed (in free air)	26 mph.
Sea Level Climb Rate	400-500 fpm. @ 35 mph.
Takeoff Run	150 ft.
Dist. Req'd. to clear 50 ft.	600 ft.
Landing Roll	200 ft.
Service Ceiling (100 fpm. climb)	12,500 ft.
Range at Cruise	100 mi.
L/D (Glide Ratio)	13-to-1 @ 35 mph.
Minimum Sink Rate	250 fpm. @ 30 mph.

Le Pelican
Ultravia Aero, Inc.
795 L'Assomption
Repentigny, Quebec, Canada J6A 5H5
(514) 585-6132 or 581-4986
Lorraine Chauvin

Warpath Aviation — *Mohawk*

Fig. 1-117. Warpath Mohawk features twin engines and quadracycle landing gear. Pilot sits in fairly well enclosed cockpit.

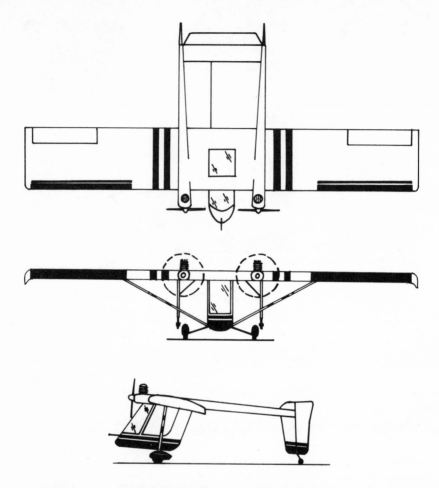

Fig. 1-118. Three-view drawing of the Mohawk shows unusual lines.

The Mohawk is a strut braced, twin engine, high wing monoplane with twin tail booms. It features an enclosed cockpit with removable side windows, fully independent three-axis aerodynamic controls, and a quadricycle landing gear.

The aircraft is constructed of foam, fiberglass, and epoxy composites. The landing gear legs are uni-directional glass rovings embedded in epoxy for added strength. The wing spars are foam, fiberglass and spruce composites. Fiberglass is used for the pre-molded pilot enclosure. Plans and a well illustrated construction manual provide the homebuilder with step-by-step procedures.

The Mohawk offers pilot comfort and good crosswind handling. In-air restarts are possible with starter ropes directly overhead. The aircraft will climb with one engine out, while separate throttles allow for enhanced ground handling. The outboard wing panels are removable for transport and storage.

All materials and hardware are available in kit form. Contact Warpath Aviation.

Specifications

Wingspan	30 ft. 0 in.
Length	13 ft. 9 in.
Height	5 ft. 2 in.
Wing Area	130 sq. ft.
Engine Make, Model, HP	2-342 Ultra engines, 30 @ 7000 rpm
Prop Diameter/Pitch	42 in.
Reduction Ratio	Direct drive
Fuel Capacity/Consumption	5 gal.
Gross Weight	550 lbs.
Empty Weight	240 lbs.
Useful Load	210 lbs.
Wing Loading	4.23 psf.
Power Loading	9.2 lb/hp.
Design Load Factors	+4, -3
Construction Time	300 to 400 man-hrs.
Field Assembly Time	20 min.
Pricing	$1,800. (Raw materials kit)

Flight Performance

Velocity Never Exceed	90 mph.
Top Level Speed	64 mph.
Cruise Speed	45 mph. @ 40% power
Stall Speed (in free air)	25 mph.
Sea Level Climb Rate	600 fpm. @ 40 mph.
Takeoff Run	150 ft.
Dist. Req'd. to clear 50 ft.	N.A.
Landing Roll	125 ft.
Service Ceiling (100 fpm. climb)	10,000 ft.
Range at Cruise	100 mi.
L/D (Glide Ratio)	14-to-1
Minimum Sink Rate	N.A.

Mohawk
Warpath Aviation Corp.
1171 W. McNab Road
Ft. Lauderdale, FL 33309
(305) 973-0355
Bob or Kay Baker

Worldwide Ultralite Industries — *Spitfire*

The Spitfire is a strut-braced, high wing monoplane with tractor engine and tricycle landing gear. It features a fully independent, three-axis aerodynamic control system, plus flaps.

The airframe is constructed primarily of aluminum tubing, with various steel fittings, and a steel tubing undercarriage. The wing is a basic ladder type frame, strut braced to the pilot cage, and jury strutted to the main struts. Ailerons and flaps are hinged to the rear spar.

A large diameter aluminum tube serves as the tailboom, which is strut braced to the pilot cage. A conventional tail group is attached to the end, providing for yaw and pitch stability and control. The moveable surfaces are actuated via teleflex cables.

The pilot cage is headed by a fiberglass pod, with instrument panel and windshield as standard. The panel includes a certified airspeed indicator as well. The pilot sits on a foam cushion seat and backrest that incorporates both seat and shoulder belts. The cage rests on a chromoly steel landing gear with steerable nosewheel. All wheels are fitted with pants.

Fig. 1-119. The Spitfire is a strut-braced monoplane with single boom tail, and tractor engine. Construction is aluminum covered with dacron sailcloth.

216

Fig. 1-120. Three-view drawing of Worldwide Spitfire.

Specifications

Wingspan	30 ft. 0 in.
Length	17 ft. 10 in.
Height	7 ft. 6 in.
Wing Area	154 sq. ft.
Engine Make, Model, HP	Kawasaki 440-TA, 40 hp
Prop Diameter/Pitch	58 in/27 in.

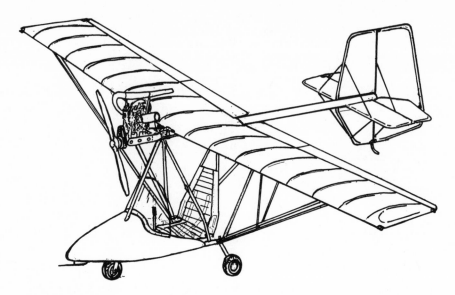

Fig. 1-121. Artist's sketch of the Spitfire.

Reduction Ratio	2.25-to-1
Fuel Capacity/Consumption	5 gal./1.8 gph.
Gross Weight	550 lbs.
Empty Weight	250 lbs.
Useful Load	300 lbs.
Wing Loading	3.57 psf.
Power Loading	13.75 lb/hp.
Design Load Factors	N.A.
Construction Time	20 man-hrs.
Field Assembly Time	15 min.
Pricing	$6,995.

Flight Performance

Velocity Never Exceed	100 mph.
Top Level Speed	60 mph.
Cruise Speed	55 mph. @ 75% power
Stall Speed (in free air)	19 mph. (with flaps)
Sea Level Climb Rate	850 fpm. @ 40 mph.
Takeoff Run	75 ft.
Dist. Req'd. to clear 50 ft.	N.A.
Landing Roll	75 ft.
Service Ceiling (100 fpm. climb)	14,500 ft.
Range at Cruise	120 mi.
L/D (Glide Ratio)	8-to-1 @ 40 mph.
Minimum Sink Rate	300 fpm. @ 40 mph.

Spitfire
Worldwide Ultralite Industries
11215 Jones Rd. West. Bldg. E.
Houston, TX 77065
(713) 890-9353
Del Martin

Z

Zenair — Zipper

Fig. 1-122. The Zenair Zipper is quite unique in that it features a ribless Princeton sailwing.

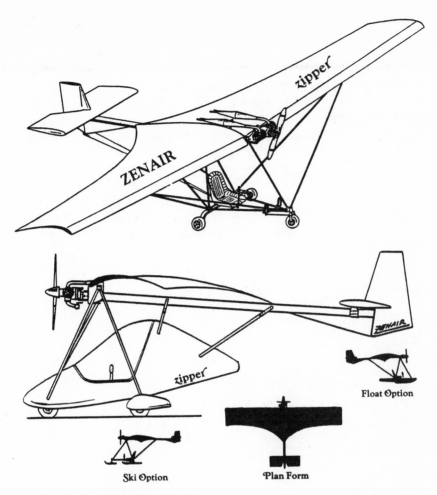

Fig. 1-123. Several different views of the Zipper.

The Zipper is a strut-braced, high wing, tractor monoplane with tricycle landing gear. It is unique among ultralights in that its wing is a Princeton sailwing, which has no ribs, and allows folding the air vehicle in two minutes for road towing.

The sailwing consists of a drooped D-section leading edge of aluminum, a tip structure, and a cable in tension as the trailing edge. The leading edge handles lift, drag and torsional loads. An envelope of stabilized dacron sailcloth fits around the leading edge and trailing edge cable. The trailing edge of the wing envelope is cut and sewn as a catenary curve, much like a suspension bridge's cables, equalizing the chordwise tension in the fabric. A single strut per wing panel, connects to the leading edge at about the 40% span location — it handles lift and landing loads. A cable from the strut to wing attack point carries the drag and some lift loads to the nose of the undercarriage. Antidrag loads are handled by the trailing edge cable.

As soon as the air vehicle starts moving and lift developes, the sail automatically assumes an airfoil shape. And, the greater the angle of attack, the greater the camber and lift — the wing automatically acts like a flap.

The tail surfaces are made of sheet aluminum, and are all flying, i.e., the entire vertical and the entire horizontal surfaces move to control pitch and yaw. Roll is controlled by ailerons located at the outer span, behind the trailing edge of the sailwing itself. The tail boom is a tapered box section of sheet aluminum. The engine is mounted on the front of the boom, which runs right through the center of the wing.

The Zipper is completely assembled at the factory, then partially dismantled for shipping. It takes only four to eight hours to bolt it back together with tools supplied with the air vehicle. The ultralight also includes tachometer, airspeed indicator, ignition switch, fuel valve, and seat belts. Optional items include: enclosed cockpit, floats, skis, propeller spinner, wheel fairings and tuned exhaust.

Specifications

Wingspan	28 ft.
Length	15 ft.
Height	6 ft.
Wing Area	140 sq. ft.
Engine Make, Model, HP	PUL 425, 22 hp
Prop Diameter/Pitch	42 in/28 in.
Reduction Ratio	N.A. - direct drive
Fuel Capacity/Consumption	5 gal./2 gph. US
Gross Weight	420 lbs.
Empty Weight	180 lbs.
Useful Load	240 lbs.
Wing Loading	3 psf.
Power Loading	19 lb/hp.
Design Load Factors	+6, -3
Construction Time	4-8 man-hrs.
Field Assembly Time	5 min.
Pricing	$5,970. Canada, $4,850. US

Flight Performance

Velocity Never Exceed	55 mph.
Top Level Speed	55 mph.
Cruise Speed	40 mph. @ 75% power
Stall Speed (in free air)	17 mph. approx.
Sea Level Climb Rate	650 fpm.
Takeoff Run	100 ft.
Dist. Req'd. to clear 50 ft.	N.A.
Landing Roll	80 ft.
Service Ceiling (100 fpm. climb)	12,500 ft.

Range at Cruise	100 mi.
L/D (Glide Ratio)	8-to-1 @ 25 mph.
Minimum Sink Rate	240 fpm. @ 20 mph.

Zipper
Zenair, Ltd.
236 Richmond Street
Richmond Hill L4C 3Y8
Ontario, Canada
(416) 859-4556
Sales Manager

Remember — Angle Of Attack Is Controlled By The Elevator, Which Governs Airspeed Via The Stick.

Section Two –
Basic Ultralight
Flight Manual

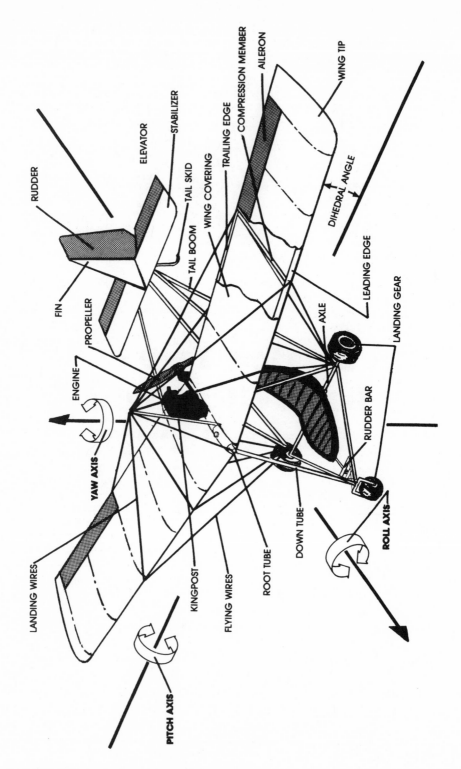

Fig. 2-1. Ultralight aircraft nomenclature and reference axes.

Ultralight Equipment - Glossary and Function

aileron The moveable control surfaces located at a wing's outer trailing edge. They deflect differentially causing the aircraft to bank and turn in the direction of the up aileron.

aircraft A vehicle of the air, generally heavier than air and supported by the dynamic reaction of the air against its surfaces.

airfoil Structure designed to obtain a useful reaction on itself in its motion through the air.

airframe Aircraft structure supporting shape and carrying equipment, payload and stresses. The fuselage, wing, tail, engine mount, tail boom, landing gear and control surfaces.

biplane An aircraft with two sets of wings, one above the other.

camber The curvature of an airfoil.

canard Lifting stabilizer at aircraft's nose. Aircraft with same.

compression strut Structural member joining leading and trailing edges.

dihedral Wide "V" angle of wing as viewed from in front.

elevator Moveable part of horizontal tail used to control angle of attack and airspeed.

elevon Dual purpose control surface on flying wings for angle of attack and roll control.

empennage The tail surfaces.

engine Power source for flight — usually reciprocating.

fin Fixed part of vertical tail.

flap Control surface on inboard end of rear of wing, used to reduce landing speed or cruise trim drag.

flying wires Lower cables connecting wing and transmitting lift loads to fuselage.

fuselage Airframe part housing pilot, with wings, tail and landing gear attached to it.

joy stick Control lever normally connected to aileron and elevator on three-axis control aircraft. Operates rudder and elevator on two control aircraft.

kingpost Tubes above wing center anchoring landing wires and transferring negative loads to fuselage.

landing gear Wheels and support structure.

landing wires Upper cables supporting negative loads.

leading edges Front of the wing.

propeller Airfoil shaped rotating wing used to convert torque into thrust. Larger diameter is more efficient.

rib Airfoil shaped part that defines wing's profile.

rudder Moveable part of vertical tail used to yaw aircraft. It balances adverse aileron yaw in independent three axis control aircraft. It is sometimes coupled to ailerons for automatic coordinated turns. Helps steer the aircraft while taxiing. It is NOT analogous to a ship's rudder and is not used like one!

ruddervator Dual purpose surface on V-tails used to control pitch and yaw.

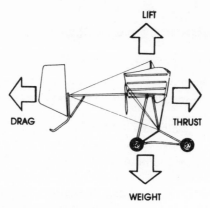

Fig. 2-2. The four forces that act on an ultralight in flight.

spar Wing's primary load carrying member.

spoiler Control surface usually located on wing's upper surface, which normally lies flush. When deflected, it reduces lift and increases drag. They roll the aircraft when deflected singly, and control glide path when deflected simultaneously.

strut Commonly refers to tubes used to brace wing to fuselage. They transmit both flying and landing loads to fuselage.

tail skid Aft fuselage member protecting tail from ground.

tail wheel Aft wheel on taildragger.

tip dragger Moveable vertical surfaces located at wing tip, used for yaw induced roll and turn.

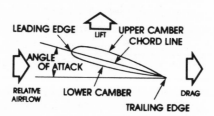

Fig. 2-3. Airfoil terminology.

trailing edge Aft part of wing.

washout Upward set of wingtip trailing edge to minimize tip stall.

Principles of Ultralight Flight

The four forces which act on an ultralight in flight are lift, weight, thrust and drag. Under straight and level, unaccelerated flight, lift = weight and thrust = drag.

LIFT is the force, generated by the dynamic reaction of the air against the wing, which acts perpendicular to the wing and the relative wind. During a turn, total lift is tilted toward the center of the turn at an angle equal to the bank angle. Therefore, more lift is required to maintain altitude so that the vertical component of that lift equals the weight. Not only must the lift support the weight, but also balance the centrifugal force generated by the turn. DRAG is air resistance, or the the force acting opposite to the direction of flight. It's main components are induced, parasite and profile drag. Induced drag is a by product of lift, and it increases with angle of attack. Parasite drag is developed by all aircraft parts (e.g. struts, cables, etc.) that are exposed to the airstream, but develop no lift. Profile drag is generated by the wing's airfoil shape. Angle of attack is the angle between the wing chord line and relative wind, and is the most important element in flying. It is controlled by the elevator and governs the airspeed. High angles of attack imply slow speed flight, while low angles of attack are required for high speeds. As the angle of attack is increased, a point is reached where the wing will stall — losing its lift and increasing its drag, because the airflow becomes quite turbulent and separates from the upper surface of the wing. Control near the stall is diminished and ailerons become virtually useless. Only a decrease in angle of attack will allow the wing to regain its lift — the control stick must go forward and the airplane must increase its airspeed by losing altitude before a stall recovery can be made. A stall can develop into a spin, especially while turning. If one wing stalls first (from a gust or a down aileron) it drops, increasing its angle of attack still more, and the airplane begins to rotate (spin) about a vertical axis while dropping toward the ground, with the wing at a stalled angle of attack. Some aircraft can recover from a stall/spin by neutralizing the controls, diving and/or by using opposite rudder. In all cases however, the angle of attack must be reduced before the wing will lift again. Essentially, the nose must be "lowered" — which is often difficult for a novice to

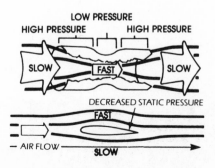

Fig. 2-4. Fast airflow reduces pressure through a venturi and over a wing.

appreciate and perform, especially when near the ground.

Center of Gravity is the point where the aircraft balances about all axes, and is most important to stable flight. Too aft a CG will result in instability and could lead to an unrecoverable spin.

"G" Loads are forces due to the acceleration of an aircraft, compared to its weight under straight and level flight in calm air. They are developed by gusts, turns, pull-outs and otherwise abrupt or aerobatic type maneuvers.

Thrust is the force developed by the propeller to overcome drag. Under full throttle, its greatest value occurs at zero airspeed (i.e., static conditions).

Weight is, of course, the force exerted on the aircraft's mass due to gravitational pull.

Wing Loading is flying weight divided by wing area. The greater its value, the higher the stall speed. Doubling the wing loading increases the stall speed by 41%.

Ground Effect occurs when an aircraft is within a wingspan of the ground and results in increased efficiency and a stall speed below the stall speed in free air. It can cause the aircraft to "float" for long distances over the landing field, especially low winged configurations.

Downwash describes the airflow behind a wing. It is caused by the wing's airfoil and angle of attack and results in the airplane being lifted.

Wing Tip vortices are "horizontal tornados" emanating from the tips of all aircraft, especially at high angles of attack and low airspeeds. The heavier the aircraft, the stronger the vortices, which can be a real hazard from other aircraft, causing an ultralight to roll over and crash. They are associated with wake turbulence from heavier aircraft (e.g. light private aircraft) and are to be avoided. When it is necessary to operate behind a heavier aircraft, remain above the flight path of the aircraft. Remember, vortices settle toward the ground along with the downwash, and they are affected by the wind. In taking off behind a heavier aircraft, plan it so you take off well before the previous aircraft's take off (rotation) was made. In taking off after a heavier aircraft has landed, plan to become airborne beyond the point where the other aircraft landed. When landing behind a heavier aircraft, be well above the glide path of the previous aircraft and touch down beyond the point where it landed. When landing after the takeoff of a heavier aircraft, make a normal landing near the approach end of the runway and be solidly on the ground before reaching the point where the large aircraft took off. Best of all, avoid operating on a runway with heavier aircraft!

Fig. 2-5. Wing tip vortices increase with angle of attack.

Principles of Flight Control

Unlike surface conveyances, which are limited to two-dimensional movement, aircraft are free to move about in all three dimensions. In addition to moving straight ahead, an ultralight is capable of making three fundamental motions, one about each of its three axes. The three axes/ motions are pitch, roll, and yaw.

Reference Axes

The pitch, or lateral, axis is an imaginary line which runs through the center of gravity, parallel to the wing. Rotation about this axis produces changes in pitch attitude, i.e., nose up-nose down. Pitch angle is controlled by the elevator, taking on a fixed degree, depending on elevator setting.

The roll, or longitudinal, axis is an imaginary line that runs from the nose of the aircraft through its CG and is parallel to the direction of flight. Motions around this axis are governed|primarily by the ailerons, which when deflected, set up a rate of roll rather than a fixed degree. Once a bank angle is achieved by aileron deflection, the ailerons are neutralized or even reversed, to maintain the desired angle. Constant aileron deflection would cause the bank angle to increase.

The yaw, or vertical, axis is an imaginary line passing through the CG perpendicular to the other two axes. Rudder controls yaw, a given rudder deflection resulting in a particular yaw rate.

Basic Elements of Flight

An aircraft is considered to be under control when the pilot is able to direct its course at will, which will be the case as long as the aircraft remains unstalled, and is moving in the desired direction at altitude. The pilot is kept informed of these events by the three primary flight instruments: airspeed indicator, altimeter and compass. These are basic to all flying, and tell the pilot what state-of-flight he's in. As necessary as they are, however, no pilot should rely solely on the information they present. After all, they are mechanical and they could fail. More important than that though, every ultralight pilot must develop a sense of "the-feel-of-flight". He should be able to judge flight by the audio and visual messages received by his brain and body — the instruments being used as a cross check.

The First Element of Flight

First and foremost, the essential element of flight is that the wing be unstalled, which implies an airspeed proper for a given angle of bank. (Remember, stall speed increases with bank angle.) This airspeed can be related to sound and feel — *the sound and feel of flight.* Under normal cruise conditions, your ultralight will produce a particular sound — the sound of the wind in the wires and struts, and over the wings. Under normal cruise you will also be able to feel a certain stick pressure with your hand. Another clue to your "degreeness-of-flight" could be the flagging motion of your pant legs — the faster they flap the higher your airspeed and the lower the angle of attack.

The stick can be a good indicator of the degreeness-of-flight because the feel of

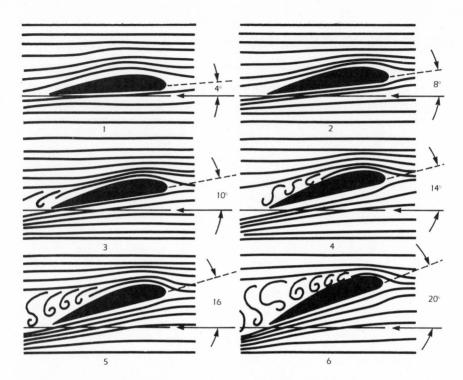

Fig. 2-6. The airflow over a wing at various angles of attack. At high angles, the airflow separates from the upper surface and the wing stalls.

the controls is transmitted to the pilot's hand. Since the control surfaces are in the airstream, the higher the airspeed, the harder the control forces become. When under high speed flight, the stick feels "hard", but only small movements are required to make the aircraft respond. Near the stall, the stick gets "soft" and large movements are required to maintain control. One must be careful, however, in interpreting stick feel. On most designs the tail is in the propwash which means it could have a greater airflow allowing for tail control surface effectiveness at low airspeeds, while the ailerons become ineffective and useless. The propwash induced hard pitch feel could be interpreted as an indicator of a high degreeness-of-flight, which in reality, doesn't exist near stall. The astute pilot will be aware of this. On canards, of course, the "tail" surfaces are not in the propwash, and so will see the freestream airflow, just like the ailerons, and give no false indications.

Another item related to pilot feel, would be indicators from the airframe itself. Under normal flight, a certain vibration will be transmitted from the engine through the airframe, to be felt by the seat-of-the-pants. The good pilot will be able to recognize the normal and abnormal vibrations. Then, too, some aircraft will buffet, or shake, when approaching the stall, a sure reminder to reduce the angle of attack.

Another very important visual cue in flying is that of aircraft attitude. What is your position with respect to the horizon? Cruising flight will present a particular aircraft attitude with respect to the horizon. Depending on your perspective, you can determine whether the nose is up or the nose is down and the wings level. For normal flying this is fine, but attitude alone cannot ultimately be used to determine your degreeness-of-flight. Your main concern is that the wing be unstalled.

Gravity and Acceleration

You will also be able to feel the effects of gravity and acceleration through your posterior anatomy. Under normal straight and level flight, you'll feel a one-'g' load, as you would sitting in a chair in your living room. If you put the airplane in a 45° bank, however, your weight will go up 41%, and you'll be able to feel it through "the-seat-of-your-pants". If you experience a negative 'g' situation, the seatbelt will tug at your gut. If your turn is less than coordinated, you'll be able to feel a side force, much like that felt in a car going around an unbanked turn, tending to slide you out of your seat. When a pilot is aware of and can sense changes with his body, he can make appropriate control corrections to restore normal flight.

The Second Element of Flight

Secondly, it is essential that you have altitude sufficient for safe flight. The altimeter is essential for this information, but after experience is gained, altitudes can be judged sufficiently so that one does not have to continually watch the altimeter. Besides, once a power setting is established and the airplane trimmed for straight and level flight, altitude should remain constant, except for updrafts and downdrafts. Proper altitude is essential. You should have enough to glide to a field in case the engine quits, and certainly enough to recover from a stall.

The Third Element of Flight

Thirdly, unless you plan on flying only the pattern or around your farm, it's nice to know the direction in which you're going — east, west, north or south. Of course, you can take visual cues from the sun, if it's out, but a compass can be a very worthwhile instrument to have. Flight must have direction.

Straight and Level

Under a given throttle setting and for a constant altitude and heading, all the aerodynamic forces are balanced, allowing the aircraft to fly "straight and level". Any deviation from this situation requires a change in the controls and results in the various basic maneuvers. A pilot must first be familiar with straight and level before he can control his aircraft precisely.

Level flight could be defined as flight that occurs at a fixed altitude above sea level. Its attitude can be discerned by making reference with the horizon and some object on the airframe in front of you — only experience will tell you where that is. Of course, setting the throttle at cruise and maintaining a constant altitude, as indicated by the altimeter, will also do it for you.

Once level flight is attained, adding power will cause the nose to go up and result in a climb, while reducing power will do the opposite. If the throttle remains at the new setting, the elevator may need retrimed, because a new attitude and airspeed will occur. Because of this, except when near the ground, the pilot must scan the altimeter during the initial leveling-off process.

Straight flight is achieved by keeping the wings level, correcting for any yaw effects with the rudder. The wing tips can be observed to see how far each is above the horizon, for a high wing, and how far they're below the horizon for a low wing. After a while, you won't need to look at the wing tips, but just straight ahead at the horizon. Aiming at a point on the horizon and maintaining a constant heading is how to achieve straight flight.

Trim

An ultralight is usually designed so that no stick or rudder control pressure need be held in straight and level cruising flight in a calm and under a given gross weight. If your aircraft is designed with the pilot at the CG, then there should be no trim changes required for different pilot weights. If your ultralight has the pilot situated at other than the CG, or you wish to fly slower or faster than cruise, then a trim change will be required.

Whereas most private planes have a cockpit adjustable elevator trim system, ultralights do not. Since they are single seaters flown typically only by the owner, there seems little need. However, some trim adjustments may be required for stick force free flight. A ground adjustable stabilizer or small metal tab at the end of the control surface, or even a spring-loaded stick, are the methods of ultralight trim.

The only way to determine if you need to re-trim your ultralight is to fly it. Get to altitude and set up a cruise throttle setting and see if the ship holds a constant altitude. If it wants to dive, the nose is heavy and vice versa. The stabilizer leading edge needs to be brought down a tad, the stick spring loaded to the rear, or the elevator tab bent down. After a small adjustment is made, take it up again and check the trim condition once more. Consult your flight instructor or dealer first, before making adjustments.

Aileron and rudder trim shouldn't be necessary however, if you feel a side force on the stick and need to hold rudder all the time, the aircraft may be improperly rigged, and out of trim. Consult your dealer or flight instructor for advice.

Stability

In order for an ultralight to be "pleasant" to fly it must possess certain handling qualities. It should be capable of being flown "hands-off" for a short period of time, which implies that it is stable.

Positive Stability

Positive stability can be defined broadly as the ability of an aircraft to return to its original flight condition, after having been disturbed from that condition. Equilibrium exists when all the forces acting on an aircraft, or any body, are balanced by equal and opposite forces. In order for an ultralight to be in equilibrium, lift equals weight and thrust equals drag. If these forces are not

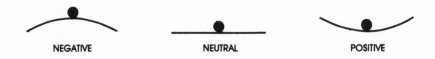

NEGATIVE   NEUTRAL   POSITIVE

Fig. 2-7. The three degrees of stability.

234

balanced, the aircraft will either accelerate or turn. A marble in a bowl would be a good example of positive stability.

Neutral Stability
Neutral stability is displayed when a body in equilibrium is disturbed and has no tendency to either return to its original position or condition, nor move further from it. It has no preference — it is neutrally stable. A marble on a flat horizontal surface would be neutrally stable.

Negative Stability
A body exhibits negative stability when, after having been disturbed from equilibrium, it has a tendency to move further away from its original condition or position. Negative stability has no place in an ultralight! A marble sitting on top of a bowling ball would be negatively stable.

Two Kinds of Stability
There are two kinds of stability: static stability and dynamic stability.

Static stability exists when an ultralight returns to its original position or condition after the passage of a disturbance. Static instability would be where, after having encountered a disturbance, the ultralight would continue deviating from its original position or condition. Most ultralights today appear to be statically stable about all axes, some more than others.

Dynamic stability is a little more complicated case since it involves oscillation, or a back and forth swinging motion, that gradually lessens or dampens out with time, until the aircraft has returned to its original position or condition. A pendulum would be dynamically stable, since the amplitude of its swing lessens with time. If the pendulum were immersed in water the period of time for it to stop oscillating would be lessened — in other words, the water dampens the motion.

Most ultralights appear to be stable with respect to pitch, the ones with tails more than the ones without tails. Basically, once an ultralight is trimmed, it tends to seek and maintain a fixed airspeed, regardless of whether it's climbing, diving or flying straight and level, depending of course on the throttle setting. An aircraft disturbed in pitch will eventually return to level flight, after going through a gradually decreasing roller-coaster ride, provided it is dynamically stable in pitch.

Most aircraft are marginally stable in the lateral and directional senses. An aircraft cruising along in level flight can return to level flight all by itself after an encounter with a side gust, so long as practically no turn is established. Once a turn sets in, though, the original state of equilibrium is upset, due to the generation of centripetal force. The situation worsens as the wing on the outside of the turn travels faster, generates more lift and increases the bank. If left unchecked, the nose will drop and a tight spiral dive will develop. Fortunately, this tendency is not noticeable in normal pilot controlled flying.

Climbing and Gliding
Climbs and glides are basically straight and level flight with power either increased or decreased from that which is required to maintain altitude. What we are talking about here is basic to performance — it depends on throttle and angle

of attack (attitude).

Under normal conditions when the throttle is fixed, such as during the climb, cruise or approach, the airspeed is controlled by the stick! Sure, pulling back on the stick while cruising will make you go up, but only momentarily. The nose high attitude will cause the airplane's drag to increase, slowing it down (the throttle may need to be advanced to prevent a stall and/or the nose lowered). Throttle controls the airspeed whenever the altitude is fixed.

While gliding, as in an approach to landing, it is important to remember that pulling back on the stick *will not* stretch your glide — it will steepen and maybe even stall the aircraft. This seems contrary to what you may at first believe, but a little thought will reveal the truth. The higher angle of attack caused by the back stick causes an increase in drag, detrimental to the maximum glide ratio you were at during approach. The angle of attack simply must be maintained below stall at all cost, for without it, you'll fall out of the air. When near the ground, keep the stick forward and maintain your airspeed. It is better to reach the ground with flying speed, than to stall out at 50 feet!

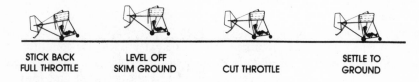

| STICK BACK FULL THROTTLE | LEVEL OFF SKIM GROUND | CUT THROTTLE | SETTLE TO GROUND |

Fig. 2-8. Practice takeoff and landing technique.

Preflight Inspection

PREFLIGHT — A thorough walk-around inspection of the aircraft, to be performed before each flight. It should be done systematically and habitually, and always in the same sequence.

First of all, assemble the aircraft for flight, being certain the ignition is off. Begin your inspection at the nose and walk around counter-clockwise to the right.

NUTS/BOLTS — Located, not stripped, secure, safetied and not compressing tubing.

POP RIVETS — Tight. No sheared heads.

CABLES — In tension, no frays or broken strands. Thimbles and Nicopress swages secure. Not wrapped around tang or bolt.

FABRIC — Secure around perimeter of flying surfaces. No tears or wrinkles. Tight and velcro sealed.

TUBES/STRUTS — Straight (or in manufactured configuration), no bends, kinks or cracks.

CONTROLS — Stick, pedals and levers operating freely, secure and safetied. Control surface hinge pins in place and safetied. Be sure controls respond properly to stick movements: moving stick toward an aileron causes it to go up, and moving the stick back causes the elevator to go up for aft tails and down for canards.

LANDING GEAR — Tires inflated and in good condition, wheels rotating freely and safetied. Control cables or struts attached to nosewheel or tailwheel.

PROPELLER — Clean surface with no cracks or missing pieces. Remove insects, mud and stones. Bolted to hub and safetied. Balanced.

ENGINE — Bolted and safetied in its mounting. Check mounting for cracks. Carb and air filter clean and secure. Spark plug cable, throttle linkage and fuel line secure and safetied. Needle valves tight.

FUEL LINE — Clamped and clean. Drain if dirty inside. Clear air bubbles before take-off. Filter clean.

FUEL TANK — Full. No water or other contamination. Proper fuel/oil mixture. Cap tight.

INSTRUMENTS — Positioned, secured and connected.

IGNITION — Battery charged. Electrical connection secure.

SEATING — Harness attachment secure. Webbing not worn. Seat secure. Seatbelt anchored and not worn.

Back away from the airplane and sight for overall appearance and trueness. Be certain it is trimmed for your weight, including clothing and accessories. Do not deviate from manufacturers recommended assembly and rigging procedure. Any alterations could seriously affect stability and flying characteristics.

NOTE: As time goes on and the airplane is used, moving parts wear and materials breakdown from exposure to the elements, as well as from flight stresses — watch for gradual deterioration. Preventative maintenance is a must for aircraft. If your airplane is newly assembled or repaired, check it thoroughly before attempting flight. HARD LANDINGS DESERVE A COMPLETE INSPECTION.

Starting and Taxiing

Before and after a flight, a certain amount of ground maneuvering is required. This is known as taxiing.

Landing Gear
There are two basic types of landing gear: conventional (taildragger) and tricycle. Some ultralights even have a monowheel arrangement, similar to a sailplane, but they are in the minority. A nosewheel can be steerable or fixed, while a tailwheel (or skid) can be steerable, fixed or free castering. A steerable nose or tailwheel turns with the rudder.

The Throttle
The throttle controls the speed of the engine. Pushing it forward opens carburetor and allows more fuel and air to be drawn into the cylinder(s), increasing the power. Pulling it out (closing the throttle), does just the opposite.

Starting
Before starting any engine, be sure that the aircraft is chocked, or otherwise restrained from movement and the propeller area is clear of spectators. Also see that the fuel tank and gasoline lines are full. If you have a transparent tank, see if there is any water or other contaminants in the bottom — water is heavier than gasoline and it stops engines! If you have an opaque tank, it should be drained and cleaned to minimize contaminating the fuel line.

After all of the above is completed, crack the throttle, i.e., open it to the idle position, so the engine doesn't race when started. See that the ignition is off, prime the engine with a squeeze or two of the primer pump, and turn it over a few times by hand to introduce some fuel into the cylinder.

Now, turn on the ignition, yell "clear" and pull the starter — the engine should start. If not, try more prime. If it still doesn't start, or even pop, perhaps the ignition system is at fault. Check the wiring and inspect the spark plug for fouling. The engine may be flooded, or have too much fuel in the cylinder.

If the engine is flooded, a soaked spark plug will tell you as well as a heavy gasoline odor, it is necessary to turn off the ignition and open the throttle wide. Then, turn the prop backward a few revolutions to draw out the excess fuel.

Keep Your Hand on the Throttle and Watch the Switch
A necessary habit to get into is that of keeping your hand on the throttle, not only on the ground, but in the air as well — you could need it at any time. Also remember to keep the ignition switch off at all times except when starting and running. If the switch were left on while turning the prop by hand during the priming period, the engine could "catch" violently striking the hand or arm, perhaps breaking it.

Keeping your hand on the throttle while starting will also tell you that it's not wide open, or closed. If opened wide and the engine starts, the airplane would

238

lunge forward and could cause all sorts of problems. If closed, the engine would start alright only to quit after the prime was burned.

Warm the Engine

After the engine is running, set it at idle rpm. and let it warm up to its manufacturer's suggested temperature. Never attempt flight with a cold engine — it is more likely to quit than a warm one. After the engine is up to temperature, point it into the wind and either chock it or have someone restrain it from moving. Now, take the throttle up and down a few times to see that it advances smoothly and doesn't backfire on the way down. If you have duel ignition, check each circuit by shorting — a small rpm.drop should occur on each. If not, one or the other or both is defective and will have to be checked before flying.

Taxiing

The ultralight student is often surprised by the difficulty he has in learning to "drive" his aircraft on the ground. It doesn't handle quite like a car! The main reason for this is that it's a flying machine first and a ground vehicle last. The controls are designed to function best at speeds above the stall, while most taxiing is done below the stall. At any rate, after some practice, taxiing becomes second nature, as you learn to feel the aircraft's responses to various control inputs at various speeds.

Taxiing techniques vary from ultralight to ultralight, but some basic rules apply. In flight, there is a strong airflow past the rudder, making yaws quick to occur. While taxiing at low speeds, the good airflow doesn't exist, and control response is slow, especially if there is no steerable nose or tailwheel. As airspeed increases, the rush of air past the rudder makes it more effective. If the rudder is in the propwash, turn response at low taxi speeds can be quickened by a momentary blast from the propeller.

On taildraggers, forward stick (i.e., down elevator) can be used to lift (assisted by momentary prop blast) the tailwheel off the ground, and allow the rudder to swing the aircraft around. Once a turn is started at higher taxi speeds, it wants to continue and requires anticipation and opposite control before straightening is desired.

On tri-geared ultralights, backstick (up elevator) will lift the nose, allowing the rudder to swing the aircraft around, as the throttle is momentarily advanced.

Aileron can also be used while taxiing at higher speeds, but gives a response opposite to that in flight. To turn left, the stick is pushed right (lowering the left aileron and raising the right) allowing adverse aileron yaw to develop a left turning tendency.

Crosswind Taxiing

Crosswind taxiing requires strict attention to wind directions with respect to the aircraft. A light wind could lift the windward wing, causing the leeward wingtip to strike the runway, resulting in a group loop, or spin around the lowered tip. Dihedral aggravates this effect due to the underside of the wing being exposed to the crosswind. In general, airplanes tend to nose into the wind, due to the side force on the tail — an effect called weathercocking.

To minimize being tipped over in a crosswind, the following stick positions are recommended for ultralights equipped with independent ailerons.

Right/Front Wind — Right Stick
Right/Rear Wind — Left Stick
Left/Front Wind — Left Stick
Left/Rear Wind — Right Stick
Nose/Tail Wind — Neutral Stick

If you analyze these positions and the winds, you'll see the intent is to deflect the ailerons so that wind pressure helps keep the windward wing down.

Practice taxiing until you are extremely confident and comfortable with the airplane's handling. Remember, when you land, you'll be in a high speed taxi situation and you'll have to be able to make a successful transition from flight control response to taxi responses. You must be ready for it before you do it!

Establishing Wind Direction

The common device used to tell what direction the wind is coming from is called a wind sock. It's actually a tapered fabric tube attached to a pole on top of a hangar or planted in the ground, where the wind can reach it unobstructed.

At first, the proper takeoff direction as indicated can be confusing, but if you remember to takeoff into the loose end of the sock you'll be right every time.

Takeoff and Climbout

Takeoff

Always takeoff into the wind, i.e., aim your ultralight in the direction from which the wind is coming. The purpose of doing this is to enable the liftoff to occur at less of a ground speed, hence requiring less distance. Taking off into the wind will also enable you to climb higher in less ground distance covered, adding to the safety of the event.

Theoretically, if you were pointed into a wind equal to your takeoff speed, and poured on full throttle, you'd rise straight up. But only a fool would try such an experiment, for unless the wind were perfectly smooth and steady, and straight on, an ultralight would not only be lifted up, but also blown away, out of control!

Takeoff is simply an extension of a high speed taxi run. The basic procedure in making a normal takeoff, is as follows:

1. Warm the engine. Let the cylinder head temperature come up to par and be able to advance to full power and back without missing or backfire. If you have dual ignition, check both circuits — as indicated by a drop in RPM. when one is shorted out.
2. Taxi to the runway, after checking for landing traffic.
3. Line up into the wind and open the throttle.
4. Hold the stick forward and accelerate to just above either the best angle of climb speed (1.2 times stall speed) or best rate of climb speed (1.4 times stall speed). If you come back on the stick too soon, i.e., before you have flying speed, the airplane will rise a little then sink, and bounce a few times before it gets up to flying speed.
5. Gently ease back on the stick, rotate and lift off.
6. Continue climbing straight ahead at either 1.2 or 1.4 times stall speed, until a few feet below the desired altitude.
7. Lower the nose to cruising speed, then throttle back to cruise RPM.

As little as 20 to 40 practice takeoffs may be enough to develop the necessary skills.

Climbout

The climbout is, of course, the natural extension of the takeoff run.

Once again, as in all phases of flight it is necessary to maintain a proper

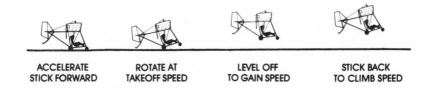

| ACCELERATE | ROTATE AT | LEVEL OFF | STICK BACK |
| STICK FORWARD | TAKEOFF SPEED | TO GAIN SPEED | TO CLIMB SPEED |

Fig. 2-9. Normal takeoff procedure.

airspeed, or more precisely, angle of attack. Rather than "chasing-the-airspeed-indicator" though, concentrate on the aircraft's attitude and takeoffs should become easy. Only small pitch corrections should be necessary once the climb is begun — maybe a half inch or less at the stick.

When you are anywhere between 5 to 20 feet below your desired cruising altitude, the ptich attitude can be lowered to slow the altimeter in anticipation of leveling off. When the desired altitude is reached, the throttle can be adjusted to maintain cruising speed. If your ultralight is properly trimmed, this is where it will show up — no stick forces should be evident. If there is a stick force, you would have to fly faster or slower to the speed where the ship is trimmed.

NOTE: If a prolonged climb is necessary, keep a close watch on cylinder head temperature, so as not to allow the engine to overheat and seize.

Engine Failure on Takeoff

When the engine fails on takeoff the first thing you must do is to lower the nose to obtain your best gliding speed, which is about the same as your best climb speed, and keep calm. If you are high enough to turn back to the field, fine, but keep up that airspeed or you'll stall and enter a spin. If you are too low, it's probably best if you continue straight ahead or initiate a very shallow bank to avoid hitting some obstructions. Do not attempt a 180° turn and downwind landing unless you are absolutely certain you have enough altitude.

Clearing Obstructions

The best angle of climb speed can be used to climb out of a confined field. Accelerate to slightly more than the best angle of climb speed, then rotate and climb out at the best angle speed. This can be dangerous as it is very near the stall, and should be used only if absolutely necessary.

Turn, Turn, Turn

Once you have successfully mastered the takeoff and find yourself cruising, you are faced with the task of either maintaining a direction of flight and/or turning. To gain a clearer picture of what is involved in controlling flight direction, let's use the example of a car traveling on a slippery road.

Suppose you are moving along on a straight and level highway at a fairly high rate of speed, as if the road were dry, and you attempt to negotiate a curve. Not long after you enter the curve, you find yourself skidding sideways off the road. If the road had been "banked" enough, it should be apparent that the skid would not have occurred.

This situation is quite similar to flying a turn. For instance, if only the rudder is deflected, say right, while the ailerons are not touched, the nose will swing toward the right, but the airplane will not come around, without skidding in the original direction of flight. To correct for the skid, the wings, (like the road) need to be banked to tilt the lift force toward the center of the turn in counteracting the centrifugal force.

Now, suppose you tried to drive your car along the bank of a slippery hill. You couldn't! The car would, of course, slip sideways until you reached the level (un-banked) bottom. No amount of turn away from the fall line would prevent the slip — only the leveling of the surface. Or, the car might be driven down, if the front wheels are steered in the direction of the level.

This situation is also similar to flying. If an airplane is banked only, with insufficient rudder into the turn, it will slip toward the low wing. If the rudder is deflected into the turn, a coordinated turn will be established and the slip will stop. Also, the wings could be un-banked, i.e., leveled, accomplishing the effect of the car reaching the level at the bottom of the hill, and the slip would be stopped!

Banking Turns the Aircraft

If you were to drive your car on a properly banked, icy racetrack at some given speed, depending on the degree of banking and radius of curvature, you would

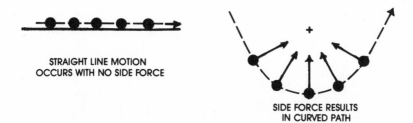

STRAIGHT LINE MOTION
OCCURS WITH NO SIDE FORCE

SIDE FORCE RESULTS
IN CURVED PATH

Fig. 2-10. A constant side force is needed to produce a turn.

neither skid nor slip — you'd be perfectly balanced or coordinated in the turn. If the slope of the bank were too steep for your speed and turn radius, you'd slip toward the center of the track. If the track wasn't banked steeply enough, you'd skid to the outside and hit the guard wall!

This situation is exactly analogous to flying, but in flying it's the bank angle that establishes the turn rate for a given speed. When a wing is banked, it tilts its lift toward the center of the turn, in essence, pulling the aircraft around the turn. The amount of pull (lift) is, of course, dependent upon the angle of attack, or pitch attitude with respect to a plane made by the longitudinal and vertical axis (not with respect to the horizon!).

While an aircraft is banked and its lift is tilted toward the center of the turn, it still needs to develop a vertical component of that lift equal to the gross weight, to keep itself up. What this means is that, unless the stick is pulled back and/or the throttle advanced, the aircraft will descend. Now remember that stall speed increases with bank, so it won't take as much back stick to stall, while banked. Stay above the stall speed for your angle of bank and you won't stall!

To increase the turn rate, it is necessary to increase both the bank angle and the angle of attack. The bank angle will determine the turn rate for a given airspeed, while back pressure (angle of attack) will allow generation of enough vertical component of total lift to maintain altitude. The turn rate can be decreased by shallowing the bank and reducing the back pressure.

As a general rule, it is a good habit to enter a turn with more speed than when you were flying straight and level. This may be done by advancing the throttle and/or pushing the stick forward. This will not only help get you away from the banked stall speed, but also make the controls a bit more responsive. Once in the turn remember that the THROTTLE CAN BE USED FOR AIRSPEED CONTROL TO TIGHTEN THE TURN WHILE HOLDING BACK PRESSURE, OR TO CLIMB AND DESCEND.

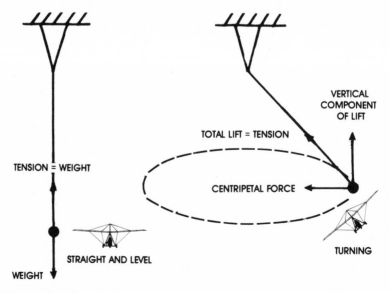

Fig. 2-11. The physics of a turn.

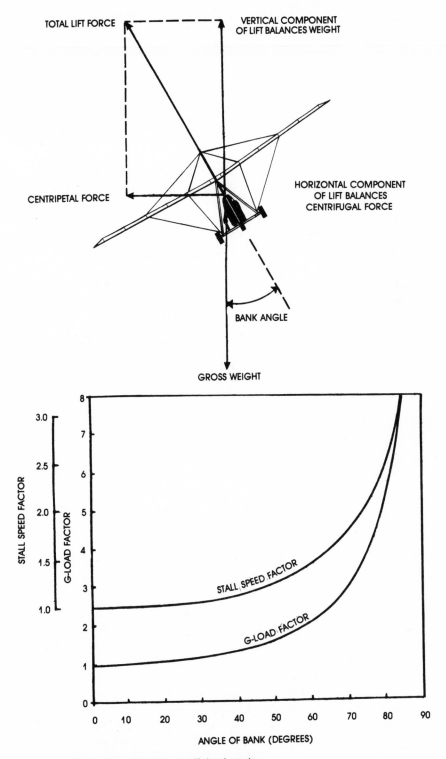

TOTAL LIFT FORCE

VERTICAL COMPONENT
OF LIFT BALANCES WEIGHT

CENTRIPETAL FORCE

HORIZONTAL COMPONENT
OF LIFT BALANCES
CENTRIFUGAL FORCE

BANK ANGLE

GROSS WEIGHT

STALL SPEED FACTOR

G-LOAD FACTOR

STALL SPEED FACTOR

G-LOAD FACTOR

ANGLE OF BANK (DEGREES)

Fig. 2-12. Load and stall speed increase with bank angle.

Throughout the foregoing discussion, you may have noticed that no mention was made of the rudder! What is its function in a turn? Simply this. The rudder is used merely to counteract any yaw tendencies that develop while the other controls are used — that is all!

But what about the so-called two control (rudder and elevator) ultralights. After all, they don't have ailerons, yet they are turned by rudder, you say. Well, to the casual observer, it certainly looks like the rudder does the turning, but it isn't so. This apparent paradox can be explained as follows.

Turns can certainly be made by using the rudder, provided enough dihedral (wide "V" formed by the wing panels) exists. When the rudder is deflected, it first causes the aircraft to yaw, and since it doesn't have any ailerons to set up the appropriate angle of bank, the aircraft enters a skid. Due to the dihedral angle, the underside of the outside wing is exposed to the skid velocity which in turn lifts that wing into a bank. The wing lift is tilted toward the center of the turn and the airplane turns! Now the elevator and throttle can be used as described above to control the turn. Properly designed, the aileronless ultralight can actually make fairly coordinated turns. However, an airplane without ailerons is quite limited in the amount of crosswind it can handle, and in its ability to be rolled. A wing simply cannot be "picked-up" right now without ailerons to roll the airplane.

Judging the Proper Angle of Bank

When the angle of bank is too steep for the airspeed and radius of curvature desired, the aircraft will slip toward the inside of the turn and the pilot will feel himself sliding sideways toward the low wing. This can, of course, be corrected by decreasing the bank.

If the angle of bank is too shallow for the airspeed and radius of curvature desired, the aircraft will skid toward the outside of the turn and the pilot will feel himself being thrown toward the outside of the turn. The solution would be to increase the angle of bank.

Without the aid of a bank indicator, which most ultralights don't have, the proper bank angle can be felt by the seat-of-the-pants. A perfectly coordinated turn will give the pilot no side force sensations. He'll just feel as though he were in straight and level flight, while observing an apparently titled horizon moving by sideways in front of him.

How a Turn is Made

In making a coordinated turn then, an airplane must be rolled, yawed and pitched in a smooth continuous motion. For the beginner, however, it is possible to perform this in steps. For example, to make a gentle turn of moderate radius to the left, start by rolling the aircraft into a moderate left bank. Push the stick to the left until the desired bank angle is reached, then move the stick back to neutral (or slightly to the right, as required to hold the bank angle). Immediately thereafter, yaw the airplane left with left rudder. Then pitch the airplane up by applying a slight back pressure. Provided the amounts of roll, yaw and pitch are in proper relation with each other, the airplane will circle at a constant bank and altitude, neither slipping or skidding — it will be in a coordinated turn.

Coming out of a turn is the reverse of entering one. Pitch and yaw must be neutralized and then the wings leveled.

Doing this in steps first requires the pitch (angle of attack) to be lowered by releasing the back pressure on the stick until it is neutralized. Next the yawing must be stopped by releasing rudder to center. Finally, roll the airplane back to level by moving the stick away from the turn, then centering it when level.

Keep in mind that the above step-by-step procedure is fine for understanding and learning the turning process, but in normal flying, these steps are coordinated into a smooth continuous motion. Coordination is, after all, the heart and soul of flying. To make a coordinated turn is to make a turn without slipping or skidding. In other words, the ball in a bank indicator would be centered constantly throughout the turn.

Adverse Aileron Yaw

Whenever the stick is moved sideways and the ailerons deflect to initiate a bank or to level the wings, the down going aileron (the high wing) creates more drag than the up going (the low wing) aileron. This has the effect of actually yawing the aircraft in the direction opposite to the intended turn, especially at slower speeds (high angles of attack)! Because of this effect, called adverse aileron yaw, it is necessary to apply rudder into the turn, otherwise, or you will be in an uncoordinated turn — slipping slightly.

Rudder Not Necessary To Turn

If an ultralight is well designed, and possesses a certain amount of weather cocking tendency, it is possible to make a coordinated turn without the rudder deflected. If there is sufficient side area aft the CG, the aircraft will tend to position itself with the circumference of the turn so that no rudder is needed. This is especially true of higher speeds where minimal aileron deflection is required to bank, thereby creating little or no adverse aileron yaw.

Understanding the Physics of a Turn

In high school we learned Newton's first law of motion: "A body persists in its state of rest or of uniform motion in a straight line unless it is compelled to change that state by forces impressed on it." And so it is with an airplane flying in

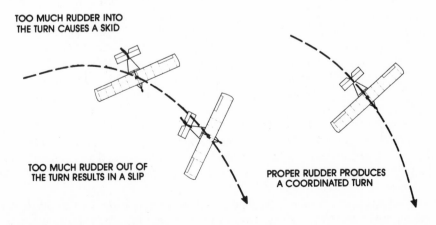

TOO MUCH RUDDER INTO
THE TURN CAUSES A SKID

TOO MUCH RUDDER OUT OF
THE TURN RESULTS IN A SLIP

PROPER RUDDER PRODUCES
A COORDINATED TURN

Fig. 2-13. How the rudder is used in a turn.

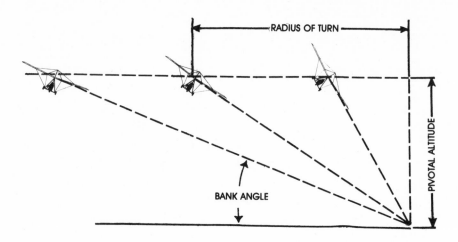

Fig. 2-14. There's a certain pivotal altitude for a given airspeed and the proper angle of bank.

a straight and level, unaccelerated flight. Unless a force is introduced to unbalance the established equilibrium, the airplane will continue doing what is was doing.

To gain a better understanding of the forces generated in a turn, we can use the example of a bowling ball. Once it is released down the alley, it will roll straight — the alley is smooth and there is nothing to interfere with the ball's trip to the pins. The only way we can alter the ball's course is to apply a sideways force. And, the only we can make it turn in a circle is to apply that side force continuously, both perpendicular to the direction of motion and toward a single point. This "toward-a-single-point-side-force" is known as centripetal (which means center seeking) force, and it counter-balances the centrifugal force, which tends to tear the ball away from the center.

Now let's take our bowling ball and suspend it from a rope. The tension in the rope is upward and opposite the ball's weight — a situation analogous to straight and level, constant speed flight where lift equals gross weight.

Unlike the bowling alley situation, the ball is now restrained. If we give it a push this time, it will move in a circle at some "bank angle" depending on its speed. Here, the rope's tension is comprised not only of the ball's weight, but also the centrifugal force! And, this is exactly as it is in a turning airplane, where the lift is equal to the tension. The lift must be greater in turning because it's not only counterbalancing the gross weight, but also the centrifugal force trying to "un-turn" the airplane. The inward pointing lift is what turns the airplane.

Pivotal Altitude and Turns About a Point

Pivotal altitude is that height above the ground, for a given speed, at which an airplane can fly around a point while its lateral axis is pointed at that point. This altitude is always the same, regardless of the turning radius. The shorter the radius the steeper the required bank.

At 50 mph, for example, the pivotal altitude would be 168 feet. At 25 mph it would be 42 feet. Pivotal altitude varies as the square of the speed, i.e., doubling airspeed quadruples the pivotal altitude.

248

Now keep in mind, if there is a breeze, the angle of bank has to be continuously varied to turn about a point. With the wind coming from the inside of the turn, a steeper bank is needed to prevent drifting with the wind, and vice versa. The faster the groundspeed caused by the wind, the steeper the angle of bank required to maintain a constant radius. Only practice will make turns about a point possible in a wind.

Steep Turns

Sometime in you flying career, you may find it necessary to do a steep turn, and anything above a 30° bank might be considered steep. At 60°, you'll experience a 2-'g' load (pressed into your seat at twice your weight), the wing will have to develop twice its normal lift, and you'll have to maintain an airspeed of more than 1.41 times your normal stall speed. While 60° of bank might not sound like much, from an airplane it looks as though you are almost vertical!

The main thing about a steep turn is that it requires power levels above those used for normal cruise. Before entering the turn, advance the throttle and build up excess speed, at least 1½ times (for a 60° bank) your normal speed, but more to move well above your stall speed at 60°. Then enter the turn as you would any other, with the correct amounts of pitch and yaw and continue banking until you're at the desired angle.

The other thing about a steep turn is that, besides the bank angle itself, pitch control will be most important. Yawing required is minimal. If you pull too much back stick, you'll stall. If you pull too little, you'll start slipping into the turn and lose your altitude.

To stop a steep turn, do as with any other turn. Reduce the back pressure to lower the angle of attack, then roll out and correct for any yawing.

Downwind Turns

In general aviation, there seems to be continual discussion about the dangers of the so-called downwind turn. And, indeed there should be, as it seems to be the focal point for a significant percentage of all flying accidents. So what extra precautions should the ultralight pilot take when turning downwind?

First of all, when flying at an altitude safe enough to recover from a stalled turn, there shouldn't be any more concern than normal: besides, a good pilot won't stall in a turn. When near the ground, however, it's an entirely different ballgame. But why should the propensity to stall be greater near the ground?

As we've said many times before, an airplane simply will not stall, provided it stays below stall angle of attack. That sounds easy enough, but in making a downwind turn near the ground a couple of "culprits" emerge. For example, let's assume you're making a forced landing in the downwind direction because there is no other alternative. After determining your perspective, you set up a base leg, with a crosswind to your right. You begin turning left onto final, and here's where you make or break the landing.

In this situation, that crosswind could tend to over bank the aircraft. Also, the turn might be a little tighter than it should be (to make the field) and the stall speed at that bank angle could be exceeded. The air near the ground is often turbulent and a sudden gust could stall a wing. Then, too, once you've turned final, the tailwind will add to your ground speed, giving the false impression of sufficient airspeed, causing a stall, as back stick is inappropriately applied.

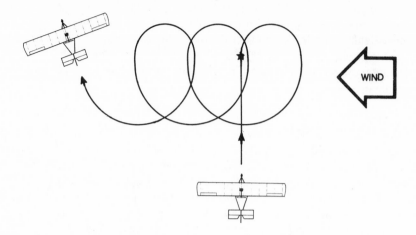

Fig. 2-15. How wind affects a constant banked turn.

To avoid the trauma and potential dangers associated with downwind turns, the rule is simple — MAINTAIN ANGLE OF ATTACK BELOW THE STALL. One way to do this is by keeping your airspeed well above the steep bank stalling speed of the airplane. It's far better to have too much airspeed than too little, especially in an ultralight.

Clearing Turns

When you wish to make a turn in a high wing ultralight, it makes good sense to "clear-the-turn" first. This is done simply by first momentarily raising the wing on the inside of the intended turn and checking for traffic in that direction. If all's clear, proceed with the turn.

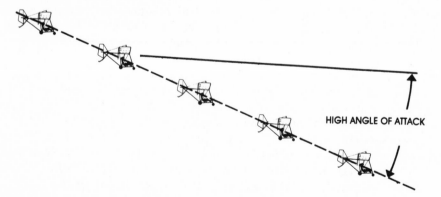

HIGH ANGLE OF ATTACK

Fig. 2-16. Mushing is dangerous, because it's done so near the stall.

Mushes, Stalls and Spins

The Mush

Many of the ultralights presented in this book are often described as being able to mush. Some are also claimed to go into a mush, rather than a stall, when the stick is pulled all the way back.

So what is a mush? Somewhere between a normal glide and the actual stall is where you'll find it. Once in a glide, if you gradually come back on the stick and stay slightly above the stall, you'll be mushing. It's a glide with a higher sink rate and/or steeper descent path, while the nose (angle of attack) is held higher than for a normal glide.

In the case of a mush, the higher angle of attack causes more drag since you're gliding below your maximum glide ratio. Mushing can be used to steepen the approach, but it is considered dangerous since it is done so near the stall. And, if you were to land in a mushed attitude, you'd certainly damage the airplane and injure yourself, because of the sink rate.

Stalls

All throughout this book we've mentioned the stall, but let's look at it in more detail. Before we do, remember that any ultralight can be made to stall. Sure, some are more resistant to stalling and require a different technique, but they can all be stalled.

A stall is that event which takes place when the wing is at such a high angle of attack that the airflow over the upper surface breaks away, diminishing the lift. As a result, the nose drops and the aircraft dives until the angle of attack is low enough for the wing to develop its full lift. The proper angle of attack for airflow reattachment coincides with an airspeed just above the stall speed.

The stall can be recognized in ways other than by what the airspeed indicator says. Some ultralights might exhibit a buffet, and shaking of the stick, as the airflow partially separates then reattaches to the wing's upper surface. That's the time to get the nose down (lower the angle of attack) before the stall breaks.

If a stall is left to occur, and the pilot does nothing, the nose will drop and the airplane will dive until it has enough speed to fly, and then it will gradually level itself out. If the pilot wants to, he can improve upon the airplane's natural recovery rate by gradually coming back on the stick after the nose has dropped, that way affecting a recovery with a very small loss of altitude — maybe within 25 feet!

Stall recovery is something every pilot must be capable of doing — his life could depend on it, especially if he's near the ground. Keep in mind that roughly half of all aviation accidents are stall related. Stalls should, of course, be practiced but only at a safe altitude, with plenty of room for recovery.

Stalls can be made with power-off and power-on. The power-off stall can be done with the engine at idle, the airplane in a glide. Gradually, pull back on the stick and try to hold the aircraft level. The airspeed will drop and the airplane will stall. As soon as you recognize the stall, push the stick forward, regain flying speed and resume your glide. (If a gradual application of back stick doesn't result

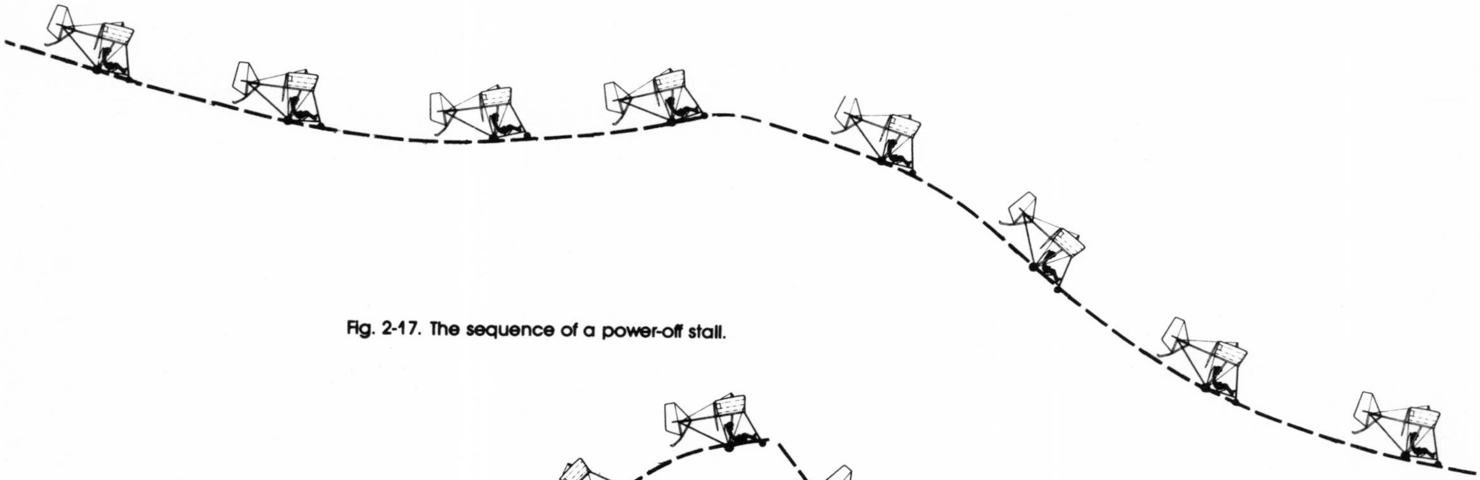

Fig. 2-17. The sequence of a power-off stall.

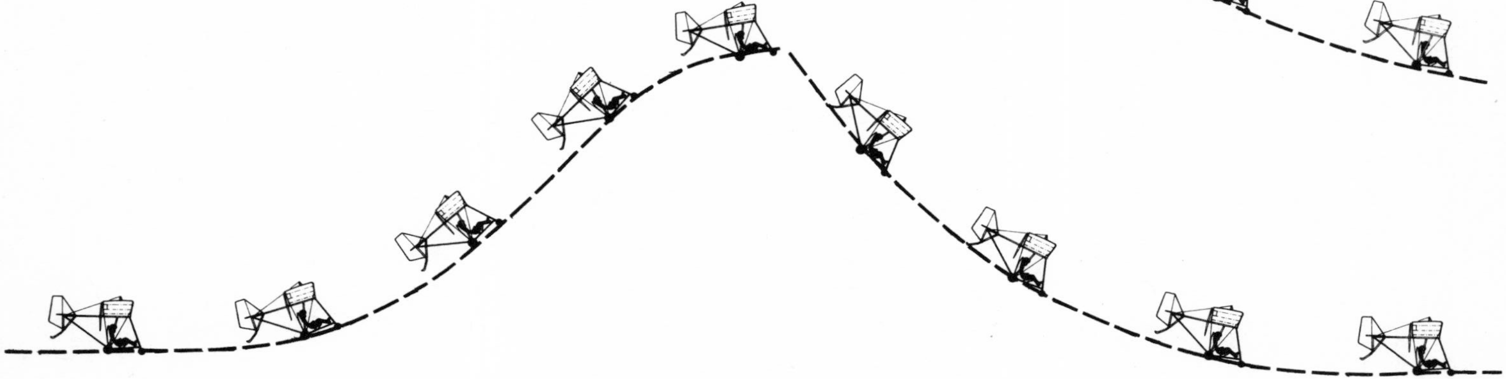

Fig. 2-18. The sequence of a power-on stall.

in a stall, you might have to come back sharply on the stick to force a break.)

The power-on stall requires a gradual application of back stick as you put the airplane into a very steep attitude, say 30°-45°, with the throttle set at cruise. After a few seconds, the stall will occur and the nose will fall through. Recover by pushing the stick foward and return to level flight as soon as flying speed is regained.

While in a stall, keep in mind that the airflow is separated from the upper surface of the wing, making the ailerons useless. In fact, if you are near a stall and wish to raise a low wing, forget it. The instant you move the stick, the low wing will stall and possibly put you into a spin. The only thing you can do is to lower the angle of attack first, regain attached flow (flying speed) and then level the wings.

The rudder, on the other hand, is the least affected by the stall and it can be used to aid in keeping the wings level, as well as in maintaining direction. The rudder is especially effective in a power-on stall, with the propwash making it so. In a power-off stall, much rudder movement is required to maintain effective control.

At this point, it is necessary to mention the canard (horizontal tail first) ultralight and its supposed stall resistance. This configuration is set up so that a stall is just about impossible — just about. Under normal circumstances, the canards do seem relatively stall resistant! If the nose is brought up to the normal stall angle, what happens is that the canard (which might be supporting only 20% or less of the aircraft's gross weight) stalls, causing the nose to drop while the main wing keeps on lifting, and the airplane does not stall. In fact, if the stick is continued to be held back, the canard will rise, stall then lower in a gentle porposing motion, with a characteristic period.

The apparently unstallable canard can be stalled, primarily by performing what is known as an accelerated stall. Here, the aircraft is put into a very abrupt pull-up that, due to its curved flight path adds an additional 'g'-load to the airplane, increasing its stall speed and forcing the upper surface canard airflow to separate.

One final word on stalling. Always remember that any ultralight will stall at any time provided its angle of attack is too high — no matter what the airspeed, throttle, setting, attitude, configuration or 'g'-load!

NOTE: As a beginning ultralight pilot, or even as a seasoned pro, it might be a good idea to rig up an angle or attack indicator of your own. It's simple. Attach a stiff wire or dowell to the aircraft so that it protrudes into undisturbed airflow. Bend the end down 90° and attach a length of string (6-12″ long) to it. And there you have it. No matter what airspeed or attitude you're in, that simple string will tell you about your angle of attack!

Spins

A spin is defined as the auto-rotation of a stalled aircraft around a vertical axis, coupled with a large altitude loss with each revolution. It happens when one wing stalls before the other, as might occur in a turn made too near the stall.

If, for instance, you're in a left turn near a stall, and you decide to level the wings before you lower the nose. The left wing's down going aileron will increase that wing's angle of attack and stall it — rather than raising it as intended. The left wing will drop further still and set-up a rotation to the left, as the nose drops below the horizon — a spin will be started.

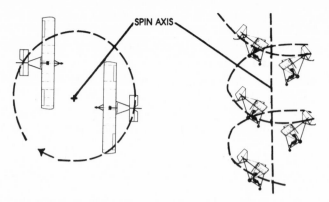

Fig. 2-19. A spin has the airplane stalled and rotating about a small radius vertical axis.

Now, even though the nose is below the horizon, the wing is at high angle of attack — due to the vertical component of velocity — and it is stalled. At this point the ailerons are quite useless and will do nothing to correct the situation. As in all other phases of flight, to be flying requires that the wing be at an unstalled angle of attack, and that means — get the stick forward. Yes, even though you are pointed down already, the stick must come forward in order to lower the angle of attack. If the engine is at an advanced rpm, the throttle must be closed immediately.

Extreme care must be taken in recovering from the dive that results from a spin recovery. After the spin rotation stops, back pressure is to be applied slowly in order to restore level flight. If the stick is pulled back too abruptly, the ultralight's airframe could be overstressed — tearing the wings off! Excessive back stick could also cause the aircraft to enter a secondary stall or another spin.

A spin could also be stopped by applying opposite rudder, but it depends on the design. It is not known how thoroughly some ultralights have been spin tested and you'd do well to inquire at the factory or dealership to find out. If the particular design you're interested in has been spin tested, the manufacturer will have a specified method of recovery. If it hasn't been spin tested, don't volunteer to be the test pilot — fly to avoid spin potential by maintaining proper airspeed, or more correctly, proper angle of attack at all times. Some designs may be claimed as "spin proof", but why tempt fate.

Landing

Landing is often said to be the most difficult part of flying, followed by takeoff, then actual cruising flight.

The actual steps involved in making a landing in a standard left hand traffic pattern, are as follows:
1. Choose the runway.
2. Enter the pattern 45° with respect to the downwind leg.
3. Turn 90° at end of downwind leg and fly base leg as you descend, with reduced power.
4. Turn 90° at end of base leg and set up final approach glide.
5. Determine your perspective and select your touchdown point, and glide toward it.
6. Break the glide as you approach the ground.
7. Level off 2-3 feet above ground.
8. Hold aircraft off as it loses flying speed.
9. Bring the nose up to landing attitude.
10. Sink to the ground for a touchdown.
11. If a taildragger, hold the stick back so the tailwheel is effective. If a tri-gear, hold the stick forward to plant the nosewheel firmly on the ground.

NOTE: Steps 9 through 11 could be modified to allow touchdown above stall speed. This would be a "wheel landing" where the aircraft is "driven-onto-the-ground". The reason being to stay well above stall and not be susceptible to stalling out from an unanticipated gust.

Now let's analyze each step of the landing procedure.

Choose the Runway

Before choosing the runway, it is necessary that you determine the wind direction. If there's traffic at the field, their takeoff direction will tell you which direction to land. If you're out in the middle of nowhere, you could look for telltale signs, such as drifting smoke or flags. If there's a windsock, check it out. You'll be landing into the free end.

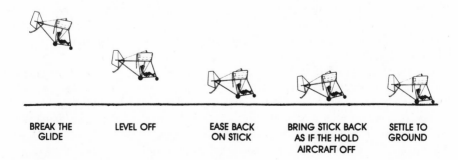

| BREAK THE GLIDE | LEVEL OFF | EASE BACK ON STICK | BRING STICK BACK AS IF THE HOLD AIRCRAFT OFF | SETTLE TO GROUND |

Fig. 2-20. Normal landing sequence.

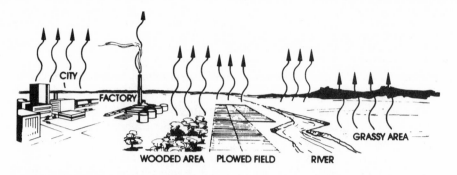

Fig. 2-21. The earth's surface heats unevenly, giving rise to convective currents of varying strength.

Enter the Pattern

A traffic pattern is a rectangular course flown over the ground at certain altitudes in a systematic procedure, allowing consistent landings to be made. While no prescribed pattern, per se, exists for ultralights, experience flying them suggests a pattern like that shown.

In conventional aviation, it is common practice to enter the pattern at 45° with respect to the downwind leg, and it makes good sense to do this with an ultralight, too. This entry might occur at 125 feet above ground and 600 feet parallel to the runway, at an airspeed of 40 mph. Fly the downwind leg maybe 250 feet downwind from the end of the runway and turn 90° onto the base leg. Come back on the throttle to say 1½ times idle speed and begin the base leg at 35 mph.

The Final Glide

Turn 90° to final at maybe 50 feet above ground and slow to 30 mph. Line up with the runway and use throttle as required. Remember, the engine could quit at any time so it's better to have a little excess altitude than not enough, in case you have come in "dead stick" (propeller stopped!)

It is important to remember that on final you are actually a glider, and unlike cruising flight your attitude will have to be lower. The nose will be aimed below the horizon to maintain that 30 mph. glide. If this isn't the case and you're at a level altitude, the airspeed will drop below 30 mph. and the airplane could stall, which would be disasterous.

It's a real good idea to keep an eye on the airspeed, as ultralights tend to lose it rapidly with a pitch up. Also, remember that you're slower now than when cruising, and the controls won't be as responsive. More anticipation is necessary. Come in a little faster if it makes you feel more comfortable. It's better to have too much speed on final than too little. Look at it as an extra margin against a gust stalling you out.

Since gliding is different than cruising, you should climb to an altitude of say 1,000 feet, and practice gliding with the engine slightly above idle. And remember to "clear" the engine (i.e., give it a shot of ¾ throttle) every 30 seconds to keep it warm. If it gets too cool, it could quit — then you would be flying a glider for sure, and be forced to land. Pick a point on the ground, and practice gliding toward it. Improve your skill with the safety of altitude. Remember, if the point you aim for is neither rising nor falling in your field of view, you'll reach it.

If your aiming point is rising, you'll undershoot and not reach it. You'll have to

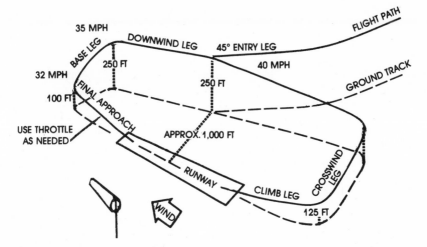

Fig. 2-22. A possible ultralight traffic pattern.

add power to maintain your present altitude or to rise. If your aiming point is dropping, you'll overshoot and touchdown beyond it. This will require going around the pattern again or slip it in, as explained in the next chapter.

Level Off

After you have mastered the glide and can accurately control it to reach the desired point, you're ready to brake the glide and level off.

In some respects, leveling off is much like parallel parking a car. If you enter the space at too much of an angle, you'll hit the curb. If you enter it at too shallow an angle, you'll be too far from the curb. And so it is with leveling off. And, as in other maneuvers, a certain amount of judgment and anticipation is required. You must be able to assess your sink rate and anticipate it being zero when you touch down.

When you are about 5-10 feet above the runway, you should break the glide. This requires coming back on the stick, while maintaining a good margin above stall speed. This will slow your rate of descent and round-out the glidepath. When you're about 1-2 feet above the ground, the round-out should be completed and you should be flying parallel to the runway.

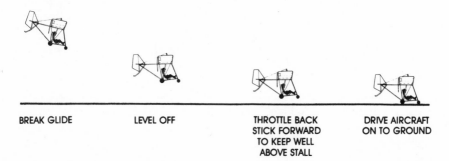

| BREAK GLIDE | LEVEL OFF | THROTTLE BACK STICK FORWARD TO KEEP WELL ABOVE STALL | DRIVE AIRCRAFT ON TO GROUND |

Fig. 2-23. Wheel landing sequence.

257

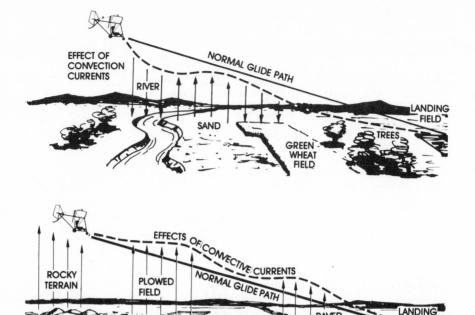

Fig. 2-24. The effect of convective currents on glide path.

If you level off too high, the ultralight could stall before it touches down, dropping and damaging the airframe and injuring the pilot. If you level off too low, the aircraft will strike the ground too hard and bounce back into the air, only to stall out on the way up. Full throttle and a go-around might be the only way to save the landing.

A good way to judge the leveling-off altitude while maintaing directional control at touchdown, is to maintain a visual focus beyond the touchdown point toward the end of the runway. Focusing too close will blur objects and cause delayed reaction or over controlling. Focusing too far away, beyond the runway, will cause altitude judgement to be off and the nose may be flown into the ground.

Losing Flying Speed to Touchdown

After you have leveled off and are skimming the runway, ground effect will be felt and tend to cause you to float. Be ready for it. Nevertheless, you will sink and your speed will drop to very near stall speed. Your height will also diminish.

As you come closer and closer to the ground, keep coming back on the stick, as if you were trying to hold the airplane off. Come back gradually on the stick, or you may zoom back up into the air, only to stall out. This zoom is called ballooning and is certainly to be avoided. At any rate, keep coming back on the stick as you sink and a good landing should result. This technique describes a so-called full-stall landing, as you are at or near stall when you touchdown. It is fine for calm and very light wind landings.

Wheel Landing

When the wind is above about 5 mph and/or gusting and/or not straight down the runway, a full stall landing could be dangerous. In these situations, it is often wise to carry extra airspeed (as much as 10 mph. above stall) as an insurance policy against having a gust cause you to lose flying speed and stall.

In a wheel landing, you effectively level off at the instant you touch ground. A taildragger would touch on its main wheels only and keep the tail up. A trike gear could touch all three wheels at the same time. What you are doing is essentially driving the ultralight onto the ground at above flying speed. The stick must be held forward as soon as you touch, so as to prevent ballooning.

Judgment and Concentration

Landing is a matter of perspective. How do objects appear from your point of view? What angles to things appear to present? A good example of how perspective can be used in landing is for you to look at an object while standing and then squat down. The object will appear to change its shape somewhat. The angular relationships will change as you move the level of your eyes for even a couple of inches! Perspective is a powerful tool for judging a landing.

It shouldn't be necessary for you to look at the wheels of your ultralight to make a good landing, but you may want to at first. Look all around, especially to the front and focus on your aiming point. Notice if it is rising or falling or steady, and after a while, you will be able to make perfect touchdowns without watching the ground directly beneath your wheels.

Landing is also a matter of concentration. Concentrate on what you are doing and don't allow yourself to be distracted from your task. Concentrated effort can go a long way in learning and save lots of time besides.

Post Touchdown Taxi

Once you have touched down you must continue to fly the aircraft, especially if you did a wheel landing. You'll be in a very high speed taxi situation requiring all of your attention. Until you're below stall speed, the airplane is still flying, and the flight controls will remain functional. "Fly" the ultralight on the ground until the speed drops below stall, then switch over to your taxi techniques. If you have to turn, remember to do it gently, or you may find yourself in a ground loop.

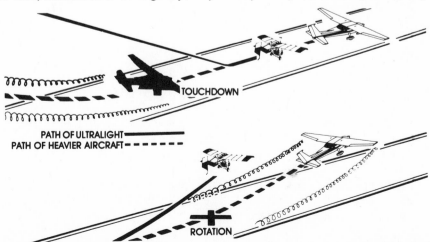

Fig. 2-25. When operating from a runway with heavier aircraft, always land in front of its touchdown point, and takeoff before its rotation point.

LANDING is a matter of perspective, not depth perception. Perspective is different for different ultralight designs, and winds. Greater head winds and "airfler" aircraft have the landing field appearing more like No. 3. Calm conditions and "cleaner" designs favor No. 1. No. 2 is about right for many ultralights.

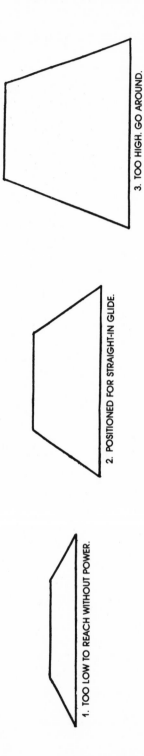

1. TOO LOW TO REACH WITHOUT POWER.

2. POSITIONED FOR STRAIGHT-IN GLIDE.

3. TOO HIGH. GO AROUND.

IF your intended landing spot appears to move up, you won't reach it. If it appears to move down, you'll overshoot. If it doesn't move at all, but only grows in size, you're on the right glide path, and you'll touchdown on the intended spot.

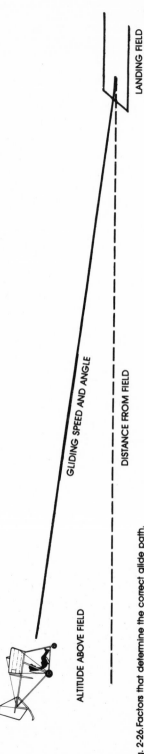

GLIDING SPEED AND ANGLE

ALTITUDE ABOVE FIELD

DISTANCE FROM FIELD

LANDING FIELD

Fig. 2-26. Factors that determine the correct glide path.

Sideslipping — A Way to Lose Altitude

Suppose you are too high on final approach and your engine has just stopped and there's no way you have enough altitude to go around. You simply must set it down, since the field below you is the only one within gliding distance — in the middle of a forest of tall trees. What do you do? Dive it in? No. You'd have too much speed near the ground and float in ground effect to the end of the field and crash into the trees at the other end.

The solution to the above scenerio is called the sideslip — a deliberate cross-controlling of your ultralight. It will allow you to decrease your glide ratio to perhaps half of what it normally is, while still maintaining good airspeed. You'll be able to drop 2 feet in 10 instead of one foot in ten, for example.

Having set up your approach to the field in a normal glide, you are ready to slip. Depress the right rudder pedal gradually and keep it depressed, while at the same time feeding in some left stick and holding it. The ultralight will assume a right heading with the left wing down, while the glidepath will steepen at the same glide speed.

By increasing rudder and aileron deflections as above, the sideslip can be increased, steepening the glide still more, for a little increase in glide speed. The nose will be pointed further right, while the left wing will be lower still.

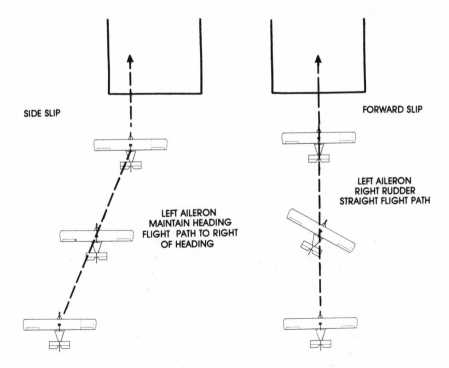

Fig. 2-27. Side slip and forward slip expose aircraft side to the flight path, increasing drag for a steeper descent, when necessary to lose altitude quickly.

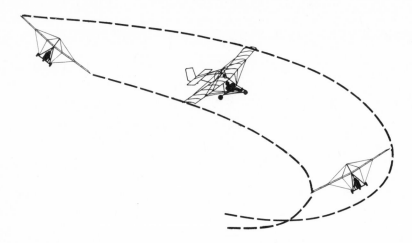

Fig. 2-28. A slipping turn.

To control the direction of the sideslip, think about how an aircraft is turned, as discussed earlier. If you'd like to direct your course to the right, to correct for drift for instance, simply raise the left wing a little, thereby directing some lift to the right. If you wish to turn left, let the stick where it is, and release some of the right rudder you've been holding.

When you get down to the point where you're ready to break the glide, release the rudder and bring the stick back to neutral. This will straighten the aircraft so that it is headed and flying in the direction of the original glide. Now make corrections are necessary to straighten the glidepath with respect to the field and touchdown going straight ahead. This is important, for if you have sideways speed, the landing gear could break on touchdown and/or the airplane could cartwheel onto its side. Always touchdown with forward speed only.

NOTE: The foregoing described a left sideslip. It is also possible to do a right sideslip by pressing left rudder and holding right aileron.

Why a Sideslip Works

At this point you might be puzzled as to why a sideslip can work. After all, aren't the ailerons supposed to roll the airplane? A sideslip works because the rolling force of the ailerons is counterbalanced by the extra air pressure under the low wing which has a sideways velocity component tending to pick it up. And, this same sideways velocity also strikes the fin, counterbalancing the yaw produced by the rudder. So, a state of equilibrium is reached with the airplane flying in a slip. And, since the controls are deflected so abnormally, and areas of the airplane are exposed to abnormal airflows, the total drag rises, steepening the glidepath.

How to Slip a Turn

If the occasion arises that you must lose altitude more quickly than normal while turning, it is useful to superimpose the sideslip technique on to your turn. Start by entering the turn as normal, using the appropriate amounts of pitch and yaw with the bank, so it is coordinated. Once that's established, increase your bank slightly while applying some opposite rudder (i.e., diminish the amount of rudder into the turn). And that's a slipping turn. To get out of it, simply restore the rudder and stick so that the turn is once again coordinated.

Fishtailing

Another way to steepen the glidepath is by fishtailing — the application of rudder, alternating right and left. Done without any aileron inputs, this results in a series of alternating slips, while maintaining the desired direction of flight. It's not as effective as a fully developed slip, but it is another method of helping you get down as desired.

Tip Draggers

Some ultralights are also equipped with tip draggers or tip rudders. These not only yaw and induce banks when deflected independently, but they can also be used to control the glidepath when they are deflected simultaneously. The basic technique is to apply some deflection to both draggers while on final. That way, if it looks like you're going to undershoot, let them both go, and your glide will increase. If you're too high, deflect them both as needed to steepen the glide.

Fig. 2-29. A series of linked left and right rudder applications, without aileron, is called fishtailing and results in a succession of alternating forward slips.

Crosswinds

Whenever you choose to fly when there is wind, you will encounter a crosswind at some point in the flight, be it in cruising, truning, takeoff or landing. Or, you might have an engine failure and be forced to land in a field that is in a crosswind. Now, since most ultralight pilots will not restrict their flying to calm conditions, it would be wise to learn how to handle crosswinds.

Crab It

Suppose you want to fly from your field over to a friend's farm, which is due south, and there's a wind blowing from the west. If you were to fly south, you would never reach the farm — the wind would have blown you east as you traveled south! This is called drift and you must crab to overcome it. For example, if your cruising speed is 40 mph, the wind is at 5 mph and your friend's farm is 40 miles away, in an hour's time you would end up 5 miles east of his farm!

In order to reach your friend's farm, your heading must actually be west of south, i.e., slightly into the wind. The greater the crosswind, the more west of south your heading must be. The ultralight would be flying sideways with respect to the ground, and you'd be aiming at a point on the ground, left of the airplane's centerline.

Being in this situation for the first time, you immediately surmise that the solution to this problem is to kick in some right rudder. So you try it — but it doesn't work! Sure, the aircraft yaws to the right, but it still drifts with the wind. Even if right rudder is held continually, the airplane would only make circles, and skidding ones at that, that would still drift with the wind.

Thinking again, you recall reading somewhere in this book that ailerons roll the airplane and tilt the wing's lift in the direction of the stick. Perhaps you can tilt the lift into that pesty crosswind and make the airplane go where you want it to? You try, and viola, it works! In effect, you are turning to compensate for drift, and that's the way it's done. A crab is simply a turn, done in the normal way with aileron, while the rudder is used to correct any adverse yaw.

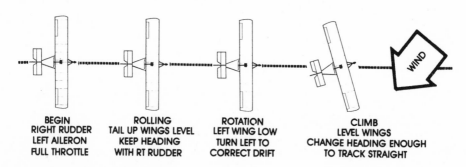

BEGIN	ROLLING	ROTATION	CLIMB
RIGHT RUDDER	TAIL UP WINGS LEVEL	LEFT WING LOW	LEVEL WINGS
LEFT AILERON	KEEP HEADING	TURN LEFT TO	CHANGE HEADING ENOUGH
FULL THROTTLE	WITH RT RUDDER	CORRECT DRIFT	TO TRACK STRAIGHT

Fig. 2-30. Crosswind takeoff technique.

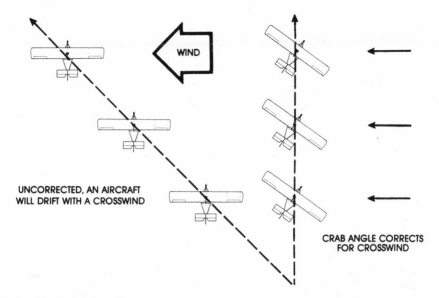

WIND

UNCORRECTED, AN AIRCRAFT
WILL DRIFT WITH A CROSSWIND

CRAB ANGLE CORRECTS
FOR CROSSWIND

Fig. 2-31. Crab to correct for wind drift.

Crosswind Takeoff

While an Ultralight is in contact with the ground it, of course, must be headed in the direction it is going. Sideways motion could damage the landing gear or tip the aircraft over and into a ground loop.

The basic technique used in a crosswind takeoff is to hold stick into the crosswind to tilt the lift toward it, while applying appropriate opposite rudder to counteract any weathercocking tendency. Sound familiar? It should, because that's exactly what a slip is. Once airborne, you can control the drift by maintaining proper aileron and necessary rudder to correct for any unwanted yaw, and, that is a crab.

Crosswind Landing

Now that the cat is out of the bag, landing in a crosswind should be easy. On your final approach you can either crab or slip, depending on whether you need to steepen the glide to get down. Then, at the end of the runway, before touchdown, straighten out by going into a slip and you'll touch down headed in the direction you're going — straight down the runway.

Basic Instruments for Ultralight Flight

While it is entirely possible to fly an ultralight solely by-the-seat-of-your-pants and the wind in your face, it is strongly recommended that you employ minimal instrumentation. Due to various accelerations not encountered in surface travel, and just plain unfamiliarity with being in the air, your senses can sometimes lead you to believe something you should not. For these reasons, and also for accuracy and safety in flight, there are four primary instruments that you should have on board: airspeed indicator, altimeter, tachometer and compass.

STANDARD AIRCRAFT
AIRSPEED INDICATOR

AIRGUIDE AIRSPEED
AND COMPASS

STANDARD AIRCRAFT
COMPASS

Fig. 2-32. Standard aircraft ASI and compass. Airguide unit is popular with ultralights.

Airspeed Indicator (ASI)

The airspeed indicator tells us how fast we are moving relative to the air, and it's the most important instrument of the group. Since the stall speeds of ultralights are so low, it can be difficult to judge exactly when the stall will occur, by such a method as sound. In this regard, an airspeed indicator is an essential piece of equipment. At best though, it is second to angle of attack as a stall indicator — but it's the best device available to relay the information.

An airspeed indicator is very useful in adjusting throttle and stick to make the airplane fly at a prescribed speed, be it for effeciency, safety or performance. As discussed elsewhere, there are *fourteen distinct speeds* at which you can fly, and only the ASI will tell you when you're there.

The ASI is also extremely useful when flying near the ground. If, for example, you are forced to land downwind for some reason, your groundspeed would be your airspeed plus the wind speed. In this instance, the ground would be rushing by faster than normal and unless you watched the ASI, you'd probably slow down and stall. Sure, your groundspeed was high, but your airspeed is what matters.

How the ASI Works

The standard aircraft ASI operates on the difference in pressure between the impact pressure caused by forward motion and the static pressure of the atmosphere. These pressures are picked up by a pitot-static tube located in front of a wing or strut, where it feels the freestream airflow. These pressures are then

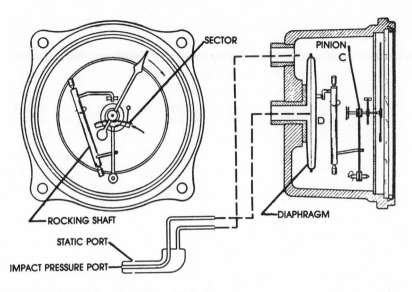

Fig. 2-33. The mechanism of an airspeed indicator.

transmitted via two tubes to the ASI itself, where the pressure difference is translated into mph.

An ASI more common to ultralights consists of a vertical tube with a foam ball inside that rises with increasing airspeed. The inside of the tube is cone shaped, allowing the ball to rise higher with increasing impact pressure. Graduations on the tube indicate mph. Other ASI's would be a small propeller attached to a small DC motor connected to a millovoltmeter calibrated in mph, and a simple spring loaded vane that angles back with increasing speed.

Another popular ultralight ASI is a unit, manufactured by Airguide, that also includes a compass. The handle is removed and the instrument is mounted to the front of the aircraft, where it sees unobstructed airflow. It is extremely important that the air inlets be unshielded and the unit must point into the relative wind. If the airflow into the device is altered, by say a cowling, the airspeed readouts would be incorrect and could spell disaster. It must be calibrated, as it is mounted on the aircraft, with a known source.

Altitude Correction

As you gain altitude, the air becomes less dense, which means for a given true airspeed, the impact pressure is less. To compensate for this, we must add to the indicated airspeed about 2% for every 1,000 feet of altitude. At 5,000 feet you would need to add 5 x 2% = 10% to your indicated. If you're indicating 50 mph, your true airspeed would be 50 + = 55 mph.

Now you ask, does stall speed change with altitude? And, the answer is yes and no. Fortunately, the indicated stall speed doesn't change with altitude, whereas the true airspeed does. But, this won't matter to you — watch the ASI. As we said recently, the air is less dense at altitude therefore, to get the same impact pressure — which is really what matters to the wing — you must go 2% faster for every 1,000 feet of altitude.

Fig. 2-34. The Hall Brothers ASI is popular with ultralighters.

The Altimeter

Unless you are quite close to the ground, it is nearly impossible to accurately judge altitude. For this and reasons of safety, we have the altimeter.

An altimeter has a clock-like face and hands, as well as a small window scale that can be set to read local barometric pressure with a small knob located on the lower left corner of the case. The hands rotate clockwise for altitude gains and vice versa. The large hand indicates altitude in thousands of feet, while the small hand points to hundreds.

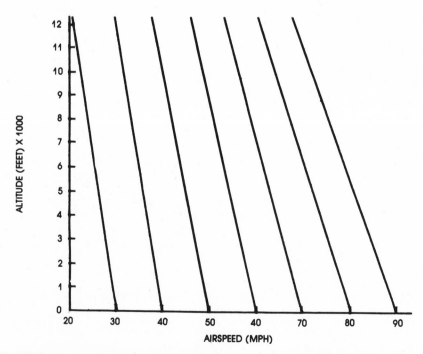

Fig. 2-35. How to correct indicated airspeed for altitude.

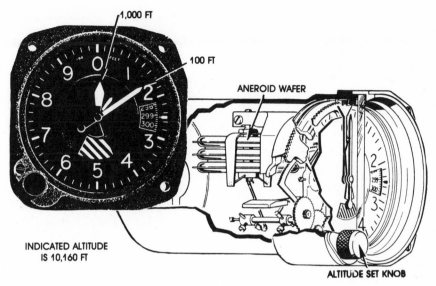

1,000 FT

100 FT

ANEROID WAFER

INDICATED ALTITUDE
IS 10,160 FT

ALTITUDE SET KNOB

Fig. 2-36. Altimeter and inner mechanism. USAF.

How an Altimeter Works

The altimeter is actually an aneroid barometer that is calibrated to read in feet. It makes use of the fact that air density decreases with altitude. A wafer-like capsule, the aneroid, is a thin wall piece sealed under a vacuum. A small spring keeps it from collapsing under outside air pressure. The meter case itself is under normal outside static air pressure. When altitude is increased, the outside air density decreases, and the aneroid-spring arrangement expands. Through a system of levers and a chain, the small expansion is magnified and turned into a rotary motion of the pointers. Thus is altitude indicated.

For local work, some pilots prefer to set the altimeter to zero, no matter what the barometric pressure, for zero will be the level of the field and serves as a convenient reference.

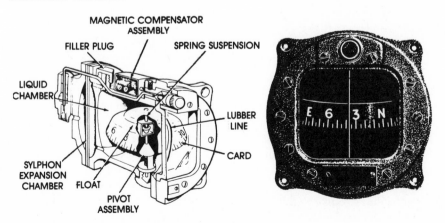

MAGNETIC COMPENSATOR
ASSEMBLY

FILLER PLUG

SPRING SUSPENSION

LIQUID
CHAMBER

LUBBER
LINE

CARD

SYLPHON
EXPANSION
CHAMBER   FLOAT

PIVOT
ASSEMBLY

Fig. 2-37. The inner workings of an aircraft compass. USAF.

The Compass

Unless you are planning to fly only around your local area, a compass is a wise investment. Besides, it is nice to have anyway, as it can be used to improve your flying skills.

An aircraft compass is very similar to a standard issue hand held type, with a few modifications. The main difference is that the numbers are on a pivoted card immersed in a damping fluid. A vertical line (lubber line) across the face of the compass, crosses the direction you are headed. The card points north at all times and the lubber line, along with the airplane, rotates around it. The "swing-of-the-card" may be confusing at first, but if you remember that the lubber line, along with your aircraft, rotates around it, the confusion should vanish.

Standard aircraft compasses have small compensating magnets to adjust the card to magnetic north under the influence of any iron and steel that may be on the airplane. Most ultralights, however, don't have this problem, since aluminum construction prevails. However, the engine is a large mass and it contains steel, which may affect the card.

There are two in-flight situations that affect the reading of a compass: northerly turning error and acceleration error.

Northerly turning error is the most pronounced. Due to the vertical component of the earth's magnetic field, when a turn is made to either side from north, the compass lags or even initially indicates a turn in the opposite direction. This is due to the north seeking end of the card dipping to the low side of the turn. Because of this, it is necessary to begin your roll-out about 10° before east or west or at 80° or 280°.

If you are heading south and turn east or west, the effect is reversed, i.e., compass leads the turn. In this case, start your roll-out only 5° ahead or at 95° and 265°.

Acceleration error is also caused by the vertical component of the earth's magnet field and the pendulum type mounting of the card — acceleration causes the card to tilt upward, deceleration causes it to tilt downward — both of which are most noticeable heading east or west. If you accelerate while on either heading, the compass card turns northward whereas if you decelerate, it'll turn southward.

What this all means is that the compass gives an honest magnetic reading only in straight and level flight. A word to the wise is sufficient.

When using a compass for navigational purposes you must be aware of the fact that the magnetic north pole does not coincide with the geographic north pole, and that the earth is not uniformly magnetized. Because of this, it is necessary to add or subtract several degrees from your compass indication, depending on your location. The proper amounts are shown on sectionals (charts used in navigation) as Isogonic lines, or lines of equal magnetic variation.

In central Pennsylvania, for instance, the Isogonic line reads "10° W", meaning the compass will actually be pointing 10° west of true north. To fly due east, you'd have to add the 10° to 90° and fly a magnetic heading of 100°!

There is one line called the Agonic line, for which true north and magnetic north coincide. It runs roughly from the Great Lakes down through just east of Florida. In this region, the compass will indicate true north.

On the western side of the Agonic line, it is necessary to subtract the Isogonic line variation values from what your compass reads, in order to determine your true heading.

Fig. 2-38. Various ultralight engine gages.

The Tachometer

Your engine speed is a primary piece of information, as your life as well as your engine's depends on it, and the tachometer is the instrument that measures it.

While experience can be used to gauge rpm, the tachometer is essential if you want to be accurate. As with the ASI, the tach will help determine your flight condition — whether you're cruising, climbing or gliding. It's senseless to fly at wide open throttle, as the engine will wear out all that much sooner. (Cruise speeds are typically quoted for power outputs of from 50% to 75 %, resulting in averages of 79% and 94% of top speed. The extra 25% of power for a 6% gain in speed is crazy!)

The tach is also quite useful for helping to determine the engine's state of tune. If you can't rev up to full rated static rpm, something is wrong — don't attempt flight. If you can't hold idle — don't attempt flight. Perhaps the plug is fouling or the needle valves are misadjusted. Maybe you have the wrong prop installed. If you have dual ignition, also short each circuit out when you run-up for takeoff, the rpm should drop for each short. RPM can tell you a lot about your engine — it can tell you not to fly!

A tachometer can be either mechanical or electrical in operation. A mechanical tach contains a governor mechanism which translates centrifugal force into a needle position via levers and gears. The more common electric tach operates from one per rev impulses from the engine which generates an alternating current from the magneto. The current flows to a millivoltmeter and is converted to DC and reads out as rpm.

Other Useful Instruments

Another useful instrument would be a cylinder head temperature gauge. The engine manufacturer has determined optimum operating temperatures which, if exceeded, could damage the engine. The CHT will tell you if you're near danger, especially in a prolonged climb or glide. A cool engine could quit easier than a warm one, and they cool down in a glide.

A bank indicator could also be useful as an aid in determining the coordination of a turn. It's simply a metal ball in a curved glass containing a damping fluid. The ball is centered in a coordinated turn. The indicator does not tell the amount of banking, but only if it's coordinated.

A fuel gauge is not needed if your tank is transparent and in view. If it is neither of these, you'll need some gauge to indicate your fuel level. It's embarassing at best, to run out of fuel and it can be hazardous to your life.

Density Altitude
and the Koch Chart

Density altitude is one subject that nobody evers seems to talk about during those great flying "bull" sessions — probably because many ultralighters simply don't know enough about it! Like most other aspects of flying, being ignorant of the facts can kill you. Knowing your density altitude and what it does to your ultralight's performanc is vitally important for every pilot to understand. Hot outside air temperatures, high field elevations, and even high humidity can change an otherwise normal takeoff or landing into an accident in no time.

The three factors that go into determining density altitude are:

Altitude — Air thins out with altitude.

Temperature — Air thins out with temperature.

Humidity — While humidity is not really considered important in its effect on aerodynamic performance, it does effect the power output of your engine. At high outside air temperatures, the atmosphere can hold a large amount of water vapor. For instance, at 96° F the air's water vapor content can be eight times as great as it is at 42° F! High humidty and high density altitudes don't necessarily go hand-in-hand, but if high humidity does exist, you'd be wise to add 10% to your computed takeoff distance and be prepared for a reduced rate of climb.

Your Owner's Manual as prepared by the ultralight manufacturer should provide you with flight performance figures under standard conditions, i.e., sea level at 59° F. But, these figures will change for consitions that are different than standard. If you don't allow for changes in density altitude, you could be in for some real surprises, or a disaster, during takeoff and climb.

The effects of density altitude are not exclusive to mountainous areas. Whenever the field elevation is above sea level and the temperature is above 59° F, density altitude increases. The main thing about the mountains is that the effects of density altitude are all the more pronounced. Takeoff distances, engine power, as well as climb rate are all adversely affected the true airspeed increases, while indicated values remain the same.

Whenever you are at density altitudes of 5000 feet or more, or at 75% throttle setting, it is imperative that your engine be leaned properly for maximum power — you need all you can get. A rich mixture setting would be detrimental to overall performance.

Keep in mind that density altitude is not to be used as a height reference, and it should not be confused with indicated altitude, pressure altitude or true altitude — it is used only in determining ultralight performance capabilities.

Whenever the outside air temperature rises above the standard value of 59° F, the density of the air decreases and the density altitude increases. This causes the engine's maximum power output to be reduced and affects the aircraft's aerodynamic performance. If the air temperature is above standard, no matter what the field elevation is, you should make it a habit of checking your aircraft performance figures and the Koch Chart.

The following chart shows "rule-of-thumb" effects of temperature of density altitude:

As far as the ultralight pilot is concerned then, increased density altitude

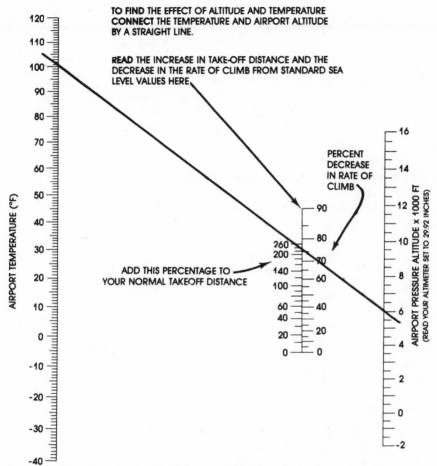

Fig. 2-39. The Koch Chart for altitude and temperature effects.

means:

1. Longer takeoff distances.

2. A rate of climb reduction.

3. The true airspeed will increase (indicated airspeed remains the same, however).

4. Landing roll increases.

STD TEMP	ELEV/TEMP	80° F	90° F	100° F	110° F
59° F	Sea Level	1,200'	1,900'	2,500'	3,200'
52° F	2,000'	3,800'	4,400'	5,000'	5,600'
45° F	4,000'	6,300'	6,900'	7,500'	8,100'
38° F	6,000'	8,600'	9,200'	9,800'	10,400'
31° F	8,000'	11,100'	11,700'	12,300'	12,800'

Often, at fields located at the higher elevation, like those in the Western United States, flight operations can be affected by density altitude to the extent that it's just about impossible to fly. What this means is that during midday, operations could become quite hazardous — you'd better plan on flying during the morning or early evening. Interestingly, these times of the day are also more suitable for ultralight operations from the standpoint of wind conditions — it's usually calm in the morning and early evening, while often blustery in the afternoon.

In order to avoid the problems and potential dangers associated with density altitude, you should refer to the performance data presented in your owner's manual as developed by the ultralight manufacturer. If this is not available, the Koch Chart, as presented in Fig. 2-39 may be used to determine how your ultralight's performance is affected in regards to takeoff distance and rate of climb.

Fly Only In Calm Or Light Wind Conditions. Avoid Gusty Conditions Like The Plague!

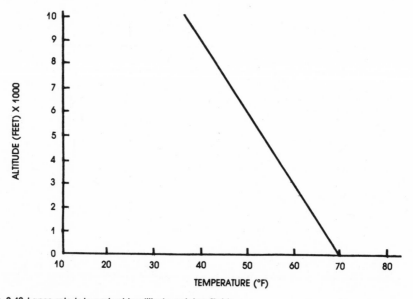

Fig. 2-40. Lapse rate is important in altitude gaining flights.

The Flying Speeds of an Ultralight

All aircraft have certain speeds at which they should be flown in order to realize maximum efficiency, economy, safety and performance. The following speeds could represent an "average" ultralight.

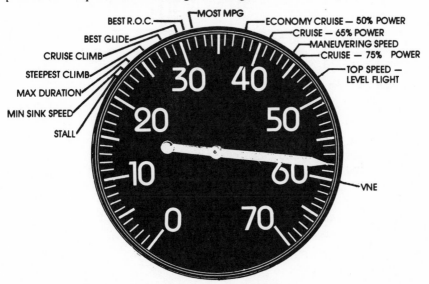

22 MPH – STALLED. Insufficient airspeed to fly. Control power lost.

23 MPH – MINIMUM SINK speed will allow an aircraft to remain airborne for a maximum period of time while gliding. It is useful for gaining altitude in soaring conditions.

24 MPH – MAXIMUM DURATION speed will enable the aircraft to remain under power for the longest period of time. It requires the minimum of the engine's power.

26 MPH – STEEPEST CLIMB speed is where the aircraft climbs at its greatest angle. It is good for climbing out of an obstructed field. Since it is so near the stall, caution should be exercized in its use. It's approximately 1.2 times stall speed.

28 MPH – CRUISE CLIMB speed occurs half way between best R.O.C. and best angle of climb, with the throttle at 75%. Provides better engine cooling and longer life. This is also the normal approach speed, which is typically 1.3 times stall speed.

30 MPH – BEST GLIDE speed is the best L/D speed providing the shallowest glide or maximum distance for a given altitude.

31 MPH – BEST RATE OF CLIMB (R.O.C.) speed will provide climb to altitude in the least amount of time. It's approximately 1.4 times stall speed.

32 MPH – MOST MILES PER GALLON (MPG) speed will provide maximum range.

38 MPH – ECONOMIC CRUISE speed provides modest fuel consumption with reasonable airspeed at 50% power.

41 MPH – CRUISE SPEED at 65% power.

44 MPH – MANEUVERING SPEED is typically set at twice the stall speed and is designed to protect against structural failure in rough air. Here, the aircraft could receive a maximum 4G load, where it will stall before loading the airframe further.

45 MPH – CRUISE SPEED at 75% power.

48 MPH – TOP SPEED for level flight at full throttle.

60 MPH – VNE (VELOCITY NEVER EXCEED) beyond which structural failure occurs.

Fig. 2-41. The "flying-speeds-of-an-ultralight".

AIRSPEED OR WIND IN MPH	OUTSIDE AIR TEMPERATURE (°F)											
	50	40	30	20	10	0	-10	-20-	-30	-40	-50	-60
	EQUIVALENT TEMPERATURE (°F)											
calm	50	40	30	20	10	0	-10	-20	-30	-40	-50	-60
5	48	37	27	16	6	-5	-15	-26	-36	-47	-57	-68
10	40	28	16	4	-9	-21	-33	-46	-58	-70	-83	-95
15	36	22	0	-5	-18	-36	-45	-56	-72	-85	-99	-112
20	32	18	4	-10	-25	-39	-53	-67	-82	-96	-110	-124
25	30	16	0	-15	-29	-44	-59	-74	-88	-104	-118	-133
30	28	13	-2	-18	-33	-48	-63	-79	-94	-109	-125	-140
35	27	11	-4	-20	-35	-49	-67	-82	-98	-113	-129	-145
40	26	10	-6	-21	-37	-53	-69	-85	-100	-116	-132	-148
(wind speeds greater than 40 mph have little additional effect)	LITTLE DANGER (for properly clothed person)			INCREASING DANGER			GREAT DANGER					
							Danger from freezing of exposed flesh.					

Fig. 2-42. Wind chill factor chart.

Considering the above speeds as a baseline, the following "rules of thumb" apply. If your airplane has a larger than average wingspan, it will be most efficient in slow flight, and all speeds will decrease. If it has a short span, it is inefficient in slow flight and all speeds should be on the higher side.

If you fly a "dirty" (i.e., cables, struts, floats, etc. in the airstream) ultralight, slower speeds are favored. On the other hand, a "clean" (i.e., streamlined) ultralight will favor slightly higher figures.

Higher wing loadings, (e.g., heavier pilots) will cause an upward shift of all speeds, and vice versa.

Basic Navigation for Ultralight Pilots

If you are not content with flying around within sight of your field and wish to go some distance away, you'll need to know the basics of aerial navigation. The two methods useful in an ultralight are pilotage and dead reckoning, which are explained below.

Charts

For the purposes of navigation, the continental U.S. is divided into 37 sections. The charts used are called Sectionals, which are drawn on a scale of 1/500,000, or about 8 miles to the inch. Each chart contains two sides, one for the northern half and one for the southern half of the section. Sectionals are designed mainly for private cross-country flying and are ideal for pilotage in an ultralight. They contain practically everything you need to know about what you're flying over. Obstructions such as TV towers, tanks and mountains are shown along with their elevations above sea level. Topographical information, like race tracks, mines and quarries, bridges and viaducts, power transmission lines (though not all), outdoor theatres, piers, cities and towns, dams and roads. Of course, complete information is also presented for all airports, private and commercial, paved and unpaved, controlled and non-controlled. Study and become thoroughly familiar with your Sectional before attempting any cross-country flight.

Pilotage

Pilotage is navigating by means of visual reference to landmarks with the help of a Sectional chart or road map. Landmarks or checkpoints could be a lake, mountain, race track, road intersection, dam or town, etc., and pilotage would involve flying from one to the other, until your flight was completed. You could also follow railroad tracks, roads, transmission lines, mountain ridges, or a river.

Plan Your Flight

Any good pilot is interested in accuracy and safety and the best way to maximize these two is by planning your flight before you get into the airplane. You can jump into an ultralight and fly around locally without too much thought, but going cross-country requires proper pre-flight planning. Below is presented a logical sequence of events in planning your pilotage flight.

Winds and Weather

Before any flight is attempted, wind and weather conditions must be known. Local radio and TV forecasts are faily accurate (75%) and should tell you what you need to know. Basically, what you want is fair weather, with calm to light winds. And remember, the higher you climb, the faster the wind speed, which also might have a different direction than the surface wind. If you need more detailed information, contact your local Flight Service Station (see your telephone book). Be aware that Flight Service gives wind speed in knots. Convert to mph by dividing knots by 1.15 (11.5 mph = 10 knots).

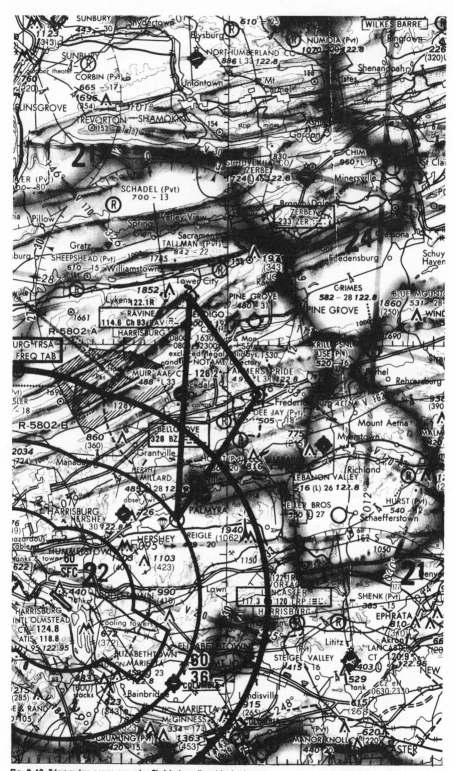

Fig. 2-43. Triangular cross-country flight described in text.

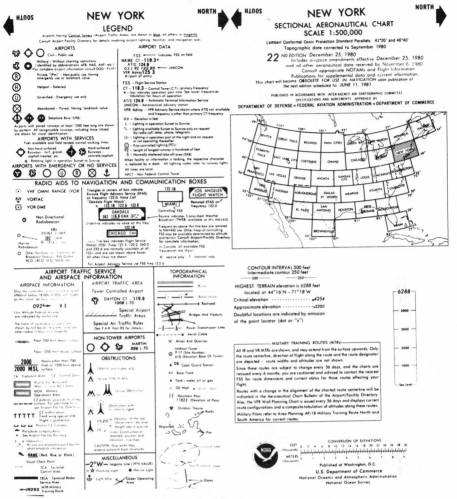

Fig. 2-44. Outer cover of Sectional Aeronautical Chart.

The Sectional Chart

If you don't already have one, you'll need the latest Sectional covering the area of your intended flight. While they were designed for easy reference at 5,000', they are still useful to ultralights.

Plot Your Course

First obtain a navigational plotter. Open the chart and spread it out on a table. Lay the plotter on the chart and draw a line from your origin to your destination. Next, mark off a small line every 5 or 10 miles. Look at the route and see if it passes over any hazardous terrain or restricted areas — such as military training areas — because their presence will necessitate another route. See if there are any landing fields along the way. Perhaps you know the area and it has plenty of farmland. Estimate your groundspeed — it'll be equal to the airspeed, only if it's calm. Now you can calculate the time enroute by dividing the air miles between departure and destination by your estimated groundspeed. Knowing your fuel capacity and engine fuel consumption at cruise throttle setting, you'll be able to

Fig. 2-45. Cross-country navigational plotter.

determine if you have enough fuel to make it non-stop. Always allow a half-hour reserve fuel.

Bracket Your Course

All this means is noting recognizable ground features that lie a couple of miles to either side of your course. Perhaps it parallels a railroad track, highway or river. These will serve as a crosscheck in keeping you on course. Note prominent features near your destination, in case you fly right over it without seeing it.

Determine True Course

Next, you will want to determine your true course. The Sectional is set up in latitude (horizontal) and longitude (vertical) lines. Lay your plotter parallel to your course and set the center of the protractor portion to intersect a longitudinal line (meridian). The degree line the meridian crosses is your true course.

Correct True Course for Magnetic Variation

Check your Sectional and you'll find the Isogonic lines as dashed lines with a degreed number followed by a W or an E. For the Sectional shown in this book, the magnetic variation is near the 10° W Isogonic line. What this means, is that we must add 10° to the true course we determined.

Correct for Compass Deviation

As explained earlier, a compass is affected by steel located in the aircraft. Since ultralights are mostly aluminum and have no radios, a compass probably reads magnetic direction like it ought to. Where general aviation aircraft have compass deviation cards, ultralights have none. An ultralight compass as installed could, however, be checked for error against a known accurate compass. Position the aircraft, with engine running and pilot in place, to magnetic north and note the aircraft's compass reading. Continue doing this for every thirty degrees and you'll generate your own compass deviation chart. These deviations would then have to be applied to the true course and magnetic variation to obtain your magnetic heading.

Compensate for Wind Drift

Unless you're flying in a calm, or with no crosswind, you'll have to crab to compensate for wind drift. In pilotage, you compensate for wind drift by noting your ground track as compared to your true course. If you're being blown to the left off your course, add some right crab. This will add degrees to your compass heading, so be aware of it. You should be able to determine your approximate drift between your first two checkpoints, and correct accordingly to get back on course and to stay there, noting the new compass heading.

For example, let's assume you have determined your true course to be 90° due east. In south central Pennsylvania, the magnetic course is 100°. Between your first two checkpoints, you estimate a 10° to the left drift angle. This means you'll have to crab right at 10°, so add 10° to your 100° magnetic course, and you'll arrive at your magnetic heading of 110°. Once back on course, from checkpoint two on, fly with the compass on 110°, and you should reach your destination.

In practice, it is customary to use the following abbreviations:

TC – true course
MC – magnetic course
WCA – wind correction angle
TH – true heading

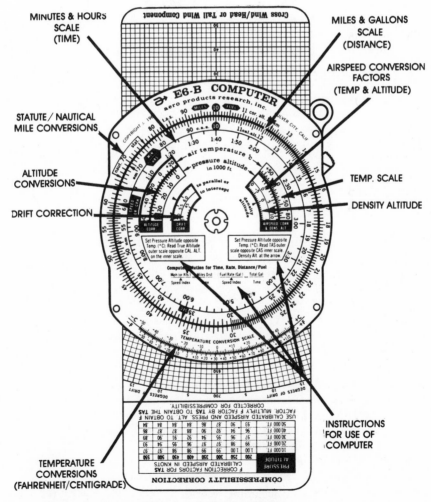

Fig. 2-46. The E6-B type "dead reckoning" navigational computer.

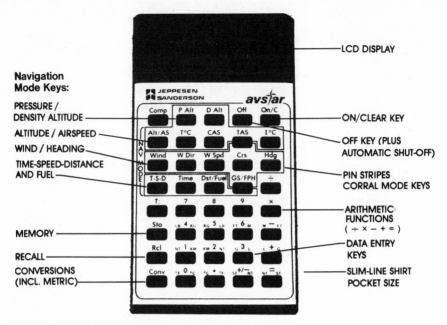

Navigation Mode Keys:

PRESSURE / DENSITY ALTITUDE

ALTITUDE / AIRSPEED

WIND / HEADING

TIME-SPEED-DISTANCE AND FUEL

MEMORY

RECALL

CONVERSIONS (INCL. METRIC)

LCD DISPLAY

ON/CLEAR KEY

OFF KEY (PLUS AUTOMATIC SHUT-OFF)

PIN STRIPES CORRAL MODE KEYS

ARITHMETIC FUNCTIONS (÷ × − + =)

DATA ENTRY KEYS

SLIM-LINE SHIRT POCKET SIZE

Fig. 2-47. The Avstar electronic navigation computer.

VAR – magnetic variation

MH – magnetic heading

DEV – compass deviation

We can summarize the above example as follows:

TC – 90°

VAR – 10° W

MC – 100°

WCA – 10° R

MH – 110°

As long as you are flying cross-country, you'll need to continually solve the above problem of determining course and heading. The standard method for converting true course to compass heading is as follows:

TC + WCA = TH

TH + VAR = MH

MH + DEV = CH

Always remember to add westerly variation and subtract easterly variation. An easy way to remember is by saying to yourself: "east is least and west is best"!

Groundspeed, Elapsed Time and Fuel Burned

Only by knowing the performance capabilities of your ultralight, can you determine these figures. Let's suppose you are flying the ultimate ultralight, with the following specifications and performance figures:

Cruise Speed – 38.5 mph indicated

Fuel Capacity – 5 gallons

Fuel Consumption – 2 gallons per hour

Endurance – 2½ hours, including reserve

Rate of Climb – 500 feet per minute

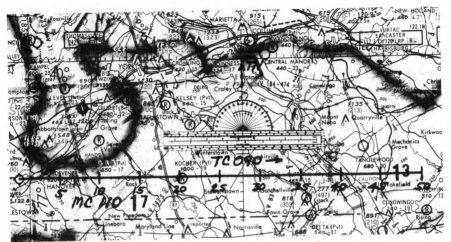

Fig. 2-48. True course plot of 50 mile cross-country flight described in text.

First of all, you must determine your true airspeed. Remember, the air gets thinner as you climb, making your ASI read low, dropping 2% for each 1,000 feet. Checking your course plot, you determine that a cruising altitude of 1,500 feet AGL (above ground level) will be safe. Since the ground is already 500 feet MSL (above mean sea level), your cruising altitude is 2,000 feet MSL. Therefore, you must add 4% to your indicated airspeed to arrive at your TAS. The answer is approximately 40 mph. That means each 5 mile checkpoint distance would take 7.5 minutes, while the entire flight would take about 75 minutes, in a calm.

But, you sleep-in, and by the time you get to the field, the wind is blowing at 10 mph, 45° from the right of your course, i.e., at 135°. It's going to require crabbing and will take a little longer. Taking off at 9 AM, you climb to 2,000 MSL (1,500 AGL). It takes 3 minutes to reach altitude, and a total of 10 minutes to reach your first checkpoint, 5 miles out. Your average groundspeed was only 30 mph because of the climbout and headwind component.

Looking at the Sectional and checkpoint two, you notice you are drifting to the left, and estimate it to be about 10°. You immediately start turning to right until you intersect your intended course, at which point you crab 10° right and maintain a magnetic heading of 110°. And, since your compass has no deviation, your compass heading is also now 110°.

By the time you get to checkpoint two, everything looks fine. You're on course, and it looks like you should pass over checkpoint three, judging by the landmarks in front of you, to either side of course. At this point, you also notice your elapsed time from checkpoint two to three took over nine minutes, and you figure your groundspeed to be 33 mph. That 10 mph wind, 45° to the right has given you a 7 mph headwind component.

Knowing your actual groundspeed, you can now calculate how long it'll take you to fly the rest of the way. Having gone by three checkpoints, that's 15 miles covered, leaving 35 miles to go. Dividing 35 miles by 33 mph tells you it'll take over an hour to finish the flight — 63.63 minutes, to be exact. The entire trip then, will take 91 minutes (10 min. climb to first checkpoint, and 81 minutes to fly from checkpont one to the destination), instead of the original 75 minutes. Since you carry 2½ hours of fuel, you'll have a reserve of 59 minutes.

If the wind conditions remain the same for the return trip, you'd have a tailwind component of 7 mph, making the total trip time approximately 65 minutes. You'll have to tank-up before returning.

Dead Reckoning

The term is derived from the phrase reckoning by deduction, and it's really an extension of pilotage. It use depends on the three primary flight instruments ASI, altimeter and compass, as well as on known wind conditions. It can be used to solve the three basic navigational problems of knowing your position, how to get to a new position, and when you'll reach that position.

Dead reckoning allows you to know what heading to fly before you takeoff. By using the principle of the wind triangle, any basic ultralight navigational problem can be solved.

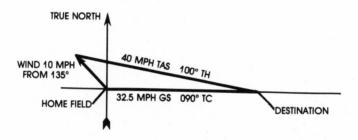

Fig. 2-49. Wind triangle for flight to a point 50 miles due east, as plotted on portion of sectional in Fig. 2-48.

Constructing a Wind Triangle

In order to get a clear understanding of what's involved here, let's use the same set of performance figures and flight conditions as we did in the pilotage example, with a few pertinent additions:

Cruise Speed – 38.5 mph (40 mph TAS)
Fuel Capacity – 5 gallons
Fuel Consumption – 2 gallons an hour
Endurance – 2½ hours
Rate of Climb — 500 feet per minute
Cruising Altitude – 2,000 MSL
Wind at 2,000 MSL – 10 mph. @ 135°
TC – 90°

Given the above information, we can find groundspeed, WCA, compass heading, time enroute, ETA and fuel required.

Starting with a clean sheet of paper, show true north and south by drawing a vertical line. Halfway down the line, put a point — that will be your departure field. Lay your plotter on the line with its straight edge at your point and draw a line to represent your TC of 90°. From the same departure point, draw another line from 135° to represent the wind direction.

Now, using the statute mile scale on the bottom of your plotter, measure up the wind line (vector) 10 mph and mark the point. Place your plotter's statute mile scale "0" at the end of the wind vector and swing it until the 40 (your TAS) intersects the TC line. Draw a line connecting the end of the wind vector with the

TC line. Measure the length of the line from your original origin to the TC-TAS intersection — that's your groundspeed and it reads 32.5 mph! You can also measure your TH as 100°, with the protractor part of your plotter.

Going back to our original data, we can determine our compass heading:

TC + WCA = TH = 100°

TH + VAR = MH – 100° + 10° W = 110°

MH + DEV = CH = 110° = 0 = 110°

CH = 110°

Since our groundspeed is 32.5 mph and our destination is 50 miles away, we can calculate our time enroute as 50 miles divided by 32.5 mph equals 1.54 hours, or 92 minutes. Having 2½ hours of fuel on board, we can safely fly the distance.

As a point of interest, go back to the pilotage example, and you'll see that our figures are in real close agreement. But, the point is, the dead reckoning approach is more accurate, gives you more assurance after you're in the air, and allows you to enjoy the flight more.

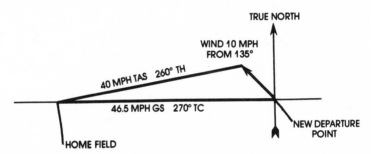

Fig. 2-50. Wind triangle for return flight as plotted on portion of Sectional in Fig. 2-48.

The Flight Back

To determine the particulars of your return flight, all you have to do is construct another wind triangle, as before. This time, your ground speed is up to 46.5 mph, since the crosswind now has a tailwind component. The compass heading is determined as follows:

TC + WCA = TH – 260°

TH + VAR = MH – 260° + 10° W = 270°

MH + DEV = CH = 270° + 0

CH = 270°

Navigating a Triangular Course — The Airspeed Circle

Navigation of a triangular course could be done by constructing three separate wind triangles, but there's an easier way — let's call it the airspeed circle method. For our example, we'll plot a course from Reigle to Farmer's Pride to Bendigo to Reigle, as shown on the portion of the Sectional in this book, Fig. 2-43.

First draw a true north-south line in the center of your paper and then a true east-west line thru the center of the first line. From that intersection, draw in your wind speed and direction (10 mph from 135°). Now, get a circle compass, and spread it to a distance equal to your TAS. Put the compass point on the end of the wind vector and draw the circle.

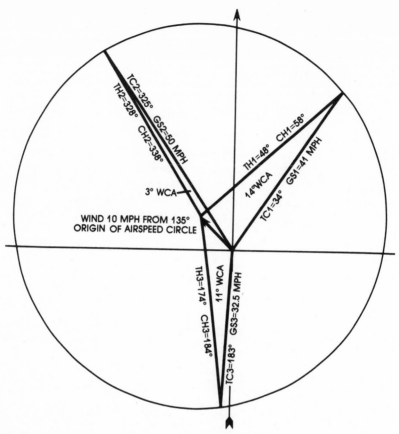

Fig. 2-51. Airspeed circle with wind triangles for three leg flight plotted on portion of Sectional in Fig. 2-43

Now, let's analyze each leg of the triangle.

Leg One, Reigle to Farmer's Pride, TC measures 34°. Draw in the 34° line from the intersection of your true N-S and true E-W lines until it hits the airspeed circle. The length of that TC line will be your groundspeed for Leg One, which equals 41 mph. Now draw a line from the point where TC 1 intersects the airspeed circle, back to the tip of the wind vector — that's your TH 1, and it measures 48°. That means your CH 1 would be 58°.

Now analyze Legs Two and Three the same way, and there you have it. A summary of the data from the airspeed circle is as follows:

Item	Leg One	Leg Two	Leg Three
Distance	12.5	10°	18.5
TC	34°	325°	183°
WCA	14°	3°	11°
TH	48°	328°	174°
CH	58°	338°	184°
GS	41 mph.	50 mph.	32.5 mph.
Time Enroute	19 min.	12 min.	34 min.

The total enroute time is 65 minutes, so there won't be any problem in making the flight non-stop.

As an aid to navigational computations, there are various flight computers available. The two basic kinds are the E6B sliderule type and the electronic type. They all come with complete instructions, and make navigation almost fun, if not easy.

CROSS-COUNTRY PLANNING AND LOG SHEET

FLIGHT _____ ALTITUDE _____ DISTANCE _____ DATE _____

FROM	TO	ALT	T	TAS	TC	WCA	TH	VAR	MH	DEV	CH	DIST.	GS	TIME	FUEL USED	ETA	ATA
											TOTALS						

NOTES: WEATHER, ETC.

Fig. 2-52. Cross-country planning and log sheet aids pre-flight planning and organizes flying.

Seaplane Operations

Float flying is a very exciting facet of ultralight aviation, opening up vast recreational areas to the pilot. This section will give you a good knowledge of the basics of operating off water. We'll begin by providing a description and illustration as an aid to recognizing the various parts of floats. These terms are used occasionally in the text and this way you can refer back to the illustration should you be in question about a certain item.

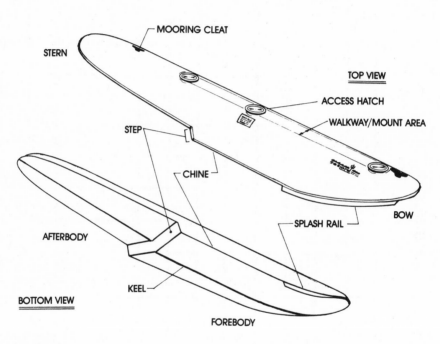

Fig. 2-53. Float terminology.

Float Terminology

Slow Taxiing — Moving through the water at a speed which does not allow the hull to plane on the surface of the water.

Step Taxiing — Moving through the water at a speed which causes the forebody to plane or ride on the surface of the water with minimum displacement.

Planning — When the float moves at a great enough speed to cause it to ride up on the surface of the water, with the afterbody completely clear.

Suction — The tendency of a float to "stick" to the water during takeoff, due to surface tension and other factors.

Preflight

A preflight check of the float system is as much a mandatory part of seaplane flying as is the preflight of the aircraft itself. Although seaplane ultralight flight is a safe and easy task, one unsafetied pin that becomes dislodged in flight could cause a float to drop out of position and wreak havoc upon landing. The preflight check is your own final assurance of a safe flight.

Check inside floats for possible water accumulation that might slosh to the back, affecting the aircraft CG.

Check that all *mounting bracket bolts* are snug.

Check all support strut *pins, bolts, nuts and safety clips* to assure they are properly secure.

Observe the movement of the floats with the waves when taxiing out for takeoff as a final check to assure their movement is not in excess of normal and that they secure and sound.

If you find a problem, correct it before flying. It's pretty hard to correct later when it begins to generate trouble in the air. Be safe.

Taxiing, Takeoff and Landing

Taxiing, Takeoff and Landing described in this section are assumed to be under normal conditions: Light wind, light chop to the water, no turbulence causing obstructions and direct into the wind site conditions. These are probably the best conditions for initial trial flights if you have no prior seaplane experience.

Get a feel for the handling of the aircraft on the water by doing slow taxiing, then step taxiing both upwind and downwind. Progress to short hop flights of about ten to twenty feet of altitude after becoming comfortable with the taxi exercises. When making actual flights, keep in mind the increased airspeeds you should use, the reduced climb rate and the steeper glide slope for approach to landing.

Taxiing: Slow taxiing is accomplished with power settings from idle on up to half or more. Since the hull of the float is displacing the water instead of planing on top, the drag of the floats (and therefore the power required to move them) is fairly high. A relatively large wake is also produced because of the displacement of the water.

Keeping the bow up by the use of back stick or aft weight shift improves the splash pattern and reduces the drag somewhat. Bow up also quickens the time and shortens the distance required to accelerate to planing speed by helping the floats to climb out of the water at a lower speed.

Slow taxi is best suited for precision maneuvering to and from the dock, and for positioning the aircraft for the initial takeoff run. The power required to propel the aircraft at the high end of the slow taxi speed range is actually greater than that needed to step taxi.

To step taxi, continue to add power while keeping the bow up. As the aircraft attains enough speed it will begin to ride much higher in the water than in previous slow taxi stages. The wake generated by the floats will also change in its pattern and become smaller. At this point some of the bow up pressure can be released and the attitude of the floats allowed to level out. Now the aircraft will actually accelerate several mph and will be planing across the surface of the water, not plowing through it.

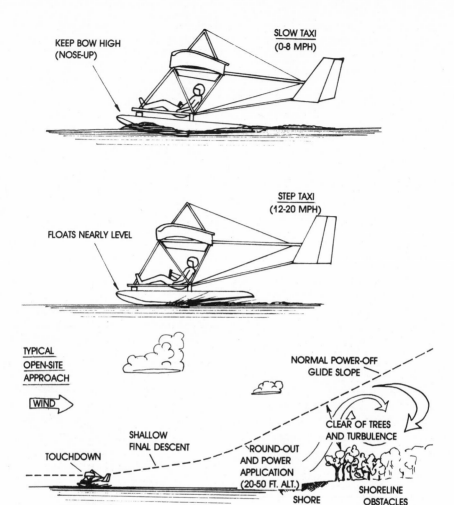

KEEP BOW HIGH
(NOSE-UP)

SLOW TAXI
(0-8 MPH)

FLOATS NEARLY LEVEL

STEP TAXI
(12-20 MPH)

TYPICAL
OPEN-SITE
APPROACH

WIND

NORMAL POWER-OFF
GLIDE SLOPE

CLEAR OF TREES
AND TURBULENCE

TOUCHDOWN

SHALLOW
FINAL DESCENT

ROUND-OUT
AND POWER
APPLICATION
(20-50 FT. ALT.)

SHORE

SHORELINE
OBSTACLES

LANDING AREA

Fig. 2-54. The basics of float operations.

Reduce power after the floats plane out since the reduction in drag from planing will be large enough to let the aircraft take off if this is not done.

Since airspeeds of ten to fifteen mph are common while step taxiing, the aircraft must be "flown" using all the aerodynamic controls. The speeds generate enough lift to make the ultralight very light on the water and therefore gusts can push it sideways or bank the wings fairly easily.

Turns can be accomplished while step taxiing by using rudder to steer while keeping the wings level. If your taxi speed is in the higher range (near takeoff speed) turns can be made more positive by using a slight amount of nose down to place the keels deeper in the water. The chines of the floats will not catch the water unless the bank angle during the turn exceeds 15°. That angle of bank will cause most ultralights to drag a tip in the water (dangerous) before the chine can catch.

Takeoff — For first flights, use a waterway that has about 1000 feet of "runway" and about 2000 feet before any tall (50 foot) obstacles. After becoming familiar with the takeoff and climb performance of your ultralight these figures may be adjusted. Normally, 400 feet or less will be required to reach liftoff and after traveling 2000 feet you may have 150 to 300 feet of altitude.

Taxi to the downwind end of the waterway and turn the aircraft into the wind. With power at idle the aircraft will want to weathervane directly into the wind, an excellent substitute for a windsock. Check to assure the takeoff area is clear of boaters, swimmers and fishermen.

Apply full power. The aircraft will plane out on the step and continue to accelerate until barely skipping across the wavetops. Use back stick or aft weight shift to rotate and lift the floats out of the water (this is done at the minimum takeoff speed to help reduce water drag at the earliest possible point). Let the aircraft accelerate to the best climb rate airspeed while flying level just above the water and then initiate a normal climbout.

Fly a standard pattern around your "field" one or more times to feel out the new handling of the aircraft. You will probably notice an increased pendulum stability. With enough altitude at hand, check out the feel at minimum control airspeed very carefully. Check the glide slope and attitude at various power settings and airspeeds.

Landing — Set up your standard approach and when turning onto final carry a little extra power to compensate for the greater sink rate with floats installed. As you near the surface of the water, level out but do not flair so as to lose airspeed. The trick is to touch down in a level attitude flying somewhat faster than you would if landing on the ground. This technique yields the smoothest landings. When you have leveled out and are at approximately a foot or two above the surface, smoothly reduce the power to idle and let the aircraft settle on the water.

After touchdown you can either carry enough power to step taxi back to the dock, or as the speed decreases and the floats begin to come down off the step you can smoothly apply full nose up which will drag the afterbody of the float causing drag in the water and rapid deceleration.

Careful experimentation with the flight techniques described can yield the best operational methods for your ultralight. Take care to approach each new trial with caution until it is proven out.

Special Flight Conditions

Special flight conditions concern realms of operation where performance or handling is affected and different piloting technique is required. Since the conditions covered in this section will occur from time to time in normal operation it is a safety oriented section and worth the time it takes to read and remember.

Since most waterways are not equipped for aircraft operations like an airport, it helps to learn a few techniques for deriving the needed information from mother nature. Wind direction can easily be determined by observing waterfowl to see which direction they are floating (they always float facing into the wind). Moored boats also weathervane into the wind. Wave direction and calm areas behind tree lines give you an indication of wind direction, too. Wind velocity is also apparent by observing the surface condition of the water — from calm to wind whipped white caps.

Crosswind technique is mostly aimed at ultralights with three axis controls, since ailerons are almost a necessity in maintaining wings level in the crosswind. If you will be doing crosswind takeoffs and/or landings it is important to be aware of turbulent air that may be blowing off a tree line, etc. upwind of your takeoff area. The rotor effect of the wind over these obstructions can severely limit your climb rate and control by blowing back down to the surface. This effect is especially apparent when flying off a river oriented in a crosswind fashion.

During the takeoff, the important thing is to cross control using the rudder to maintain a straight track across the water while using the roll control to keep the crosswind from lifting a wing. Once airborne flying the ultralight should be as usual. Landings should be made by crabbing (flying with wings level and nose pointed into the wind) to maintain a straight track over the landing area. During the level-off just above the water (1 - 2 feet of altitude), use the rudder to line the plane up with the "runway" and let it settle in immediately. Continue to steer with the rudder until slowed. This maneuver is used to prevent touchdown with the aircraft crabbing or drifting crosswind.

Takeoff from glassy-smooth water will require special techniques to be used to break loose the suction and lift off. This is because the lack of aeration under the floats increases the surface tension effects of the water. Without special takeoff techniques the takeoff run would consume long distances in order to generate enough lift to literally yank the floats from the water.

The first method is to taxi around in the water to make your own waves from the wake of the floats. Timing should be such that you ride over your own wake during the planing phase of takeoff, thereby introducing air under the floats at about the normal takeoff point.

The second method is to use your roll control (ailerons or spoilerons) to lift one float out of the water at a time. This way you are only breaking one-half of the total suction at a time making the liftoff much easier. Take care not to bank the aircraft too steeply — only a few degrees of bank are required to lift a float out.

The third method is to "horse" the aircraft fore and aft, using a pumping motion with the joystick or weight shift. When done with the correct timing, the floats will alternately sink in and spring out of the water until you reach a point when the airspeed and "spring out" will allow you to yank the aircraft out of the water. Once airborne, let the aircraft accelerate to climb speed and continue on in a normal manner.

Usually a combination of these smooth water methods will be used together. Landing on smooth water doesn't usually present a problem except for height judgement over the water.

When landing out in the open in large bodies of water or when it is nearly dark, altitude judgement becomes more difficult. In twilight conditions landing nearer to shore can provide you with an altitude reference. Out in open waters a slow letdown until contact is best since you probably have virtually unlimited space anyway.

Landing in open sea with large swells requires a different approach than the typical landing under inland conditions. Takeoffs during these conditions requires similar techniques. Runs should be made parallel to the waves in the trough between the waves to avoid premature liftoff. This will usually result in a crosswind takeoff or landing, so be cautioned to use the appropriate crosswind technique. If the swells are fairly close together it is essential that you should land parallel to them so that the bow of the float does not dangerously bury itself by piercing into the wave.

When landing in large swell conditions, pay particular attention to the wind direction — on shore or off shore. This is of concern especially in relation to the size of the body of water you're flying from (the Great Lakes or the Oceans) and your engine reliability.

Deadstick (power-out) landings should be executed with regard for the increased sink rate and steeper glide slope of the float equipped ultralight. Keep your approach altitude relatively high, using shallow dives to dissipate any excess. The airspeed for flair should be fast so a smooth, level attitude touchdown can be made as with power-on landings. Avoid making deadstick downwind landings if at all possible, especially in stronger winds.

If the need arises during overland flight to make an emergency ground landing the following technique will result in the safest landing with minimal or no damage to the floats. A normal approach is made and when making the final flair, airspeed is bled off with a nose-slightly-high attitude just above the ground. Do not slow the aircraft completely to stall speed as this results in the nose being too high. The aircraft will settle to the ground when airspeed finally decays and slide to a stop in about thirty feet. Land into the wind if possible to keep the ground speed at a minimum.

Seaplane Safety Considerations

Here's a compilation of things to know or watch for during seaplane operation.

Sea breezes on the Oceans or Great Lakes shores will change directions, from on-shore to off-shore, vice versa, or become completely calm. These changes occur near dawn or sunset, plus or minus a few hours. Watch for tell-tale signs of these shifts.

Watch carefully for *power lines* that are often strung across rivers and narrow lakes at low heights.

Watch for *boaters, skiers, fishermen and rubberneckers* that may dart into your takeoff or landing path without warning. Also watch for *swimmers* which are sometimes hard to see. In navigable waterways, *buoys* are another hazard to watch for when flying low or landing.

Submerged rocks, stumps, etc. just below the surface present a hazard and should be checked for when still in the air in the landing pattern.

Check *local ordinances* before flying the first time from resort lakes or lakes within a city limit. Sometimes they may have an ordinance against seaplane operations, and it is best to find this out without receiving a citation.

It is common sense to *carry tiedown line and tools* in the floats to provide mooring and repair capability if you should become *stranded* out in the water or on a river while flying. Carrying some money for food or phone might not be a bad idea either.

Be safe and let someone else know where you'll be flying, especially on longer trips, just in case you have trouble. A *prearranged check-in* time is a good, safe practice.

Use caution when flying in areas with large flocks of *waterfowl*. A bird strike in the prop could be dangerous if the engine is not shut down immediately to stop the vibration.

When operating in *beach areas,* watch for *other aircraft traffic* flying parallel to the beach possibly in both directions.

Always wear a *floatation jacket* or some type of life preserver, and wear *protective headgear.*

Note: When operating from a river, it is often advantageous to take off with the current, even if it's with the wind.

For further information on float flying contact Composite Industries, Flight Systems Division as listed in the Appendix.

Section Three — Ultralight Propulsion

The Ultralight Engine

Without an engine, an ultralight is just a glider, and it can certainly be flown that way. Under most circumstances, though, that mechanical wonder will be kept running. Since most ultralight flying is impossible without the engine, it is well to understand how power is produced and converted into thrust.

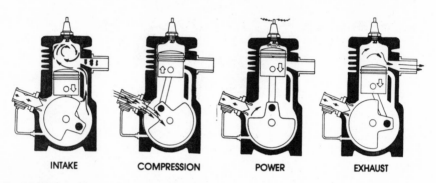

| INTAKE | COMPRESSION | POWER | EXHAUST |

Fig. 3-1. The four stages of two-cycle engine operation.

Engine Basics

The ultralight engine converts thermal energy into mechanical work by burning a mixture of fuel and air. The work is performed by turning a propeller against the air, either directly from the shaft or by a reduction drive. Today, the only type engine used in ultralights is the internal combustion reciprocating two-stroke with carburetor and spark ignition.

The fuel is gasoline, which weighs about six pounds per gallon, and it is mixed with lubricating oil in various ratios, depending on the manufacturer's specifications. Each gallon of gasoline burned in the engine uses the oxygen from 9,000 cubic feet of air to support combustion.

The heat energy content of gasoline is measured in British Thermal Units (BTU), the heat energy needed to raise the temperature of one pound of water 1° F. One BTU is equal to 778 ft-lb of mechanical energy. Complete combustion of one pound of gasoline releases approximately 19,300 BTU's, or 15,000,000 ft-lb of mechanical energy. A typical engine requires an 18 to 1 mixture, by weight, of air to gasoline to completely burn. Unfortunately, only about 25% to 33% of the heat energy contained in the gasoline is converted to mechanical energy at the engine shaft.

Horsepower and Torque

In terms of performance, these are the main ingredients, interrelated and yet distinct. One horsepower is defined as the power to lift 550 pounds one foot in one second. It is a force exerted through a distance over a period of time — a measure of the rate at which work is done. In terms of ultralight flying, work is defined as moving the weight of the aircraft and pilot through the air. The work rate is related to speed and rate of climb. All things being equal, a 30 hp ultralight

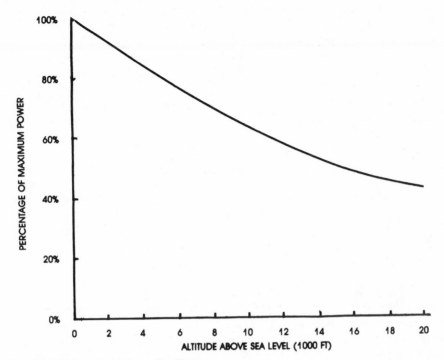

Fig. 3-2. Engine power decreases with altitude.

will be faster and climb faster than if it had a 15 hp. engine. The speed will not double, however, because of increases in drag — it will go up approximately only 25%. The rate of climb on the other hand, can be boosted significantly.

Looking closer at the generation of horsepower, we find it is related to torque. Normally expressed in foot-pounds, it is defined as a rotational force acting over a distance. One foot-lb of torque is generated when one pound is exerted against a one foot lever. For engines, torque is the twisting force on the crankshaft at a given moment in time.

Horsepower and torque can be related by assuming using our one foot lever. The distance the force would act over would be 6.28 feet — the circumference of a one foot lever — with each revolution. The foot-pounds of work per second — the horsepower — can then be calculated by multiplying rpm. times the torque and dividing by a constant, 5252.

Horsepower is the rate at which work is done, while torque is the capacity to do that work. For ultralights, torque translates into rate of climb, and the ability to turn a large propeller.

The horsepower and torque curves shown for the McCulloch engine are relatively flat with an open exhaust, but get "peakier" when the exhaust is turned. The open exhaust curves show greater values in the lower rpm. ranges as well, an indication of greater "tractability" over a wider speed range. The higher the state of tune, the more "one-speeded" an engine becomes. Pure racing engines are most efficient at only one speed, the horsepower and torque dropping off rapidly from that speed.

The Mc101A, open exhausted, produces 12½ hp at 9,000 rpm, and 9 ft-lbs of torque at 5,300 rpm. You might well question the apparent discrepency between maximum torque and peak horsepower — horsepower being a function of torque times rpm. But, torque does not increase with speed ad infinitum because of friction and reciprocating mass losses.

As a rule of thumb, torque is greatest in the mid-range speeds. Here the engine has time to "breathe" a good charge of gasoline and air and the friction and reciprocating losses are low. Both friction (from pistons, rings and bearings) and reciprocating (piston, rod and crank throw) losses increase as the square of rpm. — doubling the rpm.quadruples these loads. Other losses also occur due to the increased gas velocity flow through the intake and exhaust systems. All these items rob the engine of its torque producing capacity.

One might argue that perhaps by going to smaller pistons in larger numbers we could improve engine performance. After all, model airplane engines can put out up to 4 hp.per cubic inch! But, the problem is, they just don't produce that much torque. When we are concerned with mid-range performance and reliability, there is no substitute for displacement, primarily because more combustion occurs per revolution.

Bore and Stroke

Bore and stroke are the most basic dimensions of a piston engine. Bore is the diameter of the cylinder, and the stroke is the distance the piston moves in the cylinder from top dead center (TDC) to bottom dead center (BDC). United States practice measures bore and stroke in inches, while Europeans prefer millimeters.

All ultralight engines are said to be oversquare, i.e., their bore is greater than their stroke. The long stroke undersquare engines of the past have gone the way of the carrier pigeon because of high piston speeds and the high friction and reciprocating losses they produce. Piston speeds over 2,500 feet/min are avoided

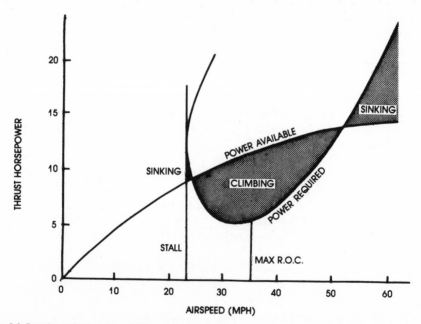

Fig. 3-3. Power required and available varies with airspeed.

by engineers, as a rule.

The displacement of an engine is found by multiplying the bore squared by the stroke by a factor of .7854 times the number of cylinders. Displacement is a measure of the swept volume. Generally speaking, the larger the displacement, the greater the horsepower.

Compression Ratio

Compression ratio is defined as the ratio of the total volume in a cylinder at BDC to the clearance volume, i.e., the small volume when the piston is at TDC. The higher the compression ratio, the more the fuel/air mixture is squeezed, and the greater the energy released. Compression ratios can go as high as 12-to-1, but problems develop.

One problem is preignition — the gasses ignite from hot spots in the cylinder — before the spark jumps. Preignition thus tends to push the piston backwards, opposite to the direction of rotation, while generating more and more heat and causing the engine to either seize or otherwise destroy itself. This backward force is hard on bearings and can break connecting rods.

Detonation is another problem of high compression ratios. It normally occurs under heavy loads at low engine speeds and is characterized by a "ping". A car climbing a hill at low rpm.in fourth gear will make its engine ping. Detonation (spark knock) is actually an abnormal combustion, which also occurs before the spark and tends to drive the piston in reverse. Unlike normal combustion, which is a rapid burning of the fuel/air mixture, detonation is more like a violent explosion. It can blow cylinder heads and break pistons. Detonation can be eliminated by using higher octane fuel, retarding the timing or decreasing the compression ratio.

Number of Cylinders

While the majority of ultralight engines are single cylinders, there are some twins and even a three cylinder in use. The main thing about a single is that it's inexpensive to make, simple mechanically, and easy to repair and maintain. Singles also exhibit good torque because they have more piston area for a given displacement, for the combustion force to act on.

The main disadvantage of the single cylinder engine is that it has no fail-safe mode. If a plug fouls a single stops, whereas on a twin, the engine will continue running even if at a reduced power level. Increased complexity buys greater reliability. Another advantage of a twin is that it's smoother in operation. There are twice as many power pulses per revolution and besides, the reciprocating mass of one cylinder can be used to balance that of the other. A twin can also dissipate more heat by virtue of the fact that it has more piston side area for a given displacement, than a single.

Arrangement of Cylinders

Multi-cylinder ultralight engines can be classified by the arrangement of the cylinders. Horizontally opposed twins have their cylinders arranged 180 degrees apart. They are compact and offer excellent cooling and good balance for smooth operation. The Skylark is a good example.

In-line twins are also seeing a wide acceptance in ultralight usage. They are easy to manufacture and adapt well to mounting on an airframe. Care must be

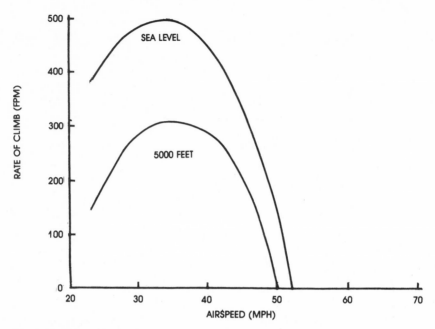

Fig. 3-4. Rate of climb decreases with altitude.

taken to cool the rear cylinder, so use of an internal fan is recommended. The Cuyuna 430-D is an in-line twin.

The radial is yet another type of multi-cylinder ultralight engine. The workhorse of military and commercial aircraft ever since the 20's until the advent of the turbojet, their use in ultralights is small. Nevertheless, they are quite

Fig. 3-5. The Mirage prototype had two Yamahas gauged into an inverted "V" to drive a single prop.

Fig. 3-6. Two Chryslers ganged in-line was an early attempt at more power and reliability.

interesting and suitable for ultralight use. An odd number of cylinders extends radially from the centerline, arranged evenly in the same circular plane. All pistons are connected to a master connecting rod and single throw 360° crankshaft, reducing the number of parts and weight.

The radial engine has the highest power-to-weight ratio of all the cylinder arrangements, and offers smooth, low vibration running. Care must be taken that it receives a good supply of cooling airflow. The Konig is the only radial on the market.

Ganging of Engines

An alternative to multi-cylinder engines is to gang a couple of singles together with an appropriate drive system. By means of belts, clutches and gears, it is feasible to put two singles together in either an in-line, opposed, or "V" configuration. The advantages are more power and increased reliability. But the disadvantages are increased mechanical complexity and weight for a given displacement.

Cooling

As mentioned previously, a typical gasoline engine converts only 1/4 to 1/3 of the fuel's thermal energy into mechanical energy. The rest is given off as heat. It transfers from the pistons to the cylinder walls and fins, and out the exhaust pipe. Combustion occurs at around 4,000° F, the exhaust gasses exceed 1,000° F, and the piston crown can also reach 1,000°. The engine would literally melt, if this intense heat were not removed.

Most ultralight engines are air cooled, transferring their heat directly to the atmosphere. Fins on the head, barrel and crankcase take the heat from the engine walls and liberate it by convection and radiation. Convection occurs when air moves over the fins and carries the heat away, and accounts for most of the cooling. Forward motion is most responsible for convection cooling. When airspeeds are low, for instance during a climbout, cooling becomes critically important. Many engines employ self-contained fans for this reason. And, even though they absorb horsepower, it's better to operate at reduced power reliably, than to overheat the engine and have it fail.

Radiational cooling, on the other hand, occurs when there is no air motion, but it accounts for only about 10% of the total cooling load. This does improve during cold weather and can be aided further still by painting the cylinder   flat black.

Lubrication

Oil mixed with the fuel lubricates two-cycle engines. The oil to fuel ratio varies from engine to engine, but some can run as lean as 1 part of oil for every 100 parts of gasoline, at full throttle. During idle, two-cycles don't need as much oil, giving it a chance to accumulate and foul the plug. This is another good reason to "clear" the engine during the approach, or during any extended idle or near idle operation, by advancing the throttle momentarily.

Oil has four main functions: minimizing friction, sealing, removing heat and neutralizing the byproducts of combustion.

Friction is minimized because oil forms a thin film between rubbing parts — the parts actually don't touch each other. As long as the film is there, even though only a few thousands of an inch thick, wear and heat build up will be prevented. Interestingly, most engine wear occurs during cold starting. When an engine is not in use, the oil has a chance to drain from the parts, leaving them dry for the first few revolutions. Priming the engine and slowly turning it over by hand might be a good habit to get into, before firing it up.

The seal function is also important, especially in starting a worn engine. The

Fig. 3-7. The ParaPlane features contra-rotating props, each with its own engine.

thin oil film will help the engine hold its compression. Oil is also important as a heat transfer medium from the moving to the stationary parts of an engine.

Lastly, oil has to withstand and neutralize the byproducts of combustion. The combustion of one gallon of gasoline will generate about one gallon of water, a small amount of unburned gasoline, and traces of hydrobromic, hydrocloric, and various sulfur and nitrogen-based acids. Also, small amounts of resins, varnishes, lead salts and soots will be released. Most of this goes out the exhaust, but some can leak by the rings and into the crankcase. Sludge can cause sticking and the acids can eat away at the cylinder wall. The unburned gasoline can breakdown the oil, leading to increased wear and the water byproduct can cause rusting.

As for the type of oil to use, consult the manufacturer's brochure for detailed information. Only oils specially formulated for two-cycles should be used.

Fuel

Gasoline is a petroleum distillate consisting primarily of hydrogen and carbon atoms with certain chemicals added to retard varnish formation, increase octane rating and enhance cold starts. Until more than 50 years ago compression ratios were limited to about 4 to 1. At that time, it was discovered that small amounts of tetraethyl lead could be added and allow higher compression ratios — as high as 12 to 1. With recent concern over the environment, however, maximum compression ratios are now down to around 9 to 1, thanks to no-lead fuel.

Most ultralight engines operate very well on regular automotive fuel and there's no reason to go to premium, as long as there's no knock. Use of premium won't do anything at all for performance or economy either. An engine's compression ratio (and therefore it's octain requirement) could possibly increase with age, due to carbon build up on the piston from too much low rpm.running. But this should not be the case with an ultralight as they get a good work-out during takeoff and climb and keep themselves relatively clean.

It is recommended that fuels with so-called carburetor cleaners not be used in two-cycles, as they tend to clean the oil from other engine parts as well, depriving them of needed lubrication.

Ultralight Engine Operation

Ultralight engines can be divided into two primary categories, reed valve and piston proted, based on the way in which fuel and air enters the crankcase.

Reed Valve Engines

A reed valve engine is easily recognized by the carburetor being mounted below the cylinder on the crankcase. The reeds are flat pieces of spring steel located at the base of the carburetor, flush with the crankcase wall. When the piston moves up in the cylinder it creates a partial vacuum, pulling the reeds open allowing fuel and air to enter the crankcase. The fuel and air trapped above the piston one revolution before is simultaneously compressed and then ignited just before TDC. After passing TDC the expanding gasses push the piston down, producing power. Near the bottom of the power stroke, the piston slides by the exhaust port, and the spent gases leave the combustion chamber. On the way down, the bottom of the piston pressurizes the fuel/air mixture (as the reed valve closes) previously drawn in the crankcase, forcing it through the transfer port and into the combustion chamber — then the process repeats itself.

The nice thing about a reed valve is that it keeps the fuel/air mixture in the crankcase and allows the engine to take in as much mixture as it can at all speeds. It is often claimed that reed valves can increase torque, because of this feature — they don't spit back fuel through the carburetor. The McColloch and Chrysler are two examples of reed valved engines.

Piston Ported Engines

A piston ported engine operates just like a reed valve engine, except for the fact that the fuel/air inlet is opened and closed by the piston skirt. Most ultralight and modified snowmobile engines are piston ported, and can be recognized as such, by the carburetor being located on the cylinder barrel. The only disadvantage they seem to have over the reed valve is that the fuel can spit back out of the carburetor at low speeds, altering the mixture and covering the engine with oil and gasoline. But under normal operation, this dosen't appear to be a problem.

Effects of Altitude

The higher you climb, the less dense the air becomes, and the lower the air mass drawn into the crankcase with each revolution. This not only enrichens the mixture, it also causes the power output to decrease. For example, at 15,000 feet, the maximum power available is 80% of the sea level value, and only 65% at 10,000 feet.

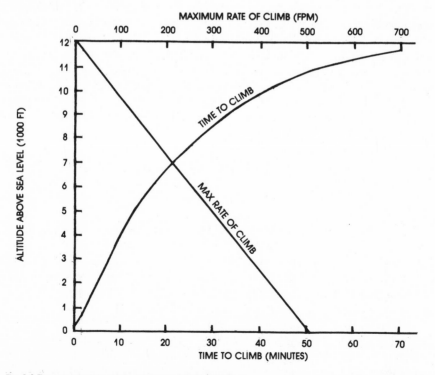

Fig. 3-8.Time required to climb and max R.O.C. vs altitude.

This reduction in power with altitude also means that the maximum rate of climb also decreases with altitude until, at some point, it is zero. This is the so-called absolute ceiling, and it is doubtful if an ultralight could exceed 15,000 feet. The point where the rate of climb is 100 fpm. is called the service ceiling.

Power Available for Flight

In order to increase airspeed and rate of climb, more power must be put into the air. The power available from the engine is roughly directly proportional to the rpm. up to near maximum power, where it rounds out, peaks then drops. Unfortunately, when we bolt a prop on to the shaft, the situation changes. Due to various considerations of prop efficiency versus forward and rotational speeds, the thrust-power available grows roughly only as the square root of two as airspeed is increased. Doubling the airspeed requires roughly five times as much power.

Rate of climb is determined by the excess power available at a given airspeed, over what it takes to fly forward at that speed. The greatest excess power available is at the best rate of climb speed.

Trouble-Shooting an Ultralight Engine

Engine Will Not Start

1) No fuel in tank or shut-off valve closed: Put fuel in tank and/or open valve.

2) Spark plug not firing: Remove plug, attach lead wire and ground plug against cylinder. Crank engine to determine if there is sufficient spark to jump plug gap. If there is no spark or spark is weak, remove flywheel and check following items: breaker points, coil, condenser, wiring, connections, hi-tension lean wire and lead wire spark plug connector.

3) Fuel not being delivered to combustion chamber: Check carbureator hi-speed and idle adjustments. Both needles should be approximately 1 to 1⅛ turns open. Remove spark plug and inspect. If plug is dry, pour a small amount of fuel into cylinder through spark plug hole, exhaust ports or carburetor. Replace plug and crank engine. If engine fires or starts but will not continue to run, check for the following: clogged fuel line, faulty fuel pump, sticking inlet needle, or dirty carburetor.

4) Engine flooded. Too much fuel in combustion chamber: Close hi-speed needle. Remove and dry excess fuel from spark plug. Install spark plug and crank until engine starts, then open hi-speed needle ¾ - 1 turn. Readjust after warm-up.

Engine Hard To Start

1) Water or dirt in fuel, stale fuel mixture, or too much oil in fuel: Drain fuel tank and carburetor. Fill with fresh fuel mixture. Be sure to strain through fine screen.

2) Weak ignition spark: Refer to "engine will not start".

3) Engine over or under choked: Refer to "engine will not start", parts 3 and 4.

4) Carburetor out of adjustment: Refer to "carburetor adjustment" section of manufacturer's instructions.

5) Gasket or seal leaks: Inspect gaskets and seals closely once engine is running.

6) Open or broken reed: Characteristic of open or broken reed: Engine will "spit back" through carburetor while idling or starting. Remove reed plate and inspect. Refer to manufacturer's instructions.

7) Spark plug fouled: Remove and inspect. Clean if required.

Engine Starts But Will Not Continue Running

1) Insufficient fuel supply: Fill tank.

2) Fuel line clogged: Disconnect fuel line from carburetor to see if fuel flows freely.

3) Carburetor out of adjustment: Refer to "carburetor adjustment" section of manufacturer's instructions.

4) Vent screw on filler cap closed: Open it.

5) Faulty fuel pump or dirty carburetor: Remove fuel pump and carburetor from engine, disassemble and inspect.

6) Air leak in fuel system: Inspect fuel system for leaks.

7) Defective or fouled spark plug: Remove and inspect, clean or replace.

Engine Misses

1) Dirt in fuel system: Clean fuel system.

2) Carburetor out of adjustment: Refer to manufacturer's instructions.

3) Spark plug fouled or defective: Remove and inspect, clean or replace.

4) Faulty magneto: Remove flywheel and inspect breaker points, all wires and connections. Test coil and condenser. Check hi-tension lead wire for leaks.

Engine Lacks Power

1) Air cleaner clogged: CLean with solvent.

2) Carburetor not adjusted properly: Refer to manufacturer's instructions.

3) Incorrect spark plug: Replace with correct plug.

4) Incorrect ignition timing: Refer to manufacturer's specs.

5) Worn or stuck piston rings or leaky head gasket: Test compression with gauge. If compression is low, replace rings or head gasket.

6) Scored piston or cylinder wall: Check compression. Disassemble engine and inspect piston, rings and cylinder wall.

Engine Overheats

1) Engine overloaded: Allow engine to cool. Reduce load.

2) Carburetor adjustment too lean: Enrichen.

3) Insufficient oil in fuel: Add for proper ratio.

4) Incorrect spark plug: Replace.

5) Ignition timing over-advanced: Refer to manufacturer's specs.

6) Scored piston or cylinder wall: Disassemble engine and inspect.

Engine Noisy or Knocking

1) Loose flywheel: Torque to specs given in manufacturer's instructions.

2) Worn bearings: Disassemble engine and inspect bearings.

3) Broken or loose parts inside engine: Disassemble and inspect.

4) Ignition timing over-advanced: Retard.

Engine Stalls Under Load

1) Carburetor adjustment too lean: Enrichen.

2) Fuel line restricted or tank vent closed: Clean line and open vent.

3) Faulty fuel pump: Remove pump, disassemble and inspect diaphragm and valves.

4) Engine overloaded: Reduce load.

Poor Acceleration

1) Carburetor out of adjustment: Refer to manufacturer's instructions.

2) Air cleaner clogged: Clean with solvent.

3) Chipped or broken reeds: Remove reed plate and inspect.

4) Ignition timing over-advanced: Retard to specs.

5) Leaking gaskets: Inspect engine closely while running.

6) Exhaust restriction: Inspect exhaust system.

7) Poor compression: Disassemble engine and inspect piston, rings, cylinder wall and head gasket.

Poor High Speed Performance

1) Carburetor out of adjustments: Refer to manufacturer's specs.

2) Low compression: Check for broken or worn rings, scored piston or cylinder wall or leaky head gasket.

3) Pre-ignition: Allow engine to heat-up thoroughly, turn ignition switch to "off" position. If engine continues to run, check for the following: dirty or incorrect spark plug, excessive carbon or foreign matter in combustion chamber, carburetor adjustment too lean, excessive back pressure from muffler, ignition timing over-advanced.

The Ultralight Propeller

The propeller's job is to transfer a maximum of the engine's shaft horsepower into the air. Depending on the task to be performed, there's a best propeller for every combination of engine and aircraft. One design will give maximum level speed. A slightly different design, with a greater diameter and less pitch, will result in maximum climb. The best propeller for all around use will fall somewhere in between these two extremes and it's referred to as a service prop.

The efficiency with which a propeller will perform under various operating conditions depends primarily on the accuracy of the performance figures (speed, hp. and rpm.) of the engine and airplane. If these figures are incorrect, the propeller will fall short of the desired performance.

A propeller is basically a wing that rotates and goes forward at the same time. A good one will convert shaft horsepower into thrust horsepower with an efficiency of 80%. Each blade has a leading and trailing edge, and airfoil sections of varying thickness greatest near the hub, gradually thinning and flattening as you go up to the tip. The airfoil sections are rounded on top and basically flat bottomed.

The reasoning behind the arrangement is simple. All blade airfoil sections (elements) face the same forward speed but have circumferential speeds directly proportional to their radius. The centerline has no circumferential speed, while the tip element is moving the fastest. The twist is established by the engineer in order to properly distribute the thrust loads across the face of the prop.

Pitch

For the sake of discussion, the blade element at the ¾ radius location is used to

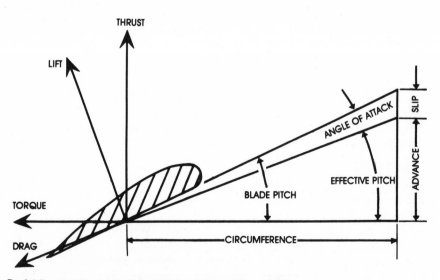

Fig. 3-9. Forces acting on a blade element and a definition of pitch.

308

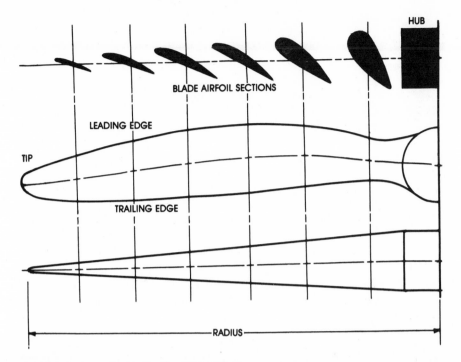

Fig. 3-10. Typical propeller blade with various sections.

describe the motion of a prop. This is where we determine the pitch, which is basically the distance the propeller moves forward with each revolution.

Pitch can be described in three ways — aerodynamic, geometric and effective. Aerodynamic pitch, also called zero-thrust pitch, is the distance the propeller has

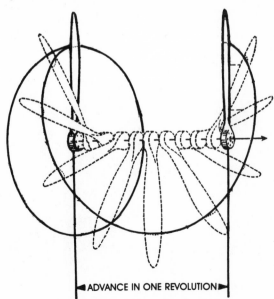

Fig. 3-11. A propeller advances its effective pitch with each revolution.

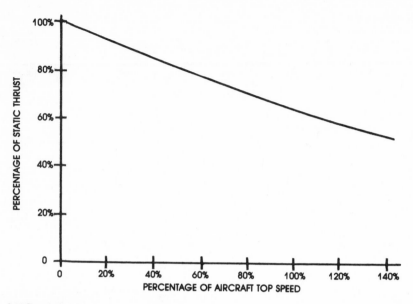

Fig. 3-12. Thrust diminishes with forward speed.

to move forward for no thrust to be developed. It would occur in a dive where the prop "unloads". Geometric pitch is the distance the ¾ radius blade element would move the prop forward if the air were a solid — this is the pitch number stamped on the prop. The effective pitch is the distance the prop actually moves forward with each revolution. "Slip" is the difference between geometric and effective pitch, and is some small percentage of the geometric pitch.

Fig. 3-13. The Lazair prototype used two chainsaw engines with direct drive.

Fig. 3-14. The prototype Hummingbird used two chainsaw engines with reduction drive.

Fig. 3-15. Kolb Flyer prototype originally mounted two Chryslers with reduction drives. Now uses Two Solos in direct drive.

Efficiency

To operate at peak efficiency, a propeller, like a wing, must generate lift at its maximum L/D ratio angle of attack. Each blade element must have a relative wind where it develops the most lift for the least drag. A typical service propeller is a compromise, designed to function over a broad range and is most efficient in cruise, since that's where most flying is done.

Under static conditions when the prop is stationary, the angle of attack of each blade element is too high, especially near the hub. Yet, thrust is greatest under static conditions. When an ultralight flies faster than what the prop was designed for, the angle of attack of each blade element is lessened and the prop's overall efficiency drops.

Fig. 3-16. Experimental single-bladed prop features automatic variable pitch and potential improved efficiency.

Section Four -
Appendicies And Lists

Appendix A — FARs for Ultralight Pilots

What You Should Know About The FARs first appeared as a series in **Glider Rider** *written by Phil McKinsey, Ultralight Chairman for the EAA Sun-N-Fun Fly-in.*

The ultralight or powered hang glider movement is enjoying an acceptance by the general public that is unparalleled in the field of aircraft manufacturing. The soaring prices of aircraft ownership have forced many a pilot to spend his weekend earthbound, longingly watching some lucky airman pass overhead. Aircraft flight instruction and rental rates have increased to the point that flying for fun is an unbearable burden for most working people. And aviation fuel cost is well ahead of auto fuel, with no end in sight. It's no wonder that this "grass-roots" ultralight movement has so captured the imagination of the flying and non-flying public.

The potentially endless flow of unregulated pilots and aircraft has presented a real headache for the people responsible for the safety of all flying machines, the Federal Aviation Administration (FAA). Not knowing quite what to do with these powered hang gliders, they wisely considered them in the same class as the foot launched unpowered hang gliders. Basically, this meant no license required for the pilot and no registration required for the aircraft owner.

This "hands off" policy was a very good move, considering the already overworked personnel and overtaxed facilities of the FAA district offices. Unfortunately for those of us who already love the sport and countless converts to come, the "winds of fortune" are beginning to shift.

Public pressure is being applied at all levels of government. The most often heard complaint is that of low flying and loud engines. Although disgruntled citizens are small in nubmer and unorganized, their cries for public safety will eventually force the FAA to try to regulate ultralight aircraft. This is a task with which the FAA is not prepared to deal. The ensuing disorder could set the sport back years.

One has only to look at the voluminous regulations for the pilots of light aircraft to see the potentially disastrous results of strict government control. Fortunately, we can, at this point in time, actually direct the future of the ultralight movement in this country. We can do so by policing our ranks and adhering to a set of rules that not only show good judgment, but are closely aligned with the rules governing all craft that use the skies.

The basis for this article will be pertinent sections of the Federal Air Regulations (FAR's), Part 61 and Part 91. Many of you who fly ultralights are already pilots and it is your responsibility and duty to inform your fellow non-pilots of the regulations that govern safe flight. Most of these regulations are good guidelines for safe flight and many will work to your advantage.

First of all, you must realize that the FAR's, as written, apply to all aircraft except moored balloons,kites on cables, unmanned rockets, and unmanned free balloons. To understand this, we must define an aircraft in the government's terms.

313

The FAA defines an aircraft (registered or not registered) as a device that is used or intended to be used for flight in the air. This means that anything you climb into to go aloft is, under international aviation law, defined as an aircraft. Defined as such, ultralights fall under the international regulations governing flight. In this country, that set of regulations is referred to as Part 91 of the Federal Air Regulations.

There is another Part of the FAR's that some powered glider riders have expressed concern about. This set of two hundred or more regs is Part 61, and is referred to as Part 61, and is referred to as Pilot Certification. Before we continue our discussion of the previously mentioned Part 91 (Flight Rules), your mind should be put at ease about Part 61 (Pilot Certification).

Part 61.3b states that no person may act as pilot-in-command of a civil aircraft of United States registry unless he has a current pilot certificate issued by the FAA. The key words here are "aircraft of United States registry". Ultralights that are *foot launchable* do not have to be registered under existing laws, so no certificate or license is needed to fly one. No license is required for an ultralight with foot-launching capabilities.

Part 61.3c goes on to state that no person may act as pilot-in-command under that certification issued to him unless he has a current medical certificate. Well, if you're not flying "under a certificate", then you don't ned a medical certificate. These two parts of FAR 61 effectively relieve the ultralight pilot of the burden of compliance — a lenghty and costly compliance.

Since we can forget about Part 61, let's move on to Part 91 called General Operating and Flight Rules. Remember, although not yet enforceable in the normal fashion by the FAA, these rules do, nevertheless, apply to all things that can carry a man into the sky. They make good sense and can offer protection as well as knowledge. If ultralight pilots adhere to these rules, even the most vocal citizen groups will not have a leg to stand on. Likewise, the ultralight movement, and the FAA, will benefit in the end.

In order to understand Part 91, you must have a clear grasp of the term "pilot-in-command". This term refers to any person responsible for the operation and safety of the aircraft during flight time. The regs do not say that this person has to be a US-licensed pilot to be covered by Part 91 (the rules of the air).

Another term that is commonly used in FAR Part 91 is airplane. Is an ultralight an airplane under the regulations? We have already established that the ultralight is truly an air*craft* but is it an air*plane*? An airplane is defined as an engine-driven, fixed-wing aircraft, heavier than air, that is supported in flight by the dynamic reaction of air against its wings. By this definition, an ultralight is a true airplane.

Armed with this information, we will proceed through Part 91 — A, B, and C — touching on only those regulations that are applicable to ultralight flying. Most of these regulations will impose little or no restriction on your flying, and may even open new avenues of flight heretofore not considered. The regulation number will be given only as a reference, if you wish to look up the exact wording. The regulation itself will be interpreted in plain language in an attempt to promote clarity while retaining the intent of the regulation.

FAR 91, Subpart A
91.3: Responsibility and authority of the pilot-in-command

The pilot-in-command of an aircraft has the final authority concerning operation of his aircraft. By the same token, he must assume responsibility for the outcome of the operations. This means that a pilot is free to deviate from any rule of Part 91 if he feels that it is in his best safety to do so.

If a rule is violated, the pilot is often asked to send a written statement concerning the circumstances of the violation. Most reasonable excuses are accepted. Ultralight pilots, who hold the unique position of not being certified, have little to fear because they have no licenses that can be suspended or removed. Certified pilots, on the other hand, must realize that they may be dealt with exactly as if they were flying a registered aircraft.

All this means is that if you have to bend a regulation to keep your aircraft out of harm's way, report the occurrence as it happened — tell it like it is. By so doing, you will have no reason to fear the entanglements that many pilots endure.

9.5: Preflight action.

This is a good, common-sense regulation. Basically, all it says is that you must check your aircraft before flying. Now, you've got to admit that even for a government regulation, that makes sense. The regulation further states that for flights away from the airport (cross-country flights), you must check the weather, determine how much fuel will be needed, and if airports en route will be adequate for your aircraft. Generally speaking, it is hard to find fault with 91.5.

Another prudent regulation, 91.7, at first seems of little concern to most ultralight pilots. Regulation 91.7 (1) says you may not leave the the controls of your aircraft while in flight. It is difficult to imagine an ultralight pilot having problems with the first part of this regulation.

However, the second part, 91.7a(2), is one that all pilots of any craft should aways heed. It requires you to keep your harness or belt securely fastened while seated in the aircraft, whether in flight or on the ground. Many a pilot has been saved by his belt, harness, and helmet . . . and lived to fly another day.

91.9: Careless or reckless operation.

You may not put another person's life or property in danger by willfully operating your machine in a careless or reckless manner. The problem with this regulation involves the definitions of careless and reckless. This regulation has been used for years as a catchall to prosecute otherwise undefinable pilot actions.

Although the federal government may have trouble in some of these cases, local governments have had good luck with both civil and criminal convictions. Unless the pilot is flagrantly reckless or downright dangerous, however, no action usually is taken. Remember, the key here is to not knowingly endanger life or property.

91.11 and 91.12: Liquor and drugs

The good old "bottle to throttle" regulation says that if you do any hard drinking, you must wait eight hours before you fly your aircraft. Most pilots, because of the way they drink, usually can't even be aroused eight hours later. This regulation unfortunately applies to all drugs; not just narcotics, but all drugs — even the drugstore variety. Most pilots follow their own consciences and use common sense when it comes to complying with this regulation. By the way, 91.12 says you can't use your ultralight to smuggle drugs, so watch it!

91.13: Dropping objects.

Any object that is not a hazard to people or property may be dropped while in flight. This is largely a judgment decision on the part of the pilot. Remember, anything can be dropped if it cannot hurt someone or damage something.

We're going to skip 91.20 (Operations within the North Atlantic Minimum Navigation Performance Specifications Airspace . . . see why it's so nice not to be regulated . . .), and move along to more pertinent regulations.

91.22: Fuel requirements for VFR flight.

By the way, VFR is simply the FAA's way of saying good weather. The Visual Flight Rules are in effect when the ground visibility, as reported by a weather observer or as determined by the pilot, is three miles or better (more on this later).

This regulation calls for a 30-minute fuel reserve on a cross-country flight in an airplane. For a rotorcraft, 20 minutes of extra fuel is allowed. There are no requirements for gliders or balloons. You can, therefore, suit yourself concerning where you think ultralights stand.

91.27: Civil aircraft — certification required.

Since the FAA has classified powered hang gliders or ultralights somewhere between birds and experimental aircraft, no certification process is needed to build an ultralight. No inspections, fees, paperwork, or registration is necessary.

As ultralights become more complex, the guidelines of "foot launchable" will constantly be in contention. Sooner or later, the industry must be braced for the inevitable "clarification" that will allow the government to reclassify and register ultralights. All of us can prevent this from happening by keeping our sport safe and inoffensive in the eyes of the public and those pilots with whom we share the air.

9.33: Instruments and equipment required on aircraft

Since this regulation applies only to U.S. airworthiness certified aircraft, it does not apply to ultralights. Therefore, no aircraft instruments are required equipment. This also eliminates the need for an ELT (emergency locator transmitter).

9.55: Civil aircraft sonic boom.

Keep your speed below Mach 1 and no one will complain.

FAR 91 — Subpart B

Just as the rules of the road are formed by trial and error, so the rules of the air are more the product of experience than regulation. Pilots have agreed upon these rules, so you should have a good knowledge of them. After all, some of these regulations are as old as flight — many were formulated by men flying machines not unlike your own. There are no legalities here. *These regulations are for all who use the air* — regardless of their method of flight.

91.65 — Operating Near Other Aircraft

Don't get so close to another aircraft that a collision could occur. However, if previous arrangements have made another pilot aware of your intentions, you may operate in close formation flight. "Sneaking up" on another aircraft may mean a bigger surprise for you than you had planned for him!

91.67 — Right-of-Way Rules

Any aircraft in distress has the right-of-way. When converging, *the aircraft on the right has the right-of-way.* But don't press your luck. Remember, you're a slow-moving small target. Because they are less maneuverable, *balloons, gliders (no power), and airships automatically have the right-of-way* over you.

When approaching head-on *each aircraft should turn to the right.* When overtaking, plan to *pass well clear on the right* side. In the landing pattern, *the aircraft that is lowest on final approach has the right-of-way.* But this should not be used as an excuse to cut ahead of someone unless you feel that you are in trouble.

Since many ultralights will now be available with floats as an option, let's look at water right-of-way rules, so that boaters will stay happy.

91.69 — Right-of-Way Rules On The Water

Stay clear of boats and try not to impede their navigation. As in the air, *the vessel to the right has the right-of-way. All passing will be to the right* and well clear. There is no better way to get into trouble with local boaters (who will surely outnumber you) than to disturb their fishing and other water sports. So no matter how great the temptation to show off your skills, stay well away from all skiers, fishermen, and sailors. They can see you from a distance — they don't have to see you face to face. If you follow these simple good sense rules, they will not mind sharing their waterways with you.

91.71 — Aerobatic Flight

In its most strict sense, the definition used by the FAA for aerobatic flight cannot be applied to an ultralight aircraft. However, it is prudent to understand the intent of the regulation.

Do not attempt flight maneuvers over a populated area, an assembly of people, or near an airport. Aerobatic flight must be above 1,500'. Stay high enough to assure effective recovery. Make sure there is at least three miles visibility.

Aerobatic flight really is not much of a problem now because of the state of the art in ultralight manufacturing. But with the advent of rigid wings and the light loadings on those wings, it's just a matter of time. So, if this becomes your "thing", stay away from people, airplanes, and the ground.

91.73 — Aircraft Lights

An aircraft operated at night needs two types of lighting systems. The first is a simple set of position lights. A red one on the left wing, a green one on the right wing, and a white one on the tail.

The other system is anticollision in nature. It consists of a red rotating beacon or strobe light. Neither of these systems is beyond the output capabilities of a small battery. Thus, the possibility exists for night flight if a suitable field away from normal air traffic can be found. A landing light is not a requirement for any aircraft unless it is used for hire.

91.77 — ATC Light Signals

Ultralight aircraft without radios occasionally get permission to operate off tower-conrolled airports. Usually the operation is off in one corner of the field, so as not to disturb the normal traffic flow. In these rare instances, it becomes necessary for the pilot to have a working knowledge of the light signal system. The tower personnel will aim a light gun at the aircraft and signal the following:

Steady green — Cleared to takeoff, or cleared to land.

Flashing green — Cleared to taxi, or (if in the air) circle to land.

Steady red — Stop (if on the ground), or give way (if in the air).

Flashing red — Taxi clear of runway, or airport unsafe (do not land).

Alternate red and green — Exercise caution (mowing equipment, ice, etc.).

As previously implied, it is unlikely that you will be granted prior permission to operate off a controlled airport. But if you are, knowledge of their rules will help assure a return invitation.

91.79 — Minimum Safe Altitude

This regulation is the most misunderstood by pilots in general. Let's take it apart and see what it actually says. We will look at 91.79(c) first. It says that you should operate at 500' above the surface when over other than congested areas. But over sparsely populated areas or over water, you may fly as low as you desire.

However, you still must *stay 500' straight-line distance from people, boats, cars, or buildings*. These are liberal restrictions and should be easy to live with. There are, of course, no altitude requirements when you are in the process of takeoff or landing.

Now a fellow has got to be crazy to fly over a congested city or town. But if you must, you are required to *stay 1,000' over the highest buildings* in your area. This may seem high for most ultralights, but, given the steep descent rate of your aircraft, this extra altitude would be ablsolutely necessary in case of engine failure. Basically, the best advice is to fly out in the boonies and to enjoy yourself.

91.87 — Operating At Airports With Operating Control Towers

As mentioned previously, you probably will not have the opportunity to fly into a controlled field. But, the question is often asked, "If I put a radio on my ultralight, can I operate it off an airport that has a control tower?" Since the regulation uses the words person and aircraft — as opposed to certified pilot or registered aircraft — the answer might be yes. It appears you cannot be stopped from operating off a tower-controlled field, at least not by Regulation 91.87, if you have an appropriate two-way radio. But the Feds make the point that airport and land owners have the final authority and right to ban any type of operation on their property.

Now, everywhere there is an operating control tower, there is an imaginary cake-shaped portion of air that extends five miles out from the airport and 2,999' above the ground. The tower wants to talk to anything flying in this block of air. This requirement covers only the field with the tower.

If another airport lies within the five-mile radius, you may operate to and from it without talking to the tower at the primary airport. This parcel of radio-controlled air is called an Airport Traffic Area. It should not be confused with, and has no relation to, a Control Zone that is shown on the sectional charts as a dashed five miles around some airports. Control Zones and their place in ultralight flying will be discussed later.

91.89 — Operation At Airports Without Control Towers

Now this is more like the operation that faces an ultralight pilot. These are not only good rules for approved airports, but should be used at all flying fields and sites.

Keep all your turns in the traffic pattern to the left. This rule may vary at some airports due to obstacles or dangerous terrain. Take precautions at your own field and design the safest possible traffic pattern. If you do fly from a "regular" airport, make it a point to check on the traffic pattern and local restrictions.

91.90 — Terminal Control Areas

If you live near a Terminal Control Area, you are to be pitied. The only advice that can be given on TCAs is to learn the boundaries and STAY OUT! There is usually enough room under and around them to find a place to fly. But *be aware that other traffic trying to avoid the TCA will be compacted into that area.*

91.95 — Restricted And Prohibited Areas

These areas are clearly marked on any aeronautical chart. They are usually military in nature, and cannot be entered for any reason. Don't take a chance. *Do not fly from or into any area that is marked restricted or prohibited.* However, these areas often do not extend all the way to the ground. Check your chart carefully to see if this is the case. You may operate with some safety under many of these areas.

91.101 — Operations To Or Over Cuba

Forget it!

91.105 — Basic VFR Weather Minimums

How bad can the weather be and still be flyable? Whereas visibility plays a very important part in determining the weather minimums, it is not the only factor. One's proximity to clouds also has a role.

For flight in controlled airspace, the *visibility must be at least three miles,* and you must be able to *stay 500' below, 1,000' above, or 2,000' horizontally from any cloud or cloud mass.* The problem here is "Where is controlled airspace?"

Across most of the USA, controlled airspace is everywhere! But wait. In their desire not to leave the little guy out, this controlled airspace does not extend to the surface of the earth except in a Control Zone. Remember, Control Zones were mentioned earlier.

In other than Control Zones that is around all instrument airports, the controlled airspace doesn't begin until 1,200'. There are some areas where controlled airspace begins at 700', but they are marked in red on charts and usually cover little territory. Below this blanket, the controlled airspace, requirements for flight are most lenient.

Outside controlled airspace the visibility only has to be one mile and is always determined by the pilot. He can fly as close to a cloud as he wants, but *may not enter one.* As long as you operate outside control zones and below 1,200', you can take advantage of the improved effective visibility offered by the slow forward speed of your ultralight. But, if you go above 1,200' or operate in a control zone when visibility is less than three miles, you will be mixing with IFR traffic . . . and those guys aren't looking out!

91.102 — VFR Cruising Altitudes

This refers to a system of separation that allows aircraft flying in opposite directions not to collide. It does not apply below 3,000' above the ground level. Below that altitude, everyone is on his own. So keep an eye out because *light planes, and even military jets, often fly at practically ground level.*

FAR 91 Subpart C

Maintenance & Alterations

Since this set of regulations is concerned with U.S. registered aircraft, it does not apply to ultralights. But, while on the subject of maintenance, let's consider a few commonsense rules:

(1) Keep all moving parts working freely.
(2) Use only aircraft strength parts.
(3) Check your flying wires and struts carefully.
(4) Safety all nuts in some fashion.
(5) Maintain your own progressive inspection.
(6) Do not fly with any cracked or jerry-rigged parts.
(7) Follow manufacturer's recommendations for assembly and storage.

What follows are good operating practices that meet the needs of the ultralight pilot.

Check Lists

It doesn't matter what kind of ship you fly, 747 or hot air balloon, you should use a check list. Check lists are especially important to those of us who fly powered aircraft. A check list should be made for assembly, preflight runup, and disassembly.

Even if you don't want the inconvenience of a written check list, at least sit down and make up a simple organized sequence that can be easily memorized. Once this list is established, do not change the sequence with which you perform the various functions. Always do everything in the same way, in the same order.

Preflight Checkout

A check of all controls, instruments, flying wires, and flying surfaces should be completed before each flight. If there is a problem, do not be tempted to "rig something up" so you can get in one more flight.

Runup the engine and make sure that you are getting full power. A hand-held tachometer like the RC modelers use may be helpful. Test the engine through a wide range of power settings and make sure you're getting a satisfactory response. Any problem the engine is having on the ground will not disappear magically in the air.

Do this runup well away from people. High rpm props — when they disintegrate — are very dangerous to people standing in their arc.

Weather Considerations

Ultralight flying normally takes place early in the morning or in the evening, when there is little or no wind. Because of the nature of normal flight, short duration and distance, it would seem that weather would play a small role in the pilot's preparations. Although the danger of being trapped by weather may not be a problem, prior knowledge of weather may save you a long trip to the flying field.

Weather information is easily obtained and will contain much that is useful to the ultralight pilot. Wind speed and direction are forecast with better than normal accuracy. Cloud conditions will indicate the stability of the air. Cumulus (puffy) clouds indicate updrafts and rough flying conditions. Stratus (smooth) clouds, or any total overcast, will produce smooth flying conditions. As you learn to match forecasts with actual field conditions, you will grow in your ability to forecast weather on the spot.

Aviation weather is easily obtainable and free to pilots. Call any Flight Service Station listed in your telephone directory under Government Offices, or listen to the weather on a Low frequency radio receiver that can be purchased from an aviation supply shop. By the way, when you call up for weather, ask for *local* conditions, surface winds only, forecasts, and forecast winds. The briefer will ask for your aircraft number — just give him your name. The important thing is that you get the information you need.

Wind Considerations

Since ultralights must operate in moderate or light wind conditions, it becomes necessary for the pilot to have a good understanding of the flow of wind across the earth's surface. Although general wind direction and strength are determined by massive weather patterns, local conditions can also produce wind.

If you are operating near a large body of water, you can expect the wind to be blowing on-shore in the day and offshore at night. This means early in the morning a wind shift will occur. The wind always blows toward a developing rain storm and away from it as its showers are dumped.

The wind flow is drastically and dangerously changed by obstructions such as hills, tree lines, buildings, and even brushy fence lines. Such obstructions can cause the wind flow to suddenly reverse, leaving the pilot without the relative wind to sustain flight.

When flying near the ground, keep your speed up while crossing or flying near these disturbed areas. Be especially carefuly to plan your approach and landing to a large open area away from the effects of turbulent airflow and wind shear. If conditions get hairy, do what any good pilot does — abort the approach before you run out of altitude and ideas.

Vortex Turbulence

As ultralights begin to operate near other aircraft, as in airshow activity, a knowledge of vortex (wing tip) turbulence and prop-wash becomes necessary. When a heavy aircraft moves through the air, its wings produce a rotating flow of air from the tips. This vortex can easily roll an unsuspecting ultralight that passes as much as one mile behind the heavier aircraft.

Stay out of the paths that airplanes leave. Never allow a helicopter to pass over you, regardless of his altitude. Inform chopper pilots in the area that their rotor wash can devastate an ultralight aircraft. Do not take off behind any airplanes that produce propwash. Any engine over 35 hp.can turn a large enough prop to give you propwash problems. If you must operate near larger aircraft, use extreme caution and plan your takeoffs and landings well away from their operating area.

Aeronautical Charts

The first question that comes to mind is, "Why do I need an aeronautical chart? A chart — Sectional Chart if possible — shows where the normal light plane and airline activity is. These are places you don't want to be. Aeronautical charts also show ground contour, small seldem-used airports, obstructions, restricted areas, military areas, and fish and wildlife reserves. If you're so inclined, they also serve as a good cross-country map.

One thing that is not shown is the military low-level training routes. These are routes that are flown by high-speed jet aircraft from about 100′ above the ground to about 2,000′. The average altitude is just about where you fly. A description of the route in your area can be as close as your phone. Cell the Flight Service Station in your area and ask if a route is in your intended flight operations area.

In Conclusion

The ultralight movement, like any new phenomenon, is really built upon all the technology that came before. For this very reason, it has a chance to offer the average working man an answer to his age-old dream of affordable flight. Or, as Mr. Piper once proclaimed, "An airplane in every man's garage." Although his dream got lost somewhere along the way, the need did not. A combination of space technology and purist desire has opened up a new world of adventure in flying. The future is a certainty.

Since the ultralight movement is new and different, it will be met with resistance from the established aviation community. Homebuilders had to go through such a trying period of adjustment. The responsibility for making the journey a smooth one lies with the aviators who are now already flying ultralights.

What I'm trying to say is, "Sure, you don't have to follow the regs. You can say, 'I don't care, there's nothing they can do to me.'" But this very attitude will only bring restrictions upon the great number of future aviators that will be entering the movement.

There are established organizations that are afraid of the impact upon the general public. Aircraft manufacturers, the FAA, and even Congress itself are waiting and watching. If we can regulate ourselves, then there will be no need for others to regulate us.

So let's close up ranks and fly by the book whenever possible. If these are the rules of the air, they are also our rules. There are few regs that are restrictive to ultralights. And no regulation can ever remove the pure joy and satisfaction of ultralight flight.

— Phil McKenzie
Olympus Ultralights

Phil McKenzie worked with the FAA in Kentucky for five years.

Appendix B —Setting Up An Ultralight Flying Club

The following was excerpted from the Liberty Field Flyers Newsletter, and is reprinted here to assist others interested in establishing a local ultralight flying club.

This group was formed specifically to encourage UltraLight Flying. We have the use of a privately owned air strip at Stoneypoint Road in Petaluma, California; which belongs to Mr. William Green.

In order to fly at this ranch with the utmost of safety (and the emphasis is on safety) we *cannot* permit entry to the flying site by the general public. Any viewing or watching must, therefore, be done from adjacent roads or areas.

The locked gate is accessible only by members in good standing. A member may allow a non-member to enter through the gate with him, but is responsible for this guest during this period and must have a release-waiver signed immediately upon entering. Any trespasser will be subject to prosecution.

It is the duty of any member to alert the local sheriff if a violation is noticed and not responded to.

We have 3 types of memberships.

FULL ACTIVE MEMBER —
Cost: $150.00 annually for flying priviledge plus $12.00 for Newsletter.
ASSOCIATE MEMBER —
Cost: $25.00 annually. This gives the member access to the field but he/she *cannot* fly. Plus $12.00 for Newsletter.
SUBSCRIPTION MEMBER —
Cost: $12.00 for Newsletter only, cannot enter flying site. (Recommended for out-of-the-area UltraLights enthusiast who does not fly or lives away from the area.)

Fiscal Year: February 1st thru January 31st.

A full member's $25.00 can be used towards the $150.00 full flying membership, when so desired. ($150.00 will be pro-rated monthly/quarterly.)

Insurance: The owner of the flying site has liability insurance to protect himself. The waiver to be signed by guests is tied to that policy.

All "Flying" members must have approved USGHA or other liability coverage, copy of policy or certificate to be on file with Club Secretary.

Flying Ability: All flying members must pass a test, both flight and written. The written test covers VFR's and pertinent aerodynamic and meteorlogical knowledge.

Flying Guests: An active member may introduce an outsider for flying priviledges at Liberty Field. It will be his/her duty to have the guest sign the guest book and liability waiver. Collect $10.00 per day for flying priviledges and make sure monies are turned over to the Treasurer. (Checks preferred, made payable to: LIBERTY FIELD UltraLight ASSOCIATION.)

All Flying guests will have to show a log or other means of competency, and must show proof of insurance.

Liberty Field Flyers Infraction Policies & Procedures
• Any member breaking any rule or by-law is subject to a Committee Inquest.

- The Committee, has the right to impose a fine of not more than $50.00; or to eliminate the member from participating in the L.F.F. permanently. Associate members may serve on the Committee. Committee will be chosen when the need arises.
- In the event of an inquest, there are two steps to handle subject of Infraction:
  1. Primary procedure.
  2. Secondary procedure.
     A. Primary procedure consists of a meeting where the infracting member presents his/her account of the events that took place. The Committee will then decide if there was just cause for the infracting member's action. If the member is cleared, the issue will be dismissed; if not, the issue will continue to secondary procedure.
     B. Secondary procedure will take place in the event that formal charges have been brought against the infracting member. The accused member, the person making the complaint, the Committee and the safety Committee will then have a meeting and deal with the problem accordingly.
- Any member not willing to meet their responsibility in the event of primary or secondary inquest is voluntarily giving up their membership in the LFUA.

Club Rules

All Club Members are responsible for knowing and abiding by all applicable Federal Aviation Regulations (FAR). No dealers are to be officers.

Take-off & Landing Procedures

1. Remember to always have someone pre-flight your aircraft after you do.
2. Take-off and land only in designated areas. (See map posted.)
3. Look to see if immediate area is clear and yell "Clear Prop".
4. When approaching take-off, look up and around to check if anyone else is preparing to depart, or is landing, or on final. *ALL* aircraft on landing and final have the right of way.
5. No downwind departures. In no wind conditions, cast-to-west departures will be observed.
6. No downwind landings, except in an emergency.

Flight Rules

1. Use designated traffic patterns. (See map posted.)
2. Do not fly over aircraft set-up area at less than 200 feet. Pattern altitudes will be at 200 feet.
3. Stay at least 500 feet above and away from all housing.
4. Absolutely no night flying. (After sunset.) No flying before 7:00 a.m.
5. No alcohol or drugs within eight (8) hours of flying for pilots. No drugs on field. Spectators are allowed to use alcohol in restricted areas, provided that they do not become intoxicated. Intoxicated individuals will be asked to leave the field.
6. No smoking, except in designated area.

Membership

1. Members must carry Club Membership Card while on field.
2. A non-member flying guest, must be approved by a Club Officer.
3. No persons may fly or be trained to fly, unless they are members, or are being trained by an authorized flight school.
4. Members are not to give out gate combination to anyone.

Appendix C
Dealers of Ultralight Aircraft

ALABAMA
Hickeyville Ultralights
5172 Kooiman Road
Theodore, AL 36582

4 Seasons Aviation
708 77th Way
So. Birmingham, AL 35206

ALASKA
Sunrise Country Ultralights of Alaska
3521 Mountain View Dr.
Anchorage, AK 99504

Arctic Sparrow Aircraft, Inc.
230 Center Ct.
Anchorage, AK 99502

Sky High Sports
4712 Kupreanof St.
Anchorage, AK 99507

Ultra Flight AK
8250 KIP CRT
Anchorage, AK 99507

Ultralights of Alaska
3521 Mt. View Dr.
Anchorage, AK 99504

ARIZONA
ARVS, Inc.
4939 E. Florian
Mesa, AZ 85206

Cactus Patch Flying Service
P.O. Box 1591 Black Cyn.
STG 1
Phoenix, AZ 85029

Fantasia, Inc.
2205 E. Fox
Mesa, AZ 85203

Phoenix Ultralight Center
21424 N. 7th Ave., Suite 2
Phoenix, AZ 85027

Southwest Ultralight Aviation
7570 N. Wade Rd.
Tucson, AZ 85743

Superstition Mountain Airpark
1901 S. Hobson
Mesa, AZ 85204

U.S. Ultralight Aviation
P.O. Box 30527
Phoenix, AZ 85046

Valley Ultralights
10302 E. Illini, #5
Apache Jct., AZ 85220

Vista Ultralight, Inc.
6232 W. Wolf St.
Phoenix, AZ 85033

CALIFORNIA
Aero-Flite
1701 W. 5th St.
Oxnard, CA 93030

Advanced Ultralights of Southern California
5362 N. Dorfee
Hangar, C-1A
El Monte, CA 91732

Best Flite Aircraft Service
Flabob Airport
4130 Mennes Ave.
Riverside, CA 92509

Bright Star Hang Gliders
3715 Santa Rosa Ave.
Santa Rosa, CA 95401

California Power Systems
790 139th Ave. #4
San Leandro, CA 94578

Central Valley Ultralights
1400 N. 9th St., Suite 50
Modesto, CA 95350

Challenge
4435 Huckleberry
Carnelean Bay, CA 95732

Chandelle San Francisco
198 Los Banos
Daly City, CA 94014

Clark Flight Center, Inc.
P.O. Box 1353
Los Altos, CA 94022

Columbia Aviation
10753 Airport Rd.
Columbia, CA 95310

Diablo Sport Aviation
Rt. 1, Box 1186
Antioch, CA 94509

Elsinore Valley Hang Gliding Center
31395 Riverside Dr.
Lake Elsinore, CA 92330

Elsinore UL Flight Park
P.O. Box 301
Lake Elsinore, CA 92330

Flight Sensations
11366 Amalgam Way
Unit K
Rancho Cordova, CA 95670

Flight Realities
1945 Adams Ave.
San Diego, CA 92116

FunFlight Center
3172 A Mission Trails
Lake Elsinore, CA 92330

Hang Gliders of California, Inc.
2410 Lincoln Blvd.
Santa Monica, CA 90405

Hang Glider Emporium
613 N. Milpas
Santa Barbara, CA 93103

The Hang Gliding Co.
391 Dolliver
Pismo Beach, CA 93449

HG Equipment Co.
3620 Wawona
San Francisco, CA 94116

Hang Gliders West
20-A Panaron Way
Ignacio, CA 94947

Hillside Aviation
2600 Gold St.
Redding, CA 96001

Inland Air ULs
Rialto Municipal Arpt.
1436 N. Ayala
Rialto, CA 92376

Inland Empire ULs
12379 Willet Ave.
Grand Terrace, CA 92324

Lite Flite
3423 Investment Blvd., #204
Hayward, CA 94545

Montague Aviation
900 Old Montague Road
Montague, CA 96064

N. California Aerolights
Gate 3, Antioch Arpt.
Antioch, CA 94509

**Northern California
Ultralights Inc.**
Route 1, Box 1202
Antioch Airport
Antioch, CA 94509

Pure Ectasy
8312 Weeks Lane
Redding, CA 96002

Rally West Aircraft Service
6301 Lindbergh
California City, CA 93505

San Diego Ultralight Park
12240 Valhalla Dr.
Lakeside, CA 92040

**Silver Wing
Flight Specialties**
2525 Park Marina Dr.
Redding, CA 96001

Skyworks Aircraft
521 Sinclair Ftg. Rd.
Milpitas, CA 95035

Sportair
769 Cessna Ave.
Chico, CA 95926

Stamp Enterprises West
15712 Sexton
Escalon, CA 95320

The Ultralight Shop
Box 756
29 Palms, CA 92277

Triflight, Inc.
P.O. Box 935
Placentia, CA 92670

UFO Inc.
1401 North C St.
Sacramento, CA 95814

Ultimate Hi
13951 Midland Rd.
Poway, CA 92069

Ultraflight
820 East Ave, Q-6
Palmdale, CA 93550

Ultraflight A/C Co.
15651 Hawthorne Blvd.
Lawndale, CA 90260

Ultralight Aircraft Co.
South Bay
15651 Hawthorne Blvd.
Suite D
Lawndale, CA 90260

Ultralight Aviation
P.O. Box 27434
Escondido, CA 92027

Ultralight Flight, Inc.
2475 Morse Rd.
Sebastopol, CA 95472

U.S. Ultralight, Inc.
3380 E. Date St.
Brea, CA 92621

**Ultralights & Education
Training Co.**
716 Dahlia
Corona Del Mar, CA 92625

UltraSport
8415-1 Reseda Blvd.
Northridge, CA 91324

Valley Quicksilver
32081 Corydon Road
Lake Elsinore, CA 92330

Vickery's Ultralight Aircraft
P.O. Box 1014
Adelanto, CA 92301

Waspair Corporation
1881 Enterprise Blvd.
W. Sacramento, CA 95691

Weedhopper of San Diego
1840A Joe Crosson Dr.
El Cajon, CA 92020

Wind N Wires, Inc.
29332 Rd. 86
Visalia, CA 93277

Windsports International
5219 Sepulveda Blvd.
Van Nuys, CA 91411

The Wright Solution
Box 1351
Vacaville, CA 95696

COLORADO
ARVs, Inc.
3920 S. Clarkson
Englewood, CO 80110

Aspen Hang Gliders Ltd.
219 Arapahoe
El Jebel, CO 81628

Continental Divide ULs
P.O. Box 259
Brekenridge, CO 80424

Feathaire Aviation, Inc.
Bldg. C, Hangar 5
Tri County Airport
Erie, CO 80516

4 Corners HGs & ULs
Box 38
Hesperus, CO 81326

Golden Sky Sails
572 Orchard St.
Golden, CO 80401

Granby UAC Inc.
2 mi. S. of Granby Hwy. 40
Granby, CO 80446

Leading Edge Air Foils
331 S. 14th St.
Colorado Springs, CO 80904
(303) 632-4959

Progressive A/C Co.
3545 S. Brentwood
Denver, CO 80235

Western Sky Ultralights
414 Neptune G
Littleton, CO 80124

CONNECTICUT
Airwise Inc.
15 Long Ridge Road
West Redding, CT 06896

Avocet UL Aircraft, Inc.
58 Old Farm Rd.
Madison, CT 06443

Bridgeport Weedhopper Sales
1 Islandbrook Ave.
Bridgeport, CT 06606

Microflite Inc.
143 Chestnut St.
Manchester, CT 06606

Tek Flight Products, Inc.
Colebrook Stage
Winstead, CT 06098

DELAWARE
Aviator World Ents., Inc.
P.O. Box 10806
Wilmington, DE 19850

FLORIDA
Aero-Mart
Nova Village Market
1104 Beville Rd.
Daytona Beach, FL 32014

Bay Ultralights
P.O. Box 4141
Panama City, FL 32401

The Aeroplane Store Inc.
6629 53rd Ave. E.
Brandenton, FL 33508

The Air Force-Ultralights Inc.
812 W. Government St.
Pensacola, FL 32501

Everglades Ultralites Inc.
154 Palm Tree Lane
Fort Meyers, FL 33905

Free Spirit Flite
Rt. 1, Box 119C
Hawthorne, FL 32640

Inflight Ventures Inc.
Route 29, Box 454-D
Fort Meyers, FL 33905

Lenox Flight School
Route 4, Box 4639
Arcadia Municipal Airport
Arcadia, FL 33821

Miami Air Sports
4636 S.W. 129th Ave.
Miami, FL 33175

No. Florida Ultralights
109 Century Park Dr.
Tallahassee, FL 32304

Phantom Aircraft, Inc.
1450 N.E. 39th St.
Ocala, FL 32671

Pioneer Aerolights
3651 Cherry Bluff Lane
Tallahassee, FL 32312

Ultraflight Aviation
c/o Ft. Walton Yamaha
421 Racetrack Rd., N.W.
Ft. Walton Beach, FL 32548

Ultralight Aviation
10726 S.W., 190th St.
Miami, FL 33157

Ultralight Sport Flying Inc.
1450 10th St. S.
Safety Harbor, FL 33572

Ultrapro ULs, Inc.
51 Royal Palm Blvd. #C
Vero Beach, FL 32960

Wilkinson Aeromarine Co.
Muncipal Airport
New Smyrna Beach,
FL 32069

GEORGIA
Aerosports, Inc.
1105 Sixth Ave.
Albany, GA 31707

Alpha Flite Sales, Inc.
13224 Hwy. 9N
Alpharetta, GA 30201

Atlanta Hang Gliders
6000 N. Unity Dr.
Norcross, GA 30371

Columbia Aviation
10753 Airport Rd.
Columbia, GA 95370

Savannah Ultralight
12426 White Bluff Rd.
Savannah, GA 31406

Ultralight Flying Objects Inc.
195 N. Main St.
Jasper, GA 30143

Southern Air-Time, Inc.
Gwinnett County Arpt.
Lawrenceville, GA 30245

Starwing, Inc.
P.O. Box 1146
Newman, GA 30264

IDAHO
Bonneville Aviation
Route 1
Indom, ID 83245

ILLINOIS
Apple Canyon UL, Inc.
RR 1, Box 6144, N. Lake Rd. #1
Apple River, IL 61001

Cloud 9 Ultralights
935 E. Tohill Rd.
Decatur, IL 62521

Collins Aviation
1182 Pine
Batavia, IL 60510

Jeff Weishaar
Box 388
Ashton, IL 61006

Linmar Enterprises, Inc.
Ultralight Division
355 Windsor Dr.
Roselle, IL 60172

Mid-America, Inc.
141 Cleveland Circle
Granville, IL 61326

Rainbow Ultralight, Inc.
P.O. Box 273
Moweagua, IL 62550

RFE, Inc.
Russ Janson ULs, Inc.
Ridott, IL 62067

Sunset Aviation Inc.
29 Richard Dr.
Urbana, IL 61801

Ultralight Adventures, Inc.
9516 Beech Ave.
Crystal Lake, IL 60014

Ultralights Unlimited, Inc.
8407 Pyott Rd., #5
Lake In The Hills, IL 60102

U.S. Ultranautics Corp.
P.O. Box 300
Itasca, IL 60143

WLS Ultralights, Inc.
1512 North Ave.
Crystal Lake, IL 60014

INDIANA
Alpha Aircraft
145 E. 14th St.
Indianapolis, IN 46202

Indiana Rec. Aircraft, Inc.
5325 Mt. Pleasant North St.
Greenwood, IN 46142

Indiana Ultralights, Inc.
3005 So. 50 East
Lafayette, IN 47905

Penguin Aviation
202 S. Jefferson St.
Madison, IN 47250

SBN Ultralight
4715 W. Progress Dr.
South Bend, IN 46628

Tri-State Kit Sales
1121 N. Locust St.
Mt. Vernon, IN 47620

Ultraflight Inc.
6410 Cornell Ave.
Indianapolis, IN 46220

Ultralights of Indiana
P.O. Box 216
Hebron, IN 46341

Windwalker UL Aircraft
RR 4, Box 231A
Angola, IN 46703

IOWA
Aerolite Sales
John Moffit
RR 1
Mechanicsville, IA 52306

Hawkeye Glider Sales, Inc.
Rt. 1, Box 33
Mt. Union, IA 52644

Hawkeye Ultralights, Inc.
RR 2
Marion, IA 52302

KANSAS
Lite-Flite Inc.
Route 1
Benton, KS 67017

KENTUCKY
Aerial Promotions Inc.
610 S. Beckley State Rd.
Louisville, KY 40223

Kentucky Aeronautics
5231 Briar Hill Rd.
Lexington, KY 40516

LOUISIANA
Freebird Flying Machine
P.O. Box 45011
408 Sunbeam Lane
Lafayette, LA 70505

Freedom Machines, Inc.
202 Thompson Dr.
Lafayette, LA 70506

Louisiana Agrilites
Rt. 1, Box 187
Welsh, LA 70591

Post Windsports
3958 Lakeshore Dr.
Shreveport, LA 71203

Rebel Airsports Inc.
115 Lisa Dr.
Monroe, LA 71203

Sky High Ultralights
3436 Wainwright St.
Alexandria, LA 71301

Southern Air Sports, Inc.
Rt. 4, Box 48
Vacherie, LA 70090

ULAC of the South, Inc.
4612 Young
Metairie, LA 70002

Ultralite Flite
Rt. 4, Box 181
New Iberia, LA 70560

MAINE
Ultraflight Sports Inc.
P.O. Box 101
Birchcroft Lane
Berwick, ME 03901

Upcountry Aviation, Inc.
RFD 2, Box 515
Carmel, ME 04419

MARYLAND
Aero Sport Inc.
P.O. Box 222
Elkton, MD 21921

Paragon Aviation
Suite 102
31 Old Solomons Island Rd
Annapolis, MD 21401

Potomac Ultralights
16009 Partell Ct.
Bowie, MD 20716

Sport Flight Inc.
9041-B Comprint Ct.
Gaithersburg, MD 20877

Sunfire Aircraft
1325 S. Phila. Blvd.
Aberdeen, MD 21001

Windstar Aviation, Inc.
3538 Aldino Rd.
Churchill, MD 21028

MASSACHUSETTS
Freedom Ultralights, Inc.
74 Garden St.
Feeding Hills, MA 01077

International Ultralights
Box 346
Uxbridge, MA 01569

The Pilot Shop
106 Access Rd.
Norwood, MA 02062

Ray's Pilot Training
North Ramp
Barnstable Municipal Arpt.
Hyannis, MA 02601

United Flyers Ultralight
Box 77, Lower Rd.
West Deerfield, MA 01342

MICHIGAN
Aerovon, Inc.
4509 Thompson Rd.
Linden, MI 48451

Almont Ultralight Sales
52551 Brenton Dr.
Rochester, MI 48063

Barnstormers Inc.
126 N. Main
Almont, MI 48003

DELTA Wing ULAC
1237 Ridgebrook Ct.
Kentwood, MI 49508

Eurimpex
4100 Howe
Bath, MI 48808

**Great American Flying
Machines, Inc.**
P.O. Box 152-C
Holland, MI 49423

Great Northern UL Co.
4379 West Section Rd.
Ottawa Lake, MI 49260

Magic Carpet Airpark
7423 Bacon Rd.
Petersburg, MI 49270

Michigan Aerolights
500 Lansing Rd.
Charlotte, MI 48813

S.E. Michigan HGs
24851 Murray
Mt. Clemens, MI 48045

S & S Ultralights
315 E. Michigan Ave.
Albion, MI 49224

Ultralight Sport Flying
2915 S. Logan
Lansing, MI 48910

Wolverine Air Motive
5150 Kimball, S.E.
Kentwood, MI 49508

MINNESOTA
Cloud 9 Sport Aviation
1902 4th Ave.
Mankato, MN 56001

Kitty Hawk North ULs, Inc.
#1 Sunny Lane
Duluth, MN 55811

Minnesota Microlights
RR 4, Box 185
Elk River, MN 55330

Northern Sun Inc.
2277 W. Country Road C
St. Paul, MN 55113

Sky Unlimited Inc.
Regional Airport
Thief River Fl., MN 56701

MISSISSIPPI
Hill Top Food Mart
Rt. 8, Hwy. 42 East
Hattiesburg, MS 39401

Ultrasports Aviation Co.
P.O. Box 0895,
Richland Sta.
Jackson, MS 39218

Wadington ULAC Co.
5436 Diamondhead Dr. E.
Bay St. Louis, MS 39520

MISSOURI
Action Gliders
Independence Memorial
Airport
20000 R.D. Mize Rd.
Independence, MO 64057

**Beaver Creek
Kasperwings, Inc.**
Rt. 1
Ava, MO 65608

EV-WISH, Inc.
Rt. 2, W. Coles Creek Rd.
Hermann, MO 65041

Festus Flying Service
Route 4
Box 240, Airport Road
Festus, MO 63028

Matthews Ultralight, Inc.
Rt. 1, Box 44
Wright City, MO 63390

Monarch Flying Machines
850 Hog Hollow Rd.
Chesterfield, MO 63017

**Simpson Midwest
Ultralights**
R.R. 1, Box 114
Fish, MO 63940

St. Louis Ultralights, Inc.
6332 N. Roseburg
St. Louis, MO 63105

MONTANA
Beartooth Ultralights
1008 Broadwater
Billings, MT 59102

Hawkinson Air Supply
519 N. Montana
Miles City, MT 59301

Tubbs ULs & HGs
5495 N. Montana #3
Helena, MT 59601

Rocky Mtn. ULAC, Inc.
P.O. Box 31153
Billings, MT 59107

NEBRASKA
Basic Aircraft Co., Inc.
5614 "A" St.
Omaha, NE 68106

NEVADA
**Ultralight Flying
Machines, Inc.**
5500 Grand Teton
Las Vegas, NV 89030

NEW HAMPSHIRE
Gossamer Wings Inc.
Hawthorne Airport
Antrim, NH 03440

Ultraflight Inc.
33 N. Main St.
Concord, NH 03301

NEW JERSEY
Acton Aerolights
Indian Mills Road
Tabernacle, NJ 08088

Birmingham Aeroflight, Inc.
P.O. Box 64
Birmingham, NJ 08011

Jersey Gliders
1528 W. Garden Rd.
Vineland, NJ 08360

Lite Flight
34 Hilltop Rd.
Berlin, NJ 08009

Mid-East Ultralights
Emil Rolando
RR 1, 22 W. Shore Trail
Stockholm, NJ 07460

Noble Sport Aviation Inc.
Hanover Airport
E. Hanover, NJ 07936

South Jersey ULs
631 Lakehurst Rd.
Browns Mills, NJ 08015

Weedhopper Flight Center
206 Main St.
Manasgum, NJ 08736

NEW MEXICO
Buffalo Skyriders, Inc.
P.O. Box 4512
Albuquerque, NM 87106

Hawk UL Aviation, Ltd.
2012 Father Sky NE
Albuquerque, NM 87112

Weedhopper West
24 Avenue F
McGill, NM 89318

NEW YORK

A & L Stationery
1290 Amsterdam Ave.
New York, NY 10057

Aerial Techniques Inc.
Route 209
Ellenville, NY 12424

Aerosports
Athens Ap.
R.R. 1, Box 200
Athens, NY 12015

Air-Park Ultralights Inc.
4500 Clinton St.
West Seneca, NY 14224

Bob Keech
9 Knollwood Dr.
Freeville, NY 13068

Brookfield Aviation, Inc.
Brookhaven Airport
Mastic, NY 11950

Elmira Air Sports
959 Oak St.
Elmira, NY 14901

Finger Lakes Airsports, Inc.
Canandaigua Airport
2440 Brickyard Rd.
Lanandaigua, NY 14424

Lite Flite International
c/o Clinton Aero
MR-16
Plattsburgh, NY 12901

Mountain Wings Inc.
Main St.
Kerchonkson, NY 12446

Ultralight Aviation
P.O. Box 63
Mayville, NY 14757

Sky Sports, Inc.
6815 Gildner Rd., Box 588
Central Square, NY 13036

Sport Aviation
222 Quaker Lake Rd.
Binghampton, NY 13903

The Aeroplane Co.
56 S. Applegate Rd.
Ithaca, NY 14850

The Sky's The Limit
P.O. Box 461
Olean, NY 14760

ULAC of C. NY
183 Wygant Rd.
Horseheads, NY 14845

UL Aviation of W. NY
P.O. Box 63
Mayville, NY 14757

NORTH CAROLINA

A & A UL Aviation
2525 S. Blvd.
Charlotte, NC 28203

A & P Sports Aviation
P.O. Box 2068
Elizabethtown, NC 28337

Atlantic Aero, Inc.
3808½ North Main
High Point, NC 27260

C. Carolina ULS, Inc.
215 N. Cobb Ave.
Burlington, NC 27215

Carolina UL Aviation
816 N. Horner Blvd.
Sanford, NC 27330

East-Way Aviation, Inc.
Rt. #1, Box 289-D
Ayden, NC 28513

Johnson Aviation, Inc.
Johnson Field Airport Rt. 1
Sophia, NC 27350

Kitty Hawk Kites
Bypass 158
Mile Post 13
Nags Head, NC 27959

Sport Flying Inc.
Route 2, Box 62-A
Jacksonville, NC 28540

The Flight Center, Inc.
3307 Mandalay Street
Fayetteville, NC 28303

N. Atlantic ULs, Inc.
P.O. Box 369
Edenton, NC 27932

Sail & Soar, Inc.
2823, Hwy. 66 South
Kernersville, NC 27284

Scott's Marine
226 Old Statesville Rd.
Huntersville, NC 28078

Upeind Ultralights
Old Fashioned Airfield
c/o Reliable Construction
Company
100 Sutherland Ave.
Monroe, NC 28110

OHIO

Aeroflite Ultralights, Inc.
9201 Seward Rd.
Fairfield, OH 45014

Blue Max Flying Machines
15525 Montgomery Road
Johnstown, OH 43031

Buckeye Ultralights, Inc.
2052 Airport Rd.
Delaware, OH 43015

Easy-Flight Aviation Inc.
P.O. Box 2022
Streetsboro, OH 44240

Don Harrop
7208 Wathill Rd., NE
Roseville, OH 43777

King's Wing's
119 Pike St.
Marietta, OH 45750

Liberty Airpark
6188 St. Route 303
Ravenna, OH 44266

Natural Flightline, Inc.
P.O. Box 17420
Arcadia, OH 44804

KC Ultralights, Inc.
P.O. Box 1533
Stow, OH 44224

Light Flight, Inc.
20032 Sixteen School Rd.
Wellsville, OH 43968

Midwest Ultralites, Inc.
145 Lakewood Dr.
Avon Lake, OH 44012

Ohio Ultralights, Inc.
7440 Reitz Rd.
Perrysburg, OH 43551

Northcoast Ultralights
9478 Valley View Rd.
Macedonia, OH 44056

Personal Planes Inc.
Huron County Airport
961 U.S. Route 20
Norwalk, OH 44857

Ultralight Sales Assn.
673 Montrose Ave.
Columbus, OH 43209

Zimmerman Airfield
Lakefield Airport
6177 St. Route 219
Celina, OH 45822

S.E. Ohio Ultralights
7208 Watt Hill Rd., N.E.
Roseville, OH 43777

Thunderbird Aviation
2525 Saxe Rd.
Mogadore, OH 44260

UFO, Inc.
855 Humboldt Dr. E.
Gahanna, OH 43230

Windance Airsports, Inc.
Wright Aerodrome
1334 N. Luthers Church Rd.
Dayton, OH 45473

Wings & Things, Inc.
7459 Fenton Rd.
N. Bloomfield, OH 44450

OKLAHOMA
Aero Light, Inc.
P.O. Box 506
Latoosa, OK 74015

C & O Enterprises, Inc.
1409 Prairie Heights Dr.
Bartlesville, OK 74003

Frisco Precision Power
1332 S. Florence Pl.
Tulsa, OK 74104

Grove Activities
Rt. 1, Box 235
Shawnee, OK 74801

Kingrey UL Aircraft
P.O. Box 895, Poteau Arpt.
Poteau, OK 74953

Weedhopper of Enid
219 Lamplighter
Enid, OK 73701

OREGON
**Christen Ultralight
Aeronautics**
763 S.E. 168th St.
Portland, OR 97233

Eastern Oregon Ultralights
500 S.W. 11th St.
Pendleton, OR 97801

Logan & Reavis Air Inc.
Medford-Jackson County
Airport
Medford, OR 97501

Sky Ryders Inc.
2167 S.E. Meadows Ct.
Gresham, OR 97030

PENNSYLVANIA
AC-DC Aviation
148 Bunker Hill Rd.
Ottville, PA 18942

Airborne
Venice Rd., R.D. 3
McDonald, PA 15057

The Bagman Inc.
c/o The Aerolight Corp.
924 Windsor St.
Reading, PA 19604

Central PA Ultralight, Inc.
RD 1, Box 170
Bellefonte, PA 16823

Championship Flight, Inc.
RD 1, Central Manor
Airport
Washington Boro, PA 17582

Dave's Hang Gliders Inc.
1416 Jennings Ave.
Scottsdale, PA 15683

Flying Colors ULs, Inc.
632 Lehigh Ave.
Lancaster, PA 17602

Freedom of Flight Inc.
835 Cedarwood Dr.
Pittsburgh, PA 15235

Freedom Flyer
Rt. 1, Box 800
Claysburg, PA 16625

Hole In The Sky, Inc.
Box 368, 5835 Main St.
Fogelsville, PA 18051

Keystone Sport Aviation
1195 McKean Rd.
Ambler, PA 19002

Keystone Ultralights
P.O. Box 44
Branchton, PA 16021

Orville's Ultralights
Box 317, RD 1
Laurel Ridge Rd.
Narvon, PA 17555

Roma Rose Airpark
Dave Denning
RD 1117
Bethel, PA 19507

Skylink, Inc.
Box 316
Martins Creek, PA 18063

Sweet Sky, Inc.
752 Norwood Rd.
Downingtown, PA 19335

**Timothy R. Martin, dba
Adler Aviation, Inc.**
Box 87
Tafton, PA 18464

Ultra-Sport Av., Inc.
RD 3, Box 317
Hollidaysburg, PA 16648

Valley Forge Ultralites Inc.
P.O. Box 593
Kimberton Road
Kimberton, PA 19442

SOUTH CAROLINA
Airborne Enterprises Corp.
500 Textile Rd.
Spartanburg, SC 29301

Carolina Ultralights
106 Brockington St.
Timmonsville, SC 29161

Clio Crop Care,
Box 422, Hangar on #9
Clio, SC 29525

TENNESSEE
Air Power Inc.
3832 Guernsey
Memphis, TN 38122

Big Boys Toys, Inc.
612 Davidson Rd.
Nashville, TN 37205

Bradford Field
Box 179
Eagleville, TN 37060

Design Ultralights, Inc.
4621 Chalmers Dr.
Nashville, TN 37215

Dream Wing Ultralights
4065 Cummings Hwy.
Chattanooga, TN 37409

E.T.Q.
Rt. 2, Box 4-A
Oliver Springs, TN 37840

Hawk Air Sports
3743 Martin Mill Pike
Knoxville, TN 37920

Midsouth Ultralights
382 Washington Ave.
Memphis, TN 38105

Mtn. Empire Aero Sports
Route 9, Box 410
Johnson City, TN 37601

Ultra-Flite Aero, Inc.
1001 Airport Rd.
Signal Hangar
Chattanooga, TN 37421

TEXAS
Alamo Aerolights
Rt. 1, Box 1236
Bulverde, TX 78163

The Aviator Shop
16948 Hwy. 3
San Antonio, TX 77598

Blue Max Ultraflight
6223 Hwy. 87 E.
San Antonio, TX 78222

Foster Ultralights
Rt. 4, Box 4953
Pearland, TX 77584

Ground Effects Inc.
1621 N. Central Expressway
Plano, TX 75075

Lite-Flight Dist.
P.O. Box 961
Euless, TX 76039

Lone Star Hang Gliders
2200C So. Smithbarry Road
Arlington, TX 76013

Lone Star Ultralights
1001 Parkwood
Friendswood, TX 77546

**Preston Hardware
Company/Ultralight**
14260 Marsh Lane
Dallas, TX 75234

Sport Ultralights, Inc.
P.O. Box 60166
Houston, TX 77205

TX Lite-Flite, Inc.
27715 Katy Freeway
Katy, TX 77450

UL Airsports
9029 Conger
Houston, TX 77075

Ultralight, U.S.A.
20803 Stuebrier Airline #15
Spring, TX 77379

Ultralite Power Gliders
Route 2, Box 523-A
Manvel, TX 77578

Ultralight Wings Inc.
6705 N. Lamar Blvd.
Austin, TX 78752

UTAH
Aero-Sports Ultralights
898 S. 900 East
Salt Lake City, UT 84102

Free Flight, Inc.
180 North, 2400 West
Salt Lake City Int'l. Arpt.
Salt Lake City, UT 84116

Ultralight Windsports, Inc.
Star Route 2, Box 4
Woodruff, UT 84086

Wasatch Wings Inc.
700 E. 12300 S.
Draper, UT 85020

VERMONT
Green Mtn. Aerolights
Post Mills Airport
Post Mills, VT 05058

**Green Mountain
Ultralights Inc.**
Village Green
Pittsford, VT 05763

VIRGINIA
Atlantic Ultralights
Route 1, Box 449
Smithfield, VA 23430

Kitty Hawk Kites
Culpepper Municipal Arpt.
Culpepper-Brandy Station,
VA 22714

Virginia Wings, Inc.
UL Flight Park
Hopewell Arpt., Box 1628
Hopewell, VA 23860

WASHINGTON
Aerolight Inc.
17910 59th Dr., N.E.
Arlington Airport, Bldg. 7
Arlington, WA 98223

Capital City Gliders
3936 Pacific Avenue
Lacey, WA 98503

Flightmaster Power Supply
1452½ N.W. 70th
Seattle, WA 98107

Four Winds
202 E. 4th
Ellenburg, WA 98926

Evergreen Ultralite Inc.
10407 Wood-Red Rd., N.E.
Redmond, WA 98052

**Fantasy Ultralight
Aviation**
Route 3, Box 726-C
Colville, WA 99114

Sunchaser & Co. Pterodactyl
7800 Perimeter Rd.
So. Seattle, WA 98108

7-11 Store
4061 Pacific Ave.
Lacey, WA 98503

Ultralight Flight
Rt. 3, Box 137
Colfax, WA 99111

**Wildrose Ultralight
Aviation**
W. 513 Hasting Road
Spokane, WA 99218

WEST VIRGINIA
Valley Aeronautical, Inc.
Rt. 1, Box 233-A
Reedsville, WV 26547

WISCONSIN
Big Timber Lite-Flight
Rt. 4, Box 460
Mosinee, WI 54455

Eagle ULs of Green Bay
2737 Wippoorwill Dr.
Green Bay, WI 54303

Eldon McDaniel
Merrimac, WI 53561

Light Flight Sales, Inc.
2168 S. 69th St.
West Allis, WI 53219

Mid-West Eagle
5729 W. North Ave.
Milwaukee, WI 53208

Midwest Microlights Inc.
1351 W. 2nd St.
Oconomowoc, WI 53066

Northland Ultralights
102 Cemetery Road
River Falls, WI 54022

Prospect News
2103 N. Prospect Ave.
Milwaukee, WI 53202

Quick-Aire, Inc.
8260 N. 38th
Milwaukee, WI 53209

Silent Wings Inc.
W. 204 N. 5022 Lannon Rd.
Memomonee Falls,
WI 53501

Stamp Enterprises
RR 1, Box 308
Lake Geneva, WI 53147

Venturecraft Aviation
915 Bloom Rd.
Eagle River, WI 54521

WYOMING
The Flite Shop
528 Country Road #2
Evanston, WY 82930

McCue Aviation
Box 1462
Cody Municipal Airport
Cody, WY 82414

Wyoming Wings ULs
P.O. Box 619
Moorcroft, WY 82721

CANADA
Ace Aerolights
General Delivery
Limehouse, Ontario
Canada L0P 1 H0

**Acfield Aviation
Supplies, Ltd.**
7040 Torbram Rd. (14)
Mississauga, Ontario,
Canada L4T 3Z4

Alpine Ultralites, Ltd.
P.O. Box 1552
Grand Forks, B.C.
Canada V0H 1H0

**Atlantic Airsport
Ultralight Ltd.**
6341-A York St.
Halifax, Nova Scotia
Canada B3H 2K6

Birdman Enterprises
7939 Argyll Road
Edmonton, Alberta
Canada T6O 4A9

**Canadian Ultralight
Aircraft Ltd.**
R.R. #2
Lumby, British Columbia
Canada V0E 2G0

Mile 'O' Microlites
709-100B Ave.
Dawson Creek, BC Canada

Omni Microlights
#9 1826 25th Ave., NE
Calgary, Alberta, Canada

Eastern Ultralight Aircraft
Box 211, Grand Bay
St. John, New Brunswick
Canada E0G 1W0

**Morning Wind Flight
Systems Ltd.**
Hangar 5, Box 1916
Fort MacLeod, Alberta
Canada T0L 0Z0

Northern Microlights Ltd.
Route 2, Conc 9/Sideroad 26
Claremont, Ontario
Canada

Ontario Microlights Inc.
50 Cedarhill Crescent
Kitchener, Ontario
Canada N2E 2H4

Sky Ryders North
27 Gertrude St. W.
North Bay, Ontario
Canada P1A 1J4

Spectralites
3556 Bell School Line
Burlington Airport
R.R. #6
Milton, Ontario
Canada L9T 2Y1

FOREIGN
**Aerolight Aviation
Company Ltd.**
The Old Control Tower
Maby Airfield Nr. Louth
Lincolnsire, Great Britain

**Aza Aircraft
Vincente Marzal Corp.**
CTVA Faitanhr
Valencia-1
Spain

Hobbybokhandeln
Box 9185
S-102 73
Stockholm, Sweden

O-Tech Pty Ltd.
P.O. Box 28721
Sunnyside 0132
South Africa

Spartalan Microlights
Box 3871
Kempton Park Transvaal
Republic of South Africa

Appendix D
Ultralight And Related Periodicals

Air Progress Ultralights
7950 Deering Avenue
Canoga Park, CA 91304

Glider Rider
P.O. Box 6009
Chattanooga, TN 37401

Ultralight Flyer Newspaper
P.O. Box 98786
Tacoma, WI 98499

Canadian Ultralight News
P.O. Box 563
Station "B"
Ottawa, Ont. K1P 5P7

Hang Gliding
P.O. Box 66306
Los Angeles, CA 90066

Ultralight Pilot
P.O. Box 5800
Bethesda, MD 20814

EAA Ultralight Division
P.O. Box 229
Hales Corners, WI 53130

Sportsman Pilot
P.O. Box 485
Hales Corners, WI 53130

Whole Air Magazine
P.O. Box 144
Lookout Mtn., TN 37350

Flight Line Magazine/BMAA
11 School Hill
Wrecclesham, Farnam
Surrey, ENGLAND

Ultralight Aircraft Magazine
16200 Ventura Blvd.
Suite 201
Encino, CA 91436

Prof. UL Retailers Assoc.
P.O. Box 133
Melbourne Airport
Victoria 3045 Australia

Bibliography for Ultralight Aircraft

(1) Abbot, Ira H. and Albert E. Von Doenhoff, "Theory of Wing Sections", Dover Publications, New York, NY
(2) Crawford, Donald R., "A Practical Guide to Airplane Performance and Design", Crawford Aviation, Torrance, CA
(3) Dempsey, Paul, "How to Repair Small Gasoline Engines", Tab Books, Inc., Blue Ridge Summit, PA
(4) Dempsey, Paul, "The Complete Snowmobile Handbook", Tab Books, Inc., Blue Ridge Summit, PA
(5) Dohm, John, "The New Private Pilot", Pan American Navigation Service, No. Hollywood, CA
(6) Hoerner, Dr. S.R., "Fluid Dynamic Drag", Midland Park, NJ
(7) Hoerner, Dr. S.F., "Fluid Dynamic Lift", Midland Park, NJ
(8) *Homebuilt Aircraft* Magazine, Santa Monica, CA
(9) Knauss, Tracy, *Glider Rider* Magazine, Chattanooga, TN
(10) Langewiesche, Wolfgang, "Stick and Rudder", McGraw-Hill, New York, NY
(11) Markowski, Michael A., "The Hang Glider's Bible", Tab Books, Inc., Blue Ridge Summit, PA
(12) McCormick, Barnes W., Jr., "Aerodynamics of V/STOL Flight", Academic Press, New York, NY
(13) McFarland, Marvin W., "The Papers of Wilbur and Orville Wright", McGraw-Hill Book Co., Inc., New York, NY
(14) McKinley, James L., "Powerplants for Aerospace Vehicles", McGraw-Hill Book Co., Inc., New York, NY
(15) Misenhimer, T.G., "Aeroscience", Aero Products Research, Los Angeles, CA
(16) Peery, D.J., "Aircraft Structures", McGraw-Hill Book Co., Inc., New York, NY
(17) Perkins, C.D. and Robert E. Hage, "Airplane Performance, Stability and Control", John Wiley and sons, Inc., New York, NY
(18) Pope, Francis and Arthur S. Otis, "Elements of Aeronautics", World Book Co., Inc., New York, NY
(19) Sherwin, Keith, "Man-Powered Flight", Model and Allied Publications, Ltd., Herts, England
(20) Simonson, Leroy, "Private Pilot Exam Guide", Simonson, Inglewood, CA
(21) USHGA *Hang Gliding* Magazine, Los Angeles, CA
(22) Von Mises, Richard, "Theory of Flight", Dover Publications, New York, NY
(23) Welch, John F., "Modern Airmanship", Van Nostrand Reinhold Company, New York, NY
(24) Wood, K.D., "Aircraft Design", Johnson Publishing Co., Boulder, CO

The Ultralight Library
Practical Aviation Books From Ultralight Publications

ULTRALIGHT AIRCRAFT - The Basic Handbook of Ultralight Aviation (Revised 2nd Edition) by Michael A. Markowski. This is the best selling (over 35,000 sold), definitive word on ultralight flying and aircraft. Divided into four sections, it covers: **Ultralight Aircraft Described,** including - Specifications to over 60 Aircraft • Performance • Handling • Drawings • Pilot Reports • **The Basic Ultralight Flight Manual** describes the specialties of ultralight flying - Principles • Stability and Trim • Low Speed Flight Control Techniques • Stalls • Spins • Landing • Traffic Pattern • Slideslipping • Crosswinds • Crabbing • Instruments • Density Altitude • The Koch Chart • Wind Chill Factors • Navigation • Flight Planning • Winds and Weather • **Ultralight Propulsion** includes - Engine Operation • Trouble-Shooting • Engine Reviews • Propellers • **Appendicies** cover - Test and Study Guide • FARs • Manufacturers and Dealers Lists • Plus much, much more. Ultralight Aircraft is highly recommended and endorsed by industry leaders. "Every aspect of ultralight aviation is covered by a professional who knows!" 320 pgs., 220 ill., 6x9 in.
Order No. 1 . . . . **Hardbound $22.95** . . . . **Paper $15.95**

ULTRALIGHT AIRMANSHIP - How To Master The Air In An Ultralight, by Jack Lambie. What can you do after you've learned the basics of ultralight flight? What's next? This exciting new book spells it out in clear, concise language— how you should fly to make use of, avoid, and operate in various atmospheric conditions, with specific advice and flight descriptions by experienced flyers. Large weather systems and circulation patterns, as well as the intricacies of micrometeorology (airflows around valley passes, mountains, behind trees, buildings and other obstructions) are described in detail. Learn how to handle turbulence and fly practically anytime you want tb — you don't have to limit yourself to just mornings and evenings. If you know what's in this book! ULTRALIGHT AIRMANSHIP is your ticket to total mastery of the air — your "roadmap-to-the-sky." 144 pgs., 110 ill., 6x9 in.
Order No. 2 . . . . **Hardbound $18.95** . . . . **Paper $10.95**

ULTRALIGHT FLIGHT - The Pilot's Handbook of Ultralight Knowledge, by Michael A. Markowski. Covers the new world of ultralight aerodynamics, stability and control, design and performance, plus a fascinating history. If you want to be the most complete pilot you can be, you must know more than just how-to fly! The competent pilot needs to know the hows and whys of flight, as well as how ultralights evolved. His natural curiosity and quest for self-improvement, safety and his ultimate enjoyment of flying drives him to learn as much as he can about his machine's interaction with the air. Like none before, this book presents a vitally important subject in an easily understood manner. Lift, drag, thrust and weight, as well as stability, control and design are described in detail - without math! Learn why your ultralight flies the way it does. Be able to predict how any design will handle. Discover the intriguing early days of ultralights to gain an appreciation of why they are built the way they are. ULTRALIGHT FLIGHT is your key to unlocking the mysteries of flight - your guide to "intelligence-in-the-sky," written as only Markowski can! 224 pgs., 110 ill., 6x9 in.
Order No. 3 . . . . **Hardbound $20.95** . . . . **Paper $13.95**

ULTRALIGHT PROPULSION - The Basic Handbook of Ultralight Engines, Drives and Propellers, by Glenn Brinks. If you expect to fly with utmost confidence, you must know your power system — its characteristics, and idiosyncracies — inside out. The two-cycle ultralight engine is a stranger to most pilots, but it must be thoroughly understood before flying can be done with any degree of safety. ULTRALIGHT PROPULSION describes the incredibly important details of power — how it is produced and transmitted into the air to provide performance — from a pilot's point of view. The book describes ignition systems, carburetors, starters and starting, spark plugs and how-to read them, exhaust systems, break-in and trouble-shooting, teardown, inspection and reassembly, modification, accessories and controls. The various drive methods are reviewed — belts, gears and direct. The practical aspects of propeller operation, care, balancing, tracking and safety are presented. ULTRALIGHT PROPULSION tells you what power is all about — from a drop of gasoline to a rate of climb. It tells you how to get maximum performance, reliability and life from your power system. It's your most important *"tool"* for a good running engine. 224 pgs., 110 ill., 6x9 in.

Order No. 4 . . . . **Hardbound $20.95** . . . . **Paperback $13.95**

ULTRALIGHT TECHNIQUE - How To Fly and Navigate Ultralight Air Vehicles, by Michael A. Markowski. This is the book that lets you in on the "secrets" of flying ultralights properly and legally. It's an operations manual and a complete reference to the new recreational flying. ULTRALIGHT TECHNIQUE gets into the "nitty gritty" aspects of ultralight, "seat-of-the-pants" flight control techniques. It explains in clear, concise language, the details of how ultralights are controlled. It tells you how specific maneuvers are done and why they work. It deals with the peculiarities of operating from water and snow, and tells you how to protect yourself from hypothermia. The vital importance of "angle-of-attack" - the very essence of flight - is presented so anyone can understand it. The stall is analyzed in depth. The various methods of pilotage and dead reckoning are described so you can pre-plan your flights away from your home field. Everyone who reads this exciting new book should gain a deeper understanding of what ultralight flying is all about. 256 pgs., 107 ill., 6x9 in.

Order No. 5 . . . .**Paper $14.95**

THE ULTRALIGHT LOG BOOKS

Designed with the ultralight pilot in mind, each has space for over 500 flight entries. Each is bound in a beautiful, colorful, heavy leatherette cover for long wearing durability. Fits in hip pocket! These log books are the only way for you to keep track of your valuable flight experience, aircraft usage, and engine operation. Know your proficiency level as well as your ultralight's condition.

THE ULTRALIGHT PILOT FLIGHT LOG, includes: Pre-flight inspection procedures, load factor and stall speed vs bank angle chart, ultralight traffic pattern, density altitude/Koch chart, landing factors and field perspectives, wind chill chart, and the flying-speed-of-an-ultralight.

Order No. P-1 . . . .**$3.95**

THE ULTRALIGHT ENGINE LOG, includes: Trouble-shooting guide.

Order No. E-1 . . . .**$3.95**

THE ULTRALIGHT AIRCRAFT LOG

Order No. A-1 . . . .**$3.95**

ULTRALIGHT CROSS-COUNTRY PLANNING AND LOG SHEETS (50 forms)

Order No. C-1 . . . .**$1.95**

BUMPER STICKER: FLY AN ULTRALIGHT AIRCRAFT - DISCOVER A NEW DIMENSION IN FLIGHT (3" x 12": Yellow & Blue on White)

Order No. BS-1 . . . .**$1.59**

T-SHIRT (Same wording as bumper sticker, S, M, L, XL - four color)

Order No. TS-1 . . . .**$10.95**

TO ORDER: Put your name and address on a sheet of paper. List the book title and order number, and include cash, check or money order to cover book cost plus $2.95 for postage and handling of total order. A **FREE** catalog is included with each order. **Send to: Ultralight Publications,** P.O. Box 234, Dept. UP, Hummelstown, PA 17036 USA.